Neat Pieces

Atlanta History Center / The Madison-Morgan Cultural Center / The University of Georgia Press *Athens and London*

Neat Pieces

The Plain-Style Furniture of Nineteenth-Century Georgia

WITH A NEW FOREWORD BY DEANNE D. LEVISON

Published in 2006 by the University of Georgia Press
Athens, Georgia 30602
in conjunction with the Atlanta History Center
and the Madison-Morgan Cultural Center
Designed and typeset by Sandra Strother Hudson and Walton Harris
Set in Adobe Caslon with Giza display
Printed and bound by Kings Time Printing Press, LTD.
The paper in this book meets the guidelines for permanence and durability of the Committee on
Production Guidelines for Book Longevity of the Council on Library Resources.

Printed in China
10   09   08   07   06   P   5   4   3   2   1

Library of Congress Cataloging-in-Publication Data

Neat pieces : the plain-style furniture of nineteenth-century Georgia / with a new foreword
by Deanne D. Levison.
        p.   cm.
Reprint of the catalog of the exhibition held Dec. 9, 1983–June 10, 1984
at Atlanta Historical Society.
Originally published: Atlanta, Ga. : Atlanta Historical Society, 1983.
Includes bibliographical references.
ISBN-13: 978-0-8203-2805-8 (pbk. : alk. paper)
ISBN-10: 0-8203-2805-7 (pbk. : alk. paper)
1. Country furniture—Georgia—History—19th century—Exhibitions.
I. Atlanta Historical Society.
NK2435.G4N4 2006
749'.09758'074758231—dc22   2005019682

British Library Cataloging-in-Publication Data available

Photography for the catalog was funded in part by a grant from the Georgia Council for the Arts
and Humanities. Photographs of the furniture were taken by Arthur Vitols, Helga Photo Studio,
with the exceptions of the frontispiece, Figure 19, and the details for Figures 76, 101, 107, and 121,
which were taken by William Hull, Atlanta Historical Society.

Neat Pieces was originally published in conjunction with an exhibition of the same name, which ran
from December 9, 1983, to June 10, 1984, at the Atlanta History Center, 130 West Paces Ferry Road
NW, Atlanta GA 30305-1366.

Title page image: A mid-nineteenth-century safe (Figure 67). The design motif seen in the piercing
of the tin panels was a popular one in nineteenth-century Georgia. It is the so-called Georgia Arch,
derived from the design on one surface of the Great Seal of Georgia adopted by the state in final
form on December 5, 1799, just prior to the dawn of a new century. The 1799 design was the creation
of Daniel Sturges, surveyor-general of Georgia.

The Atlanta History Center gratefully acknowledges the financial support of Mr. and Mrs. Frederick A. Hoyt Jr., who made the publication of this new edition possible.

Contents

Foreword to the 2006 Edition

Over twenty years have passed since the exhibition and eponymous accompanying catalog *Neat Pieces: The Plain-Style Furniture of Nineteenth-Century Georgia* were produced at the Atlanta History Center. The stated objective of the catalog was to illustrate the predominant surviving furniture genre. Objects selected for inclusion were subjected to as thorough a documentary review as possible. Of more than 2,000 pieces recorded during the five-year research survey, 126 were selected for publication. In addition to descriptive entries, the catalog included a comprehensive introduction and social history placing the objects in context. A checklist of more than one thousand nineteenth-century Georgia furniture craftsmen indicated their occupations, towns and/or counties, ages (when known), places of birth (when known), and dates of life and work.

Among the earliest studies of Georgia furniture was the 1967 publication *Savannah Furniture: 1735–1825*, by Will H. (Mrs. Charlton M.) Theus, in which she identified the work of fifty area cabinetmakers, as well as other pieces attributed to coastal artisans. That same year, Katherine Wood Gross (later Farnham), at the University of Delaware's Winterthur Program, wrote her master's thesis on "The Sources of Furniture Sold in Savannah, 1789–1815." Nine years later, in 1976, as curator of decorative arts at the High Museum of Art in Atlanta, Farnham edited the catalog *Furniture of the Georgia Piedmont before 1830* for the most important exhibition to date devoted exclusively to Georgia furniture. This exhibition and catalog, written by Henry D. Green, were the culmination of years of work by this pioneer collector. The present Henry D. Green Center for the Decorative Arts at the Georgia Museum of Art in Athens is named in his honor.

Subsequent to the *Neat Pieces* exhibition and catalog in 1983 was the 1985 Georgia Museum of Art exhibition and catalog entitled *Georgia's Legacy: History through the Arts*, curated by Jane Webb Smith, in which objects, in addition to furniture, gave further details about the history and works of Georgia artisans from pre-European (Native American) occupation through the 1860s.

In 1989, the High Museum's *Georgia Collects* illustrated a few pieces of Georgia furniture not previously published. In 1990, through the support of the Colonial Dames of America in the State of Georgia, the High hosted the exhibition and published the catalog *Hidden Heritage: Recent*

Discoveries in Georgia Decorative Arts, 1733–1915. Curated by Pamela Wagner, this exhibition included newly discovered examples of plain-style furniture, as well as examples of late-nineteenth and early-twentieth-century styles.

In 1995, *Classical Savannah,* an exhibition at the Telfair Museum of Art that Page Talbott curated and wrote the catalog for, exhibited imported as well as northern and southern furniture of the first decades of the nineteenth century. Those attributed or identified to be of local manufacture were described as "generally quite plain."

The research set forth in *Neat Pieces* and the studies that followed influenced the organization of exhibitions and publications outside the state as well, such as *Made in Alabama: A State Legacy,* held at the Birmingham Museum of Art, and *The Art and Mystery of Tennessee Furniture and Its Makers through 1850.* The research also impacted the very localized study of Stewart County, Georgia, furniture.

Today, active study persists at the Henry D. Green Center, where symposia papers continue to be published. In addition, the renowned Museum of Early Southern Decorative Arts, in Winston-Salem, North Carolina, as part of its overall study of southern decorative arts, continues to build on decades-old research on surviving old Georgia furniture and has recently extended the boundaries of its study to the 1860s.

Interest in the story revealed in the furniture made by both trained and untrained craftsmen in Georgia has led to restoring this catalog to print. My hope is that making *Neat Pieces* available again, with rich color photographs replacing over 150 of the original black-and-white images, will inspire others to delve into further study of this intriguing subject. Although each of the above catalogs and exhibitions opened doors of discovery, much remains unknown. If this new edition stirs interest and, hopefully, action, then the work to produce *Neat Pieces* will have served its purpose.

DEANNE D. LEVISON
Atlanta

Foreword

Twas said that o'er the hills, and far away
Towards the setting sun, a land there lay,
Whose unexhausted energies of soil
Nobly repaid the hardy lab'rer's toil;
Where men were worth full twice their weight in gold.
And goodly farms were for almost nought sold;
Prairies of flowers, and grassy meads abound,
And rivers everywhere meander round.
James Kirke Paulding, *The Backwoodsman. A Poem.* Philadelphia, 1818.

Firmly entrenched in literature and the popular image of the Old South
has been the legend that southern society was comprised of courtly planters, degraded poor whites, and Negro slaves. This incomplete, stereotyped,
and sometimes distorted image of the South of stable folkways, leisurely
living, and an aristocratic society ignores a large segment of the population, the common people of the Old South. Their voice has been silenced
in the conventional history books by what the British historian E. P.
Thompson has called "the tremendous condescension of posterity." It is
no problem to identify and portray the prominent, the rich and successful, or even the notorious. Yet the ordinary, the "forgotten" or "historically
voiceless," people of our past are easily lost in the fragmentary documentation that survives the attrition of time.

In this exhibition and catalog, by focusing attention on the plain furniture of Georgia, the authors and curators ingeniously recover something
of this lost dimension of a part of the lives of these "miscellaneous and
unknown" plain folk, many of whom, in a virgin environment, were able
to rise from "rags to riches." In actuality, the most common agricultural
unit in Georgia was the farm, not the plantation, and the largest group of
white southerners in prewar Georgia were yeoman farmers with few or
no slaves, not aristocratic planters living a life of leisure and pleasure on
vast inherited estates. The "plain folk of the Old South" lived in unpretentious wooden houses and derived a sense of independence and self-re-
spect from the ownership of land. They firmly believed that through toil
and perseverance they could build their farms into plantations. In their
religious orthodoxy they tended to be deeply conservative, believing in
a God who could and did intervene daily in the lives of men. Humor-

ists have written vivid and often authentic accounts of these common people: their weddings and funerals, country dances and quilting bees, corn shuckings and log rollings, hunting and fishing, camp meetings and singing schools, mule swapping and grudge fights. They were men who worked hard, played hard, laughed loudly, and aspired to improve themselves both materially and spiritually. Household activities centered around the hearth, where the hardy farmer's wife cooked a monotonous diet of hog and hominy, wove the cloth and made the family clothes, boiled them in a huge black pot over an open fire outside, raised chickens, tended the family vegetable garden, and even helped in the fields at harvest time.

The yeoman farmer was chronically and everlastingly short of money. Yet since he was engaged in more subsistence agriculture than the planter, who depended upon a cash crop, he tended to be more economically self-sufficient than was his more prestigious neighbor. He built a utilitarian house that was considered temporary, assuming that he and his family would move west when the fertility of the land he was then farming wore out. He was a restless man who lived with great expectations. He furnished his home with furniture of local woods, sound construction, restrained decoration, and conservative style. Call it backwoods baroque or artisan mannerism, when viewed together, as in this exhibition, the pieces add up to a powerful statement of the vernacular tradition of cabinet-making and chairmaking in rural America. The plain furniture of Georgia lends support to the thesis that antebellum southern society was more diverse, dynamic, and democratic than former stereotypes would admit.

WENDELL GARRETT

Preface

Five years ago it was the thought and vision of two of Georgia's most avid students of its social history and material culture, William and Florence Griffin, to find an organization and body of people interested in undertaking a systematic study of plain-style furniture of nineteenth-century Georgia. Under the auspices of the Atlanta Historical Society, the Steering Committee accomplished this research project with the support of a Statewide Committee and the advice of scholars in the field of decorative arts. The end product of this undertaking is the first in-depth study of documented Georgia furniture, presented in the catalog and exhibition entitled *Neat Pieces: The Plain-Style Furniture of Nineteenth-Century Georgia*.

The context of viewing this furniture through the social history of the men and women who made, used, and passed on these "neat pieces" is a very real attempt to put each of us in touch with the roots of a much simpler nineteenth-century society. To view the times and circumstances during which this furniture was made is not at all impossible. It can be done in several ways. First, we can read what they wrote in their letters and diaries or what was written about them. We can observe the faces of the makers and owners of many of these pieces, captured for history by the ambrotype, daguerreotype, and glass-plate negative. Finally, we can view this plain-style furniture with an eye to its construction, degree of decorative detail, as well as the human touches that graft it indelibly to a person, place, and time.

Any research project of this nature which attempts to gather all available data, even with several years' lead time, can only gather that which is uncovered given the manpower and resources made available to it. Under the aegis of the Atlanta Historical Society, efforts were made at all levels to solicit information on furniture and makers. Given the sheer size of the state of Georgia with its 159 counties, the task of gathering information, let alone disseminating information about the study, was enormous. It was the consensus of the Steering Committee that press releases sent out by the Atlanta Historical Society with a carefully thought-out survey information form would be the most efficient way of reaching furniture owners or collectors.

Press notices were sent to all of the newsletters, newspapers, and magazines on the Atlanta Historical Society's extensive mailing list.

Letters and survey forms went out to all of the state's county historical societies, parks and historic sites, public libraries, colleges and universities, museums, local chapters of the Colonial Dames of America, selected garden clubs, some genealogical societies, and Georgians listed on MESDA's roster for Southern Decorative Arts. A great many replies led us to friends, neighbors, and relatives of those originally contacted. In all, approximately 2,000 pieces, all recorded on survey forms, were inventoried for our files. From these, 126 pieces were selected.

In studying the two thousand pieces of furniture, submitted from all over the state and beyond, several things became evident. First, the material, for the most part, fell into the period of 1820–60. Although it was the intent of the Steering Committee to find representative examples that spanned the nineteenth century, there was simply less available to document the first decades. Secondly, in the aftermath of the Civil War, furniture tended to be manufactured and lacked the plain-style country character that had marked the growth of the state prior to 1860, the period of Georgia's great internal development that epitomized the philosophy of a fundamental work ethic around one's family and kin.

Thirdly, because of the 1820–60 time frame, the bulk of the 126 exhibited pieces would have to fall within this period. It may seem awkward to deal with the century through little more than a forty-year segment, and yet historically these were the determining years for much of the economic development and growth of the state in both rural and urban areas. It is during this period that the Creek and Cherokee Indians were deprived of their lands, thereby opening this Georgia territory to settlers. The concurrent development of an extensive railroad network crisscrossing Georgia was completed; at its hub the town of Terminus, later to become Atlanta, was created. This concentration of commerce and transportation in the South would later mandate its destruction by the Northern Army in its effort to win the war. Lastly, it is in this period that the role of the farmer and planter was firmly stratified, since his lifestyle and labor force were directly locked to the slave system and "King Cotton."
In each and every case the Georgians had to come to grips with their land, its economics, and a way of life dictated by climate, soil, and settlement patterns. The furniture and other cultural artifacts are the product of this agrarian frontier and, like its people, are marked by simplicity and sturdiness.

It may be noticed that at least one regional area is scarcely touched upon—that of coastal Georgia. This occurred because very little was submitted by those counties and area organizations to whom the survey forms were sent. It may be that because this region had direct access to the sea, furniture could be easily imported from more northern cities. It may also be that the formal coastal city of Savannah, with its fashionable inhabitants, tended to desire the more elegant furnishings of established cabinetmakers from centers like Charleston, Philadelphia, New York, and Boston.

Throughout the development of this catalog, the working committees have been concerned about the historical context through which the readers would view this body of information. From the introductory essay to the explanatory notes relating to the various furniture groups, great care has been given to clarity of thought, uniform descriptions, and terminology, as well as content flow. In addition, at least one major academic tool has been produced as a result of this project that should prove useful in future scholarly research. This is an extensive checklist of Georgia furniture makers from a variety of sources published in this catalog.

It is the sincere hope of all those who have worked on this project that the catalog with the checklist, as well as the volumes of research data and photographs collected, will lead to future projects on the study of Georgia furniture.

In all, this project is the work of more than a hundred individuals, but six people deserve very special credit for their unselfish and untiring efforts to see it through. Five of these, William and Florence Griffin, Paul and Sally Hawkins, and Deanne Levison provided the structure for the exhibition, including its complete historical and physical content, with their ideas, research, and examination of the pieces and writings. The sixth is Atlanta Historical Society Project Coordinator Adair Massey, whose professional standards and persistent efforts at collecting, organizing, and following through on hundreds of details with everyone involved kept the work on schedule and made this exhibition catalog a reality. These six are the Georgians in whose homes and offices this project has been accomplished.

It is interesting to note that in 1983 at least one other modern-day Georgian is making a name for himself at his home and in his shop producing pieces of furniture in the same plain-style fashion of a century ago. James Earl Carter, thirty-ninth President of the United States and former Governor of Georgia, continues the tradition of "Neat Pieces" for yet another story.

JOHN HARLOW OTT
Director, Atlanta Historical Society, 1983–1991

Acknowledgments

This exhibition and catalog were conceived and directed by the Steering Committee. The many hours spent together in meetings and on the road to examine each piece of furniture under final consideration and individually to research and write the catalog material were all volunteer. Without the dedication and perseverance of this group, the project would never have come to fruition.

William Griffin wrote the introduction. William and Florence Griffin wrote "Georgians at Home." Deanne Levison and Sally Hawkins wrote the physical descriptions of the furniture and "Explanations to the Catalog." The introductions to the furniture categories were written by William and Florence Griffin, Deanne Levison, and Sally Hawkins. Histories of the individual pieces were compiled through the survey effort and archival research.

The Statewide Committee provided specialized support and regional liaison.

Invaluable advice and critical evaluation came from the Professional Advisory Committee.

We are grateful to governmental, institutional, and private lenders who have generously agreed to be without their furniture for more than six months.

Technical advice and expertise were freely given by Bradford Rauschenberg, who was responsible for all microanalysis of woods; by Norman Davenport Askins, who provided architectural consultation for the exhibition; and by Mary Ellen Brooks, Dale Couch, Anthony Dees, Patty Carter Deveau, Louis De Vorsey Jr., David Estes, Franklin M. Garrett, Richard H. F. Lindemann, Morton R. McInvale, Edwin S. and Norma K. Seiferle, Kenneth H. Thomas Jr., Edward Weldon, and Robert M. Willingham Jr.

Particularly valuable editorial assistance has been provided by William Nathaniel Banks, John A. Burrison, Wendell Garrett, Charles F. Hummel, John H. Ott, Jessie J. Poesch, William L. Pressly, Andrew Sparks, Olive Ann Burns Sparks, and Jane Campbell Symmes.

The least visible and most tedious work was done by a team of researchers. Those who spent several months in the archives and libraries gathering information on furniture makers were Lisa Earwood; Governor's interns Jeanne Symmes, Julie Carithers, Lethea Quin, Sally Schiller, and Lois O'Shea; and Emory intern Jody Fain. Volunteers who generously contributed their time and effort were Nancy Reeves, Rosemary Brandau, and Rosemary Turner.

Some compilation of this raw data was accomplished through the efforts of Elizabeth Wilson and volunteers Lynn Pickering, Jane Floweree, and Dorothy Howells. Cynthia Freeman is responsible for the formidable task of pulling together in the final form the material for the list of furniture makers for the catalog.

Lisa Reynolds, former Curator of the Atlanta Historical Society, was responsible for coordinating the earliest stages of the project.

John H. Ott, Director of the Atlanta Historical Society, has been extremely generous with his time in guiding our path through the final stages of the catalog and exhibition. Bob Kothe, Director of Museum Services, contributed his expertise primarily to the installation of the exhibition. Cynthia Freeman, Jean Marchman, and Laurel Wemett helped prepare the final catalog text for the printer. The following people on the staff of the Atlanta Historical Society contributed to our effort: Cady Ferguson, Public Relations Director; William Hull, Staff Photographer; Jacquelyn Kavanaugh, Museum Shop Manager; Elaine Kirkland, Visual Arts Archivist; Madeline Patchen, Curator of Education; Michael Rose, Collections Manager; Jane Powers Weldon, Director of Publications.

The W. R. C. Smith Publishing Company, whose staff demonstrated patience beyond the call of duty, published the catalog.

The exhibition installation was designed by Nancy Braithwaite of Nancy Braithwaite Interiors, who worked countless hours in creating a design that interpreted the goals and purposes of the exhibition.

Grateful acknowledgment is made to Cousins Properties Incorporated for underwriting the cost of the catalog, to the Georgia Council for the Arts and Humanities, to the magazine *Antiques* for the color transparencies, and to William Nathaniel Banks and other individuals for their generous contributions toward its production.

Through the efforts of the above individuals and institutions, the vision of this catalog and exhibition, *Neat Pieces: The Plain-Style Furniture of Nineteenth-Century Georgia*, has been fulfilled.

ADAIR MASSEY
Project Coordinator

Neat Pieces

Counties of Georgia and Some Important Cities

Introduction

Neat Pieces: The Plain-Style Furniture of Nineteenth-Century Georgia

[The plantation carpenters] constructed the wash-hand stands, clothes-presses, sofas, tables, etc., with which our house is furnished, and they are very neat pieces of workmanship—neither veneered or polished indeed, nor of very costly materials, but of the white pine wood planed as smooth as marble—a species of furniture not very luxurious perhaps, but all the better adapted therefore to the house itself, which is certainly rather more devoid of the conveniences and adornments of modern existence than anything I ever took up my abode in before.

Frances Anne Kemble, *Journal of a Residence on a Georgian Plantation in 1838–9.*[1]

The Exhibition

Furniture in this exhibition is from Georgia homes of the last century, a century of drastic change but one in which old virtues and values were universally respected. These are neat pieces. The word "neat" is derived from the Latin *nitidus*, meaning shining or fine. In 1854 Webster defined "neat" as trim, tidy, free from tawdry appendages. This is particularly descriptive of much of the handmade furniture of the nineteenth century in Georgia, whether made by black or white craftsmen at home or in cabinet shops. Because it was made in town and country, the term "country" furniture is inappropriate. It was developed and refined for utility and comfort from furniture forms of a much earlier genesis and, therefore, is not "primitive." "Indigenous" and "vernacular" are appropriate words for this furniture but have little meaning to many. It is furniture of a plain style as opposed to a high style.

From a corpus of more than 2,000 pieces of furniture examined in a statewide survey, items were selected for exhibition to convey the range of typical handmade furniture in Georgia homes of the times. Every effort has been made to eliminate furniture made in other states, but certainty as to the place of manufacture is in some cases impossible. All of the pieces were used in Georgia homes shortly after their manufacture. Many of them were made by known Georgia craftsmen, and therefore can serve as benchmarks for further studies and comparison.

These pieces are documents. They can convey to us nonverbal impressions of the past, which we can utilize now or in the future. They should be viewed with these premises in mind:

1. Furniture is and has been "the stuff of everyday life," used by all in a continuum from ancient to contemporary times.

2. Everyone living today has been biased aesthetically from earliest childhood and should recognize this fact and attempt to purge taste prejudices in any study of cultural history through artifacts.

3. Nevertheless, through the ages, all societies, including our own, seem to have developed certain standards of beauty and, if judgments are to be made, these standards cannot be overlooked.

4. Furniture and, for that matter, most artifacts can communicate history from a non-literary maker or user of the past to the student of today.

5. Nonverbal impressions from examination of artifacts must be weighed with literary source material and behavior patterns to draw historical generalizations.

6. Specific artifacts and facts lead one to conclusions and judgments, but such conclusions or judgments are subjective and personal.

7. The people of each state and region have certain cultural characteristics that set them apart from the people of every other state or region.

8. These characteristics are sometimes difficult to describe by words alone, just as it is impossible to describe a face or a voice even though that face or voice when seen or heard is instantly recognized.

9. Artifacts, particularly furniture, made or used in any geographical area afford a broad insight into that area's cultural past that cannot be transmitted by verbal documents alone.

When viewing this furniture, bear in mind the people it served and the homes it equipped. Think of hard, regular work habits and a less hurried life; think of order in the home; think of homespun wit and humor; think of laying down your possessions for the Lord; think of simplifying.

A Thumbnail History

Georgia, last of the original thirteen colonies, was founded in 1733, a scant forty-three years before the Declaration of Independence from England. The settled portion of colonial Georgia consisted of the tidewater area along the coast and a narrow strip west of the Savannah River. Savannah and Augusta were but small towns. At the close of the Revolutionary War, settlers from the Carolinas and Virginia poured into eastern Georgia. By 1800 the population of the state was 162,101 and the settled portion covered approximately one-third of the present state, extending from the Savannah River to the Oconee River and its western tributaries. Savannah had a population of 5,166 and Augusta 2,476. They were the principal trading centers.

As the new century began, Georgia ceded to the United States its lands granted under colonial charter that today comprise Alabama and Mississippi, and new territories to the west were opened for settlement. Many earlier settlers moved on and many more came into the state. Georgia was a stepping-stone to the West. By 1838 the Creek and Cherokee nations had ceded all of their Georgia lands to the state, the Indians had been removed, and the boundaries of the state were substantially as they are today. By 1850 the population was 906,185 and all of the principal modern cities had been founded. The population of Savannah was 15,312, Augusta 11,753, and Atlanta 2,572; but the bulk of the population continued to live on farms. Georgia at midcentury crested in its economic and cultural development in comparison with other states of the nation.

By 1900 the population of Georgia was 2,216,331; Savannah, 54,244; and Atlanta, 89,872. Atlanta, a railroad hub, had burgeoned into the commercial, as well as political, capital of the state and had much in common with northern cities such as Chicago and Cincinnati. Savannah had insulated itself from the rest of the state. Throughout the nineteenth century, it had looked to Europe or the great seaboard cities of America for its style and sustenance. These two urban areas were atypical of the bulk of Georgia, however. At century's end 85 percent of the people of the state still lived on farms or in small towns.

The event of the century was, of course, Sherman's "March to the Sea" in 1864. The effects of military invasion, defeat, willful destruction of the built environment in dimensions never before or since experienced by any American state, and the sudden collapse of the system of slavery were profound and long lasting for both whites and blacks. Despite the fact that the population continued to increase after the Civil War, Georgia regressed in many ways. A sharecropper system of tenant farming, perhaps as pernicious as slavery, developed to replace the antebellum slave system of agricultural labor. Mill towns for the textile industrialization of the "New South" were beginning to spring up throughout Piedmont Georgia in the late nineteenth century. The cheap labor afforded by a prostrate people was attractive to capitalists in both North and South and was exploited. Poverty, ignorance, bitterness, and despair were commonplace. Georgia and other states of the deep South could not keep pace with the rest of America.

The People

Nineteenth-century Georgians were predominantly of British or African descent. Eighteenth-century colonial settlers included Moravians, Salzburgers, and Jews, but these elements of the population either emigrated or insulated themselves in enclaves in or near Savannah. The Great Wagon Road from Pennsylvania had its southern terminus at Augusta, and in the last half of the eighteenth century large groups of Scotch-Irish, English, and Welsh settlers migrated from the older states into the Georgia up-country. A few Germans accompanied them, but most Germans by the time they reached Georgia were second-generation, thoroughly assimilated Americans. Except for the Salzburger settlements near Savannah, there were no German-speaking Georgia communities.

As the western two-thirds of the present state was opened to settlement after Creek and Cherokee land cessions in the early nineteenth century, people moved in from the eastern part of Georgia, South Carolina, North Carolina, and Virginia. Surprising numbers from northern states came in to assume influential roles in education, industry, commerce, journalism, and agriculture. The 1850 and 1860 censuses show that Georgia had two or three times as many persons of northern birth as either of the Carolinas.[2]

Agriculture was the principal occupation of the people of Georgia in the nineteenth century. By 1800 cotton was beginning to replace tobacco as the principal staple crop of the up-country, and for the rest of the century it remained "King." Rice was produced in the tidewater Atlantic counties throughout the century but production declined dramatically after the Civil War. Subsistence farming predominated in the mountainous sections of northern Georgia, in the upper Piedmont, and in many sections of the coastal plain where poorer soils would not support a large plantation economy. According to Mills B. Lane IV:

Immense plantations were not the mainstay of Georgia agriculture before or after the Civil War, despite the moonlight and magnolia mythology which has since obscured the plain realities of Southern life. . . . The portrait of an average Georgia "planter" which emerges . . . is a small proprietor, who works alongside his dozen slaves on his hundred acres of land and shares with them a simple, strong and rather difficult life.[3]

Georgia did have some large plantations, however, in the "plantation belt" across middle Georgia straddling the fall line, down the western portion of the Coastal Plain, and in the tidewater coastal counties. Owners of these large plantations were frequently absentee planters living in nearby towns such as Sparta, Madison, LaGrange, or Columbus and employing white overseers to supervise their slaves.

A few contemporary descriptions of the character of Georgia people are enlightening. George G. Smith Jr. said of Georgians of the antebellum period:

The people were generally plain and generally with but little education, but they were men of sturdy character. There was now and then a home of elegance, but mostly the homes were simple. Industry and prudence were the chief virtues next to piety. There was no want in all the land.[4]

Near the end of the century William Peterfield Trent, a Virginian, for many years professor of English Literature at Columbia University, in an essay characterizing people of the several southern states wrote of Georgians:

[The Georgian] has long been called the Southern Yankee. . . . Though possessed of a strong, clear intellect, he is more particularly a man of five senses, of which he makes as good use as he can. He may not always taste the sweetness or see the light of the highest civilization, but he has a good healthy appetite for life. In fine, the Georgian is the Southerner of all others who comes nearest to being a normal American. There are, to be sure, varieties of Georgians, and different phases of civilization are represented in different sections of the state, but the features of character that make for uniformity are more numerous and important than those that make for divergence. The various elements that compose the population—original settlers, incomers from Virginia and the two Carolinas—seem to have been fused, save perhaps on the coast about Savannah, rather than to have preserved their individuality, and the result is the typical Georgian, energetic, shrewd, thrifty, brave, religious, patriotic, tending in the extremes of society to become narrow and hard, or self-assertive and pushing.[5]

In common with people of all predominantly agricultural states in America, Georgians were conservative. Traditional values and methods prevailed. Conservative taste in home furnishings and attire surely followed. Thomas E. Watson recalled his grandfather's antebellum farm in McDuffie County near Augusta:

Everything was regular, everything was systematic. A man of settled, thrifty habits, my grandfather had drilled his slaves to his orderly methods and thus the old routine went on from year to year. The same slaves allotted to the same tasks, working the same fields with the same tools, raising the same crops in the same way, with never a material change from year to year, naturally gave to the plantation the character of a vast machine, well oiled, well managed, and doing its work without noise or friction—unhasting yet unresting, like some steady law of nature.[6]

Georgians were hard workers despite many comments to the contrary by travelers whose observations were generally limited to stagecoach stops or railroad stations and who generally had a preconceived notion that the slave system encouraged indolence in both races. Rebecca Latimer Felton speaks of her grandmother in the 1840s:

The mother of eleven children, all reaching maturity, except two that lived to eleven and twelve years, her industry, her management and her executive ability in caring for and carrying on her household affairs are still wonderful memories, and have continually lingered with me as examples in the progress of my own extended life. . . . It was grandmother's skill as a home-maker, with an eye single to her domestic duties and diligent attention to home economies, that impressed me most in that early time of my life when I trotted around after her as she went from the dwelling to the garden, and to the milk dairy, to the poultry house, to the loom house, to the big meat house, where rations were issued once a day, and to the flour and meal house where there was always a super abundance of supplies for white and colored.[7]

Three noteworthy factors influencing the daily lives and tastes of Georgians and possibly contributing to their furniture preferences should be mentioned. The first was religion. Georgia was in the heart of the "Bible Belt." The Baptist, Methodist, and Presbyterian churches were particularly influential. They afforded social intercourse among neighbors at camp meetings, revivals, and regular Sabbath services. The clergy of Georgia was particularly strong in the nineteenth century. The people, both black and white, were devout and God-fearing as evidenced by their speeches, writings, and songs. Surely the farmers of northeast Georgia felt prouder of their unpretentious homes after listening to the words of Henry W. Grady, champion of the "New South," at an old-fashioned barbecue in Elberton in June 1889:

Surely here — here in the homes of the people is lodged the ark of the covenant of my country. Here is its majesty and its strength. Here the beginning of its power and the end of its responsibility. . . . Let us honor God in our homes — anchor them close to His love; build His altars above our hearthstones, uphold them in the set and simple faith of our fathers and crown them with the Bible — that book of books in which all the ways of life are made straight and the mystery of death is made plain. The home is the source of our national life.[8]

A second important ingredient in Georgia life was humor. In the nineteenth century, Georgia's most learned judges and lawyers injected humor into the courtrooms. Backwoodsmen, housewives, even the clergy enjoyed a good joke and the dry humor of sly innuendo in conversation. Augustus Baldwin Longstreet started a literary genre now known as the "Humor of the Old Southwest" with the publication in Augusta in 1835 of *Georgia Scenes,* sketches of life in Georgia in the first fifty years of the republic. William Tappan Thompson, Francis James Robinson, Richard Malcolm

Johnston, Charles H. Smith (Bill Arp), Joseph Addison Turner, and Joel Chandler Harris, to name other Georgia humorists, followed suit. Georgia was the "cradle of Southern humor."[9] The literary genre culminated with the work of Samuel L. Clemens (Mark Twain) of Missouri, but the direct influence of these writers is seen on such twentieth-century giants as Erskine Caldwell and Flannery O'Connor of Georgia.

A third factor more prevalent in Georgia than in most states in those days was democracy. As John Donald Wade has suggested, the great barrier between black and white people tended to put all men and women of the same race on equal social footing.[10] Georgia in the nineteenth century was too young to have developed an aristocracy. To be sure, class structure based on wealth and family existed, but the relationship between classes was always open and unstrained. Joel Chandler Harris, creator of the world-famous Uncle Remus stories, was born out of wedlock in the small middle Georgia village of Eatonton in 1848, a fact well known to everyone in town. He said:

. . . [My] lot was cast among the most democratic people the world has ever seen, and in a section where . . . the ideals of character and conduct are held in higher esteem than wealth or ancient lineage.[11]

Possibly this democratic spirit compelled even the wealthiest Georgians to spurn elaboration. At the 1839 funeral of Augustin S. Clayton of Athens, a man of means, large numbers of people gathered to pay their last respects to the great lawyer and judge. An English traveler commented:

The coffin was made of oak and quite plain, there being neither handles, escutcheon, gilt or silver nails, covering or pall of any description, but everything was characterized by the extremest simplicity.[12]

Later in the century James Monroe Smith of Oglethorpe County became one of the most successful planters in the South, a multimillionaire who built a railroad to connect his farm empire, "Smithonia," to existing rail lines. He was described in 1900:

He wears plain loosely fitting garments, is absolutely without ostentation, and his home without and within is as plain and simple and as free from all luxuries as almost any farmer's in the land.[13]

Nineteenth-century Georgians, the great bulk of them, both black and white, worked hard and lived simply. They surrounded themselves with children. They were deeply religious. Humor was a part of their lives. They were democratic. They were, in the main, a plain-style people living in plain-style houses equipped with plain-style furniture.

The Houses

Georgians did not enter the nineteenth century housed in grand mansions. As the eighteenth century drew to a close, Georgia had approximately 15,800 houses. The 1798 nationwide tax survey lists only 3,461 valued at more than $100. Only four were valued at more than $6,000; three of these were in or near Augusta in Richmond County and the other was in adjoining Burke County. Savannah and Chatham County had no houses valued over $3,000; however, 236 out of the state's total of 391 houses valued from $1,000 to $3,000 were in Chatham County and 92.2 percent of that county's white males 26 years or older were housed in dwellings valued at more than $100. In 1800 the frontier county of Hancock had 1,375 white males age 26 and over—more than any other county in the state—but only 12.4 percent lived in houses appraised at more than $99.[14] Many of the settlers moving into the rich agricultural lands of middle and south Georgia early in the nineteenth century knew full well their sojourn would be short and they would be moving westward again in a few years.

Even by the 1840s when all corners of the state were settled and there was a measure of prosperity, it does not appear that Georgians attached as much importance to their housing as did northerners. A few excerpts from the letters of New Hampshire schoolteacher Emily Burke concerning various sections of Georgia in 1840–41 afford insight:

In answer to the question "Why the planters have no better dwellings" I would reply that they are under the necessity of changing their places of residence so often on account of the soil, which in a few years becomes barren, owing to the manner in which it is cultivated. If they invested much property in buildings they would be obliged to make great pecuniary sacrifices. Therefore they have but little property that is not movable.

A Northerner, who is accustomed to judge a farmer's property by his buildings, would suppose that many of great wealth [in Georgia] were poor men, their buildings are so miserable. The manner of estimating a planter's pecuniary circumstances is by the number of his slaves.

In building their houses they change little, if any more, from one generation to another than the robins do who build their nests now just as the first robin did—in the Garden of Eden.[15]

In the first half of the nineteenth century nearly all houses were of wood. A majority were of log construction. Here and there, principally in Savannah and the larger towns, brick or stone houses were built, but they were the exception. These wooden houses ranged from the one-room log cabin to the classic revival columned mansion. As fortunes were accumulated by some in agriculture, commerce, or the professions, more and more refinements in domestic architecture appeared. The great body of housing remained simple, however. Four typical vernacular Georgia favorites in the first half of the century were (1) the double-pen dogtrot log house with sleeping loft, (2) the one-story frame house with two front rooms and loft above and two shed rooms at the back, (3) the two-story frame house with two bedrooms over two principal downstairs rooms and with two shed rooms at the back, and (4) the four-room over four-room Greek Revival mansion. The dogtrot house had an open breezeway. Most of the other houses had a central hall or, lacking this, had front and back doors aligned to allow a breeze through the center of the house. Most had a veranda on one side at least to shade the rooms. Most were on piers from one to five feet above the ground to allow air circulation under the house. Most had high ceilings to allow the hotter air to rise above head height. Many had windows on at least two sides of every room, particularly every bedroom. Many had louvered shutters to allow free air passage while shading the windows. Most had outside chimneys. Many had detached kitchens and, of course, detached necessary houses. There were few cellars and few central chimneys. There were few closets and no bathrooms. Houses were sited to take advantage of shade trees and prevailing breezes. Ventilation and air circulation in a Georgia house were as important as heat retention in a New England house.

In the 1850s, as Georgia reached economic parity with many other states, more elaborate houses were constructed, particularly in the cities. Several dozen grand homes in the Italianate or Gothic Revival styles made their appearance. Perhaps the most opulent antebellum Georgia house was the William B. Johnston mansion, now known as the Hay House, in Macon. It actually had a bathroom with running water. A three-story, twenty-four-room, brick Italianate home designed by New York architect James B. Ayres, it was far ahead of its time in many ways. These homes were, however, alien to local taste and inclination, which remained conservative and traditional. If embellishments were desired to enhance status, most Georgians preferred to use patterns established by Greece or Rome and used by Washington, Jefferson, or Jackson.

In the 1860s the Civil War and Reconstruction changed patterns of life and thought. Georgia lost much housing through wanton and needless destruction by both northerners and southerners. For the rest of the century the more eclectic Victorian styles of housing became dominant in town and country. Except in Savannah, where brick row-houses had gained popularity as the century advanced, detached frame houses with air space on all sides remained predominant. Traditional southern architectural elements designed to make living more comfortable in a hot and humid climate continued to be incorporated. Vernacular houses such as dogtrot log houses continued to be built through the end of the century.

The Furniture

Most furniture forms used in Georgia in the nineteenth century were used throughout the United States. No exclusively Georgia forms are known, although several that were more frequently used in the South than in the North were found here. These include the huntboard, the lazy Susan table, the cellarette, the sugar chest, and the hide-bottomed slat-back chair.

Styles and fashions of much earlier vintage persisted in Georgia furniture throughout the century. Accordingly, it is frequently impossible to date a piece by style alone with any degree of accuracy. This lag resulted from (1) the normal delay in newer designs reaching most rural Georgia craftsmen from the style centers of the world, (2) the natural reluctance of Georgia craftsmen to adopt and utilize newer designs for their products, and, more importantly, (3) the reluctance of a conservative consuming public to accept and purchase furniture to which it was unaccustomed. Georgians liked what they had grown up with.

From examination of the entire corpus of furniture submitted for the exhibition, a few generalities may be drawn. Simple pieces without ornamentation or elaboration predominate. Little carving was used. Where inlay was used it was usually geometric and spare. Painted furniture was usually in monochrome earthy colors—brick red, brown, dark blue, green, black, or ochre. Grained pieces were also in earthy colors. If inlay was simulated on a grained piece, it too was simple. Verticality is a frequent quality in these pieces. Many sideboards, tables, desks, and bedposts are taller than their northern counterparts, possibly to better fit the high-ceilinged rooms of nineteenth-century Georgia. Many pieces have long legs, probably to elevate the case or table top to allow free air circulation. Much of the furniture is idiosyncratic. No two huntboards exactly alike were found in the survey. The furniture was designed to fit the houses and to work for the people who used it.

Nineteenth-century nomenclature for many forms of furniture was different from that now in general use. Inventories, sale records, advertisements in newspapers, wills, letters, and conversations with older Georgians reveal this. Chests of drawers were usually, though not always, termed "bureaus." The form we now call a "blanket chest" was usually termed a "chest" and by many it was pronounced "chist." Some old-timers still refer to it as a "quilt chest." The tall sideboard with long legs and shallow case which in this century has become known as a "huntboard" was called a "slab" or simply a "sideboard." No entries of huntboards were found on nineteenth-century inventories. Numerous entries of slabs appear on inventories throughout all parts of Georgia. In one estate record, the inventory included a single sideboard, value $4, but did not list a slab; when the sale occurred shortly thereafter, no sideboard was listed, but one slab was sold for $3. Inventory entries such as "slab (sideboard)" and "slab or sideboard" indicate that the names were synonymous; and numerous entries of "slab and contents," "slab and bottles," "slab and glassware," and "slab and crockeryware" suggest that the form frequently had drawers or cupboard space. Of course, a tall, long table may also have been classed as a slab. Corner cupboards were called "three-cornered cupboards" or simply "cupboards" or sometimes "safes." Pembroke tables were frequently "folding tables." Lazy Susans were "turn-top tables" or "round tables." The term "cellarette" was not found on any Georgia inventory examined; however, entries of stands, boxes, cases, or chests preceded by words such as liquor, whiskey, gin, wine, cordial, brandy, spirit, or refreshment do occur. The form was not too common. Sugar chests, often called "sugar boxes," and occasionally "sugar cellars" or "sugar stands," appeared in inventories, although few have survived. An interesting 1803 inventory entry in Hancock County refers to a "Japand [*sic*] sugar chest."

Furniture may be grouped functionally into furniture for sleeping (bedsteads, cradles, cribs); furniture for sitting (benches, stools, sofas, chairs); furniture related to food and drink (certain tables, liquor stands, sugar chests, sideboards, slabs, safes, cupboards); furniture related to textiles (chests, bureaus, linen presses, wardrobes); furniture related to reading, writing, or record keeping (desks, bookcases, some tables); multipurpose tables and small stands (candle stands, washstands, various other tables); and accessory furniture (clocks, looking glasses, picture frames). Some pieces serve in more than one capacity.

Many accessory furniture items used in Georgia were not made in Georgia. Clocks are an example. Although the census records reveal the presence of clockmakers in Georgia, no nineteenth-century Georgia-made clocks were found in this study. New England clocks were a principal stock item for the Yankee peddler of the early years of the century in the South. In 1812 Georgia enacted a peddler's license law to exact a little revenue from the numerous northern itinerants coming into the developing areas. However, in the 1812 statute, to encourage local enterprise, wares manufactured in Georgia could be sold by peddlers without necessity for procurement of this license.[16] As the license fees were increased subsequently, items manufactured in Georgia continued to be exempt. By 1831 this license fee became a serious impediment to the New England peddlers. That year the fee was increased to $2,000 for each county in which a horse-drawn wagon operated, with a fine on violation of not less than $3,000 nor more than $10,000.[17] To counter this confiscatory license, several Connecticut clock manufacturers moved to Georgia, where they would assemble northern clockworks in northern-made cases, gluing thereon their own "Manufactured in Georgia" labels. Numerous surviving mantel clocks of the 1830s and 1840s bear the labels "Dyer, Wadsworth & Co., Augusta, Georgia," and "Davis & Barber, Greenesborough, Ga." They were peddled all over this state. Sometimes peddlers themselves affixed their own "Georgia-made" labels to northern-made clocks.[18]

In addition to clocks, many looking-glasses appear on Georgia inventories. Undoubtedly, some frames were fashioned by cabinetmakers for looking-glasses, but no mirror glass was manufactured in Georgia until the last of the nineteenth century. Georgia woodworkers definitely made picture frames.

The woods used in Georgia furniture in the nineteenth century are surprising in many respects. Well before the advent of railroads, woods from the West Indies and northeastern states were shipped into Savannah and other ports and thence transported overland or up the rivers to fall-line towns and even farther. Ellis, Shotwell & Co. advertised in Macon in 1826, three years after the city's founding:

MAHOGANY. Just received by the American Eagle a quantity of Mahogany, consisting of plank, boards, shaded and crotch veneers. . . .[19]

Thomas W. Dutton advertised in Columbus five years after its founding that he would make and keep constantly on hand a general assortment of cabinet furniture "made of mahogany, walnut, birch, cherry and pine."[20] The next year in Columbus E. Sigourney Norton, auctioneer, advertised a sale including a "large lot of Mahogany and Maple Veneirs [*sic*], King's Curled maple, Black Walnut, Cherry, and Poplar Lumber for Cabinet making."[21] In Athens, Samuel Hammond announced in 1845:

that he has laid in a handsome assortment of TIMBER, consisting of mahogany, plain and curled maple, plain and crotch walnut, poplar and birch, which he will work up to order, at very reduced prices.[22]

Some primary woods regularly used for cabinetwork—black walnut (*Juglans nigra* L.), black cherry (*Prunus serotina* Ehrh.), red or soft maple (*Acer rubrum* L.), and red or river birch (*Betula nigra* L.)—are native to Georgia and generally distributed throughout the state. Yellow birch (*Betula lutea* Michx.), a favorite furniture wood in New England, grows in this state only on high mountains in northern Georgia. Black birch (*Betula lenta* L.), another New England favorite, grows only in the mountains and on the banks of rivers down into the upper Piedmont.

The sugar or rock maple (*Acer saccharum* Marsh.), another hard, strong, close-grained wood, also occurs in Georgia only in the northern counties. Planks of these last three species could also have been shipped into middle and south Georgia from more northern states just as mahogany (*Swietenia* spp. Jacq.) was shipped in from the West Indies. Microscopic wood analysis revealed a surprisingly large number of pieces of birch furniture from the mountain and Piedmont sections of Georgia. The birch wood was identified as to genus (i.e., *Betula*), but it was not possible to determine the exact species of birch (i.e., *nigra, lutea,* or *lenta*) from which the pieces were made.

The red bay (*Persea borbonia* L.) is native to the coastal plain of Georgia and the lower Piedmont. Red bay, greatly prized for cabinet work, was frequently mentioned in furniture advertisements in Georgia newspapers, but little furniture of red bay seems to have survived. The chinaberry or Pride of India (*Melia azedarach* L.) was planted as an ornamental in many parts of the South and spread throughout Georgia in the nineteenth century. Its wood was used in cabinetmaking and was said to have had insect repellent qualities. *The Albany Patriot*, Albany, Georgia, February 16, 1848, gives an account of rice stored, free from insects for more than 20 years, in a desk made from the Pride of India tree, and asks:

Will not our bedstead makers take a hint from this suggestion and rid the world of sleeping mankind from the annoyance of bedbugs and scalding ablutions for their destruction?

A number of beds made from this wood survive and are still in use in Georgia. Sweet gum (*Liquidambar styraciflua* L.), beech (*Fagus grandifolia* Ehrh.), white ash (*Fraxinus americana* L.), the oaks (*Quercus* spp. [Tourn.] L.) and the hickories (*Carya* spp. Nutt.) occur commonly throughout the state. Ash, hickory, and white oak were particular favorites of Georgia chairmakers. Based on the surviving examples of furniture it would appear that black walnut was the favorite hardwood for Georgia cabinetmakers. It is interesting that a number of advertisements in the mid-nineteenth century referred to furniture of "Georgia walnut," implying that the wood used in these pieces was definitely of local origin.[23]

The favorite softwoods in Georgia were the yellow pines and yellow poplar. Both of these were frequently used as primary woods in Georgia furniture and even more frequently as secondary woods. Sometimes pine and poplar were used in combination. The yellow pines having the hardest, heaviest, strongest, most durable, most resinous wood are the longleaf pine (*Pinus palustris* Mill.) found throughout the coastal plain, lower Piedmont, and nearly to the Tennessee line in the westernmost counties; the slash pine (*Pinus elliottii* Engelm.) of the lower coastal plain; and the short-leaf pine (*Pinus echinata* Mill.) growing throughout most of the state. The wood of the quick-growing loblolly or oldfield pine (*Pinus taeda* L.) is weak, brittle, coarse-grained, and not durable. Nevertheless, its wood was frequently used in furniture making. The tree is abundant throughout most of the state. Another yellow pine, the pond pine (*Pinus serotina* Dougl.) is found in the lower coastal plain, but not commonly. It was sometimes used in cabinetmaking because its wood is very heavy, resinous, and frequently has a contorted grain. The yellow poplar or tulip tree (*Liriodendron tulipifera* L.) grows abundantly throughout Georgia. Its wood is light, soft, brittle, and not strong, but is easily worked or turned and, accordingly, was frequently used. The cucumber tree (*Magnolia acuminata* L.) and the Atlantic White Cedar (*Chamaecyparis thyoides* [L.] B.S.P.) have limited ranges in Georgia but were sometimes used in furniture. Both were utilized in cabinetmaking where they could be obtained. The bald cypress (*Taxodium distichum* [L.] Rich.) grows throughout the coastal plain. The white pine (*Pinus strobus* L.) grows in Georgia only in the mountains, the Ridge and Valley province, and the upper edge of the Piedmont, but its wood was imported to Savannah from New England throughout the nineteenth century. Both of these trees have soft, easily worked wood. Cypress wood is very durable. Chestnut (*Castanea dentata* [Marsh.] Borkh.) formerly occurred in the mountain areas and the upper Piedmont and was sometimes used as a secondary wood in those areas. Dogwood (*Cornus florida* L.) and American holly (*Ilex opaca* Ait.) grow throughout Georgia. Both have a light-colored, close-grained wood that was used for inlay in fine cabinetry. Possibly, some of the other hollies of the coastal plain, such as Yaupon (*Ilex vomitoria* Ait.), which has a very hard, close-grained, nearly white wood, were used for inlay.[24]

Obtaining hardware for furniture in Georgia was sometimes a problem in the nineteenth century. Blacksmiths were available to forge nails, staples, hooks, and hasps; but locks, hinges, pulls, bails, and plates were usually imported from England or the northern states. Makers could purchase hardware and paints at stores in the trading centers. In 1831, John H. Oldershaw of Macon, for example, ran an advertisement announcing that he was "connected with an establishment in New York,"[25] and a few years later offered among other items:

all his stock of furniture and materials consisting of Mahogany Boards, Planks and Venniers [*sic*], Glue, Varnish, Lookin-Glass [*sic*] Plates, a good assortment of hard Ware, Glass Knobs, Locks, Patent Joints, Springs for Sofas and Chairs, Work Benches, Tools, Cramps [*sic*], Hand Screws, Mahogany Table Legs, Carved Pillars, Hair Cloth, Silk Plush and a variety of articles suitable for manufacturing.[26]

Hall & Moses, a hardware store in Columbus, advertised:

Have just received an assortment of Veneering, together with a splendid assortment of Cabinet Hardware.[27]

Marble-topped furniture was advertised at least as early as 1842 in Madison, Georgia.[28] Thereafter, marble works sprang up. In Columbus J. H. Madden and P. Adams announced:

New marble yard—will include making marble [or granite] table tops.[29]

In 1860, S. B. Oatman made at his Marble Works in Atlanta "center table, pier tables, and bureau tops."[30] Marble was being quarried in Cass, Cherokee, and Gilmer counties by 1849.[31]

The Makers

The craftsmen who fashioned handmade furniture in nineteenth-century Georgia were legion. Settlers frequently made a few essential pieces such as beds and benches for their families, especially in the first half of the century. At midcentury, many Georgians still made their own furniture. The following entries in the diary of David Thurman chronicle the manufacture of a table by one early Atlantan, a gunsmith by trade:

Fri., September 13, 1850	Turned a set table legs to carry home with me
Wed., September 25, 1850	Bought a piece of walnut lumber from Mr. Rushton paid 40 cents
Sat., September 28, 1850	Went to I.O. & P.E. McDaniels bought one quart of varnish[32]

Reading between the lines, we see that David Thurman turned the legs on a lathe at a turner's shop near his home, made the table top and skirt of walnut at his home, and had the table ready for varnishing in two weeks' time.

Later in the century shop-built or "store-bought" furniture was more readily available, but homemade furniture was still being produced. On February 3, 1890, Luther Hopkins, working for a railroad in Atlanta, wrote to his father:

Pa, would you let me have some poplar lumber enough to make me a safe, wardrobe and table? If so, I would like to come home in time to build them before you want us to begin the cleaner work.[33]

Frequently the part-time furniture maker became very proficient. William Simpson (1778–1838) of Wilkes County, Georgia, made good furniture for himself and his close friends.[34] He was not a cabinetmaker as such. He was a planter, a landowner, and a prosperous and influential citizen.[35]

Full-time furniture makers plied their trade in Georgia just as in all other states. Usually persons earning their livelihood in a furniture-making craft would classify themselves as cabinetmakers or chairmakers. These craftsmen moved into towns shortly after initial settlement. New towns needed carpenters and furniture makers. Athens was founded in 1801 and Warham Easley, a cabinetmaker, had one of the first houses there. Dr. Henry Hull mentions this home in his earliest recollections of the town in 1803.[36] "Captain" Easley advertised in 1808:

PLANK Wanting to purchase several hundred feet of Birch, Walnut or Cherry Plank for which a liberal price will be given. Furniture can be had of any kind on the shortest notice, by applying to Warham Easley of Athens.[37]

Atlanta was a village called Marthasville in 1845 when William Whitaker, a native of Buncombe County, North Carolina, opened his cabinet and coffin shop at the corner of Walton and Spring Streets in what is now downtown Atlanta, His was the first such shop in Atlanta.[38]

Sometimes the cabinetmakers preceded white settlement. The following ad appeared in New Echota in northwest Georgia ten years before the removal of the Cherokees to Oklahoma:

J S W White — House Builder and Cabinet Maker from the City of New York, respectfully informs the Cherokee Nation that he intends carrying on the business of House Building and Cabinet Making in a manner superior to any that has been done & in the most fashionable manner. . . . N.B. He will take apprentices in the above business. Any native who will come with good recommendation, and of steady habits will be received and taught in the above business. For further information apply to Messrs. David Vann and John Ridge.[39]

Cabinetmakers came to Georgia from states to the east and north and from Europe. Accordingly, a melange of stylistic influences was felt. In 97 selected Georgia counties in the 1850 census, 290 persons listed their occupation as cabinetmaker, cabinetworker, joiner, turner, bedmaker, or chairmaker. Of the 290 total, 60 were chairmakers. Only 1 of the 290 was a woman, Elizabeth Reynolds of DeKalb County, and only one was black, Robert Richards of Chatham County. Of the total, 87 were born in Georgia or gave no state of birth, 56 were from South Carolina, 42 from North Carolina, 13 from Tennessee, 12 from Virginia or Maryland, 24 from northeastern Atlantic coast states, and 1 from Florida. Thirty were born in Germany, 19 in the British Isles, and 5 in other European countries. One was from Santo Domingo. None were natives of states to the west of Georgia. Generally, the foreign-born craftsmen established their shops in the larger towns. For example, of the 30 German-born furniture makers in the 1850 census list, 22 lived in Savannah, Augusta, Macon, or Columbus, the largest cities. Southern-born craftsmen seemed to prefer the smaller towns and villages.

Many of the furniture makers settled permanently in one location, but a goodly percentage moved their cabinet shops from time to time. A number advertised their shops for sale, as did William Powers in 1836:

To Cabinet Makers—Thomaston Cabinet Warehouse for Sale—The subscriber being desirous of leaving this part of the country, offers for sale the well known stand in the town of Thomaston, including shop, lot, benches, lathe, lumber house, etc. etc. with every convenience for carrying on the above business. For further particulars enquire of the subscriber in Thomaston. William Powers. January 28. 1836.[40]

Some of the furniture makers were itinerant. Joseph Lash advertised as follows:

Joseph Lash (Morgan, Ga.) offers services in making or repairing any kind of cabinet work—can make new materials whenever lumber can be procured at "your own house & at your own notion."[41]

Furniture makers who found themselves confined to the state penitentiary in Milledgeville were not idle while serving time. Between 1817 and 1868, 17 cabinetmakers and 10 chairmakers or turners were listed in the Register of Convicts at the state penitentiary. The inmates on November 1, 1826, included four shop joiners, two cabinetmakers, two turners, and one Windsor chairmaker.[42] Products of their labor were used in state facilities and were also sold to the public. A typical newspaper notice reads:

Penitentiary, Milledgeville. We have for sale: tables, slabs, washstands and chests, spinning wheels, clocks, reels, and looms, bedsteads, cradles, cribs and Windsor chairs.[43]

Describing the state penitentiary in Milledgeville, which she visited on her southern tour in 1831, Mrs. Anne Royall wrote:

The Prison is the best kept, and best regulated of any State Prison this side of Boston. . . . All the convicts are kept at work. . . . Those who have trades work at them, and all seem to be happy, cheerful and comfortable. I saw some very neat stage coaches manufactured here, and carriages of every kind are neatly finished, and ready for the road. The painting is extremely well done. The shops are perfect warehouses. . . . I never saw more industrious, modest, or better-behaved people than in this prison.[44]

The apprentice system of teaching and learning was utilized throughout the century, though not in as formal and rigid a manner as practiced in the eighteenth century. Jeremiah Burdine of Elbert County advertised in the straightforward Georgia way in the early years of the nineteenth century:

Wanted, an apprentice to the joining and cabinet making business. Jeremiah Burdine.[45]

The 1860 census lists among others John Engle, age seventeen, as bound to a cabinetmaker in Augusta, an urban setting, and Lexington Maund, age twenty-one, as an apprentice cabinetmaker in Talbot County, in rural, west-central Georgia. In 1813 Charles Martin Gray was bound out at the age of thirteen to J. Pew, maker of fancy and Windsor chairs in Augusta. The War of 1812 had broken out and young Gray enlisted in a volunteer company to march in the defense of Savannah. Pew was enraged and

overtaking him at the Oglethorpe Barracks, reclaimed him as his property and carried him back dejected and crest-fallen to Augusta, where he remained busily plying his trade, until his master, about a year afterwards, having failed in business, [set him] at large, and permitted [him] to control his own actions.[46]

Undoubtedly the role of the black craftsmen in furniture manufacture in Georgia before and after emancipation was important. A number of pieces of furniture surveyed carried a strong family tradition of having been slave-made. Documentation is difficult, and more research is required in this area.

No exhaustive or comprehensive study of all of the nineteenth-century cabinetmakers of Georgia has been undertaken. For the purposes of this exhibition a list of makers has been compiled from selected sources and is included in the catalog in the hope that the names will encourage further investigation. A few notes follow on some of the known makers whose work has been tentatively identified.

Joseph Morgan, 1800–1854, Enoch Morgan, 1804–43, and Lawrence Sterne Morgan, 1806–62, natives of Brimfield, Massachusetts, settled in Decatur, DeKalb County, Georgia, in 1832. Joseph married Jane Kirkpatrick, daughter of James H. Kirkpatrick, a native of Ireland, who after immigrating to America eventually settled in DeKalb County in 1827. The community of Kirkwood was named for him. Enoch never married. Lawrence Sterne married Martha Jane McNeill, daughter of Colonel James McNeill, a soldier of the Revolutionary War, who settled in DeKalb County in 1830, establishing a saddlery shop.[47] In 1844 when the first Masonic Lodge for Decatur was established, Joseph and Lawrence Sterne Morgan made, painted, and sold to Pythagoras Lodge a lecture stand, three light stands, an altar, a ballot box, three squares, three trowels, and one rule, all for $46.00.[48] At the 1849 Fair of the Southern Central Agricultural Society held at Stone Mountain, the Morgans exhibited the only furniture to win a premium:

The Cottage and Walnut Chairs, made by J. & L. Morgan, of Decatur, are excellent specimens of their kind,—good and strong . . . $2.00.[49]

The following year Joseph Morgan was awarded another premium by the Society with the Report of the Committee on Manufactured Articles and Machinery citing:

No. 23 & 24 were specimens of Native Walnut Furniture—a Bedstead and Dressing Bureau,—made by J. Morgan of Decatur, which in style and finish would be creditable to the best warehouse of the city of New York. We award to him a premium of $10.00.[50]

After the death of Joseph in 1854, Lawrence Sterne went into business with William N. Kirkpatrick, a brother of Joseph's wife. The firm of Morgan, Kirkpatrick & Co. advertised in Atlanta in 1857 that they had opened "a new Ware-room on Peach Tree Street," had enlarged their manufacturing shops at Decatur, and could supply:

Morgan's original Cottage Chairs, Hindley's Patent Bedstead, together with all articles of Cabinet Ware, of their own manufacture in any quantity desired.[51]

Shortly thereafter essentially the same advertisement appeared under the name of William N. Kirkpatrick in a Rome, Georgia, newspaper.[52]

Caleb T. Shaw was another Massachusetts cabinetmaker who migrated to Georgia. Shaw was born in Massachusetts in about 1804. By 1850 he had settled in Franklin County, Georgia, near the Habersham County line. Here he lived through the 1850s, being listed as a mechanic in the 1850 census and as a cabinetmaker in the 1860 census. He made furniture for Devereaux Jarrett of Traveler's Rest near Toccoa in present Stephens County and for the Jarrett sons and daughter whose homes were nearby.[53] The furniture attributed to him by Jarrett descendants is invariably skillfully made.

A cabinetmaker known only by his surname, Vitenger, was brought in by Colonel James Caldwell Sproull to build the furniture for "Valley View," a brick Greek Revival house built circa 1850 in the Etowah River Valley of Bartow County, Georgia. Colonel Sproull's daughter, Rebecca Sproull Fouché (1844–1918), recalled in 1912:

The heavy furniture in the house was made by Mr. Vitenger (we called it Witey), a German cabinet maker Father brought here for the purpose. He had a bedroom, a workshop, a place to keep and dry his lumber, and always a seat at our table. Sister and I resented that sometimes, especially when we had company, for truly he was far from ornamental. . . . So for years Mr. Witey lived with us free of charge, making furniture for many of our neighbors. When we "refugeed" Father left everything in his care to do the best he could for us.

General Scofield, U.S.A., had his headquarters in the house for three months—his officers upstairs and his horses in the parlors, where they tore out the keyboard and strings and used Mother's piano to feed horses in. It seems that our sharp-shooters pestered them so they had to bring the horses inside. Well it didn't take long to get all the lighter pieces of furniture, books, etc., to Kingston to ship North, and here is where Father's bread cast on the waters came in.

Mr. Witey had never been naturalized, and so appealed to General Rozencrantz, (likewise a German), for protection of his property. He had the furniture returned and Sister and I own it to this day.

No record of Vitenger could be found in the 1850, 1860, or 1870 censuses or the deed or estate records of Bartow County. Mrs. Fouché's recollections, fortunately preserved, contain the sole known written account of him. After the war he continued to live at Valley View until he married. He was later drowned at Milam's Ferry on the Etowah River while trying to save his frightened horses.[54] Two massive bedsteads, a massive bookcase, and a massive china press, all in walnut with yellow pine secondary wood and all skillfully made with but little adornment, together with many smaller items, survive at Valley View, preserving the workmanship of this craftsman.

Samuel Frost was a cabinetmaker in Athens, Georgia. His advertisements appear in the 1830s and 1840s in the Athens newspapers.[55] The early chronicler of life in Athens, Augustus Longstreet Hull, gives us some information on Frost, including an amusing anecdote:

Sam Frost was not only an auctioneer but he was an excellent cabinetmaker and some of the old wardrobes and bureaus made by him are still doing service in Athens. He was also a Justice of the Peace and his place of business was the old house known as Gaukold's shop, which stood at the corner of Hull and Hancock Streets. The shop belonged to General Harden and it was suspected that the tenant paid his rent in verdicts for his landlord. When Howell Cobb was young at the bar he had a case before Frost with but little chance of success and with Gen. Harden representing the other side. He stopped by the shop one day and said, "Squire, do you know what some of your enemies are saying?" "No, what?" said the squire stopping to spit on his hands. "Well they say that you pay your rent to Gen. Harden in verdicts for his clients." "Well, it is a lie," said Frost. "I know it is;" said Mr. Cobb, "but that is what they say." When the case came to trial and was decided for Mr. Cobb, Gen. Harden, who ought to have gained it, was utterly dumbfounded. But when he heard how it happened he enjoyed the joke too much to move for a new trial.[56]

Frost was one of the founding trustees of the Mechanics Mutual Aid Association incorporated in Athens in 1837 to foster mutual improvement of workers.

The group hoped to help widows of members, visit the sick, help settle disputes, and when they had enough money to start a school. By 1844 members had opened a reading room in their hall over Dr. Alexander's drug store and offered non-members an opportunity to subscribe.[57]

A scroll-footed bureau of walnut with walnut-veneered drawer-fronts and yellow pine secondary wood bears glove drawers and a large mirror on top and carries on the bottom of one of the glove drawers the pencilled inscription: "Sam Frost, Maker, Athens, Georgia, Sept. 1844."

Thomas Jackson Maxwell was born in Elbert County, Georgia, May 31, 1804, and died there March 3, 1869. He married Annie Banks Adams (1814–86) on May 31, 1831. They had thirteen children between 1832 and 1862. A family tradition has it that Maxwell said bringing up so many children "was a lot of trouble, but it was *sweet* trouble." He was a cabinetmaker, a chairmaker, and a farmer. All of the furniture attributed to him is skillfully made, suggesting that he had learned his craft from a knowledgeable teacher who probably plied his trade in Elbert County in the early nineteenth century.[58]

Bird Isaac Moon (1845–82) of Madison County married Mary Evelyne Sarah Tiller (1844–1912) of Oglethorpe County. Their first home was in Harmony Grove, now Commerce, in Jackson County, Georgia. They had no children. Moon set up a cabinet shop at his home shortly after the Civil War. One of his ledger books still survives and shows that he conducted a small but steady business. Surviving furniture is in the mid-nineteenth-century style. For about fifteen years following the war until his early demise at age thirty-six from dysentery, Moon worked in a one-man cabinet and turning shop making traditional forms of plain-style furniture.[59]

Charles A. Platt, born in New York in about 1814, came to Georgia in the early 1840s and settled in Augusta. In 1851 he announced publicly that he was "now prepared to manufacture anything in the cabinet line." He had carpet ware-rooms and "a large and handsome assortment of Furniture, of the best manufacture & latest styles."[60] At the Eighth Annual Fair of the Southern Central Agricultural Society held in Augusta, October 18–21, 1853, C. A. Platt was awarded a $10 cup for the "best Secretary and Bookcase," a $5 cup for the "best Bureau," and a $5 cup for the "best Invalid Chair."[61] On April 8, 1854, he advertised that he had connected a coffin and undertaking business with his establishment; mentions having his own "steam cabinet manufactory"; and advises customers on Sundays or nights to leave orders at the residence of his brother, J. B. Platt, in the rear of the store.[62] A few months later, a notice of the formation of a partnership with Jacob B. Platt and Horton B. Adam to be known as C. A. Platt & Co. was announced.[63] An ad in 1857 of C. A. Platt & Co., "The Long Established Furniture and Carpet Wareroom," stated:

it is not necessary for us to enumerate our stock, for we shall keep constantly on hand everything in our line, from the cheapest article to the finest.[64]

By 1865 the name had changed to Platt Brothers, and the establishment was referred to as a Furniture Store, 710-712 Broad Street, Augusta.[65] This firm was still flourishing as late as 1884 when it was agent for Artistic Furniture and Household Decorations.[66] In 1873, ads appeared for a Platt & Co. on Whitehall Street in Atlanta.[67] Whether this furniture store was connected with C. A. Platt or his family has not been determined.

Ben Dismuke came to Gibson in Glascock County sometime in the late nineteenth century and set up his chairmaking shop. He died about 1934. He came from Richmond County, evidently from a family of chairmakers. The 1850 census reveals a Joseph Desimick, then nineteen years of age, as a chairmaker of Richmond County, Georgia; and the 1860 census lists Reuben Dismuke, then sixty-six years old, born in Georgia, as a chairmaker in Richmond County.

According to Nelle Swint and Frances Lamb of Gibson, who remember Ben well, he used a pole lathe to turn the posts and rounds, which were usually made of ash. He seasoned the rounds but used green posts so that the shrinkage would hold the seasoned rounds solidly in place. He preferred bottoming his chairs with cowhide. He bought cowhides from farmers when cows were butchered, salted them down, kept them in barrels for three or four months, then set them in the sun to cure. Before bottoming chairs he would tie the hides in Rocky Comfort Creek to get the salt out and make the hides pliable. One hide would bottom two or three chairs at least. In addition to side chairs he made armchairs, rocking chairs with or without footrests, children's chairs, table legs and tables, and turned columns for porches. The columns for the veranda of the Swint Hotel in Gibson were turned by Ben Dismuke. Sometimes, Arnold McAfee, a black basketmaker of Gibson, would bottom Dismuke's chairs with white-oak splints. In the 1900s Ben taught Walter Thigpen how to make chairs. Ben's work in the twentieth century was a continuation of nineteenth-century chairmaking—the same methods, materials, and tools. He was a craftsman of the nineteenth century by birth, training, and mind-set. The inverted "bowling pin" finials on the back posts of his chairs are distinctive. A ride through Gibson and the nearby towns today will reveal many a Dismuke chair on front porches. Chairs with a large ball finial found in McDuffie County have been attributed by their owners to an early-twentieth-century chairmaker named Dismuke who had a shop in Dearing, Georgia. This chairmaker was undoubtedly a relative of Ben.

John Reynolds of Warren County, Georgia, made chairs with a ball finial resting on two rings separated by a short neck. According to his grandson George Nicholas (Nick) Reynolds, born August 16, 1892, of Warrenton, he also used an inverted cone (steeple-shaped) finial. He, too, bottomed his chairs with cowhide. He preferred maple posts and made the slats and rounds from hickory. He cut the maple tree into blocks to season and then turned the blocks on a lathe into chair posts. He made looms, spinning wheels, wooden screws for cotton presses, gun stocks, and a variety of wood-turned items. He made his own tools. He also hammered rings from coins and made rifles and was reputed to be a superb marksman. Family tradition had it that John Reynolds always shot a wild turkey in the head in order that all of the meat would be edible. He lived with his wife, Prudence, who was part Indian, and six daughters and five sons on a five-acre tract several miles south of Warrenton. Although John died before 1892, these facts were passed on to Nick by his father, Joseph Henry Reynolds, one of John's sons. The 1860 census lists John Reynolds, age forty-six, of Warren County, born in Georgia, as a wood machinist. None of his children became chairmakers, according to Nick Reynolds.

Jesse Peyton Pierce (1872–1956) was another nineteenth-century chairmaker who survived and practiced his craft well into the twentieth century. He lived all his life in Wilkinson County. His father, Alfred Jesse Pierce (1842–1915), was a chairmaker also. According to family tradition, Jesse's grandfather Walter W. Pierce (1814–59) and his great-grandfather Thomas Pierce, whose will was dated 1853, were also chairmakers. Thomas first appears in the 1820 Wilkinson County census. Both Jesse and Alfred made the vernacular slat-back chairs with cowhide bottoms. Each had a distinctive finial for the back posts. Alfred's finial was a small ball surmounting a somewhat elongated neck. Jesse's was an urn-shaped finial on a shorter neck. Sometimes Jesse terminated the round posts without a finial. Both chairmakers made children's chairs, straight chairs, armchairs, and rockers. The work of Thomas and Walter has not been identified. Pierce chairs are now scattered throughout Georgia. Jesse's younger brother Harvill E. (Suge) Pierce, born in 1877, also made chairs. His work has not been identified.

W. P. (Billy) Barton was a chairmaker of Walton County, Georgia. He was a soldier in Company B, 25th Georgia Battalion, during the Civil

War. His home was in the Between community, halfway between Atlanta and Athens. According to his grandson, Oscar Barton, and other members of the family, Billy made straight chairs, rocking chairs, bedposts, cribs and cradles, baseball bats, and tops. His wife usually bottomed his chairs with white-oak splints. One son, William Pulaski (Shad) Barton, learned to weave bottoms but never made chairs. The slats of most of Billy's finial-tipped chairs were shaped in a fashion somewhat reminiscent of the "wavy line ladder back" of the north of England in the early eighteenth century, one of which appears in a Hogarth print of 1730.[68] An incised wavy vine-like design graces elements such as the top flattened surfaces of arms, the flattened surfaces of back posts of mule ears, and rounded surfaces of front posts of some chairs attributed to Billy Barton. Billy died in the early 1920s and is buried in an unmarked grave near Between. Censuses of Walton County list in 1830 a Presley Barton as a head of household and in 1840 and 1860 a Sarah Barton as a head of household. Living family members are unable to confirm or deny the relationship of either of these to Billy Barton. The family Bible burned in a house fire some years ago.[69]

Conclusion

This exhibition and catalog are but a suggestion of a field of scholarly work yet to be completed. Southern furniture studies in the past have concentrated on earlier or more elaborate furniture with little emphasis on social history. The focus here is not on artifacts as works of art or examples of superior craftsmanship — though, like Fanny Kemble, we, too, consider them neat pieces — but on furniture that best conveys impressions of the everyday life of representative Georgians of the nineteenth century.

WILLIAM W. GRIFFIN

Notes

1. Frances Anne Kemble, *Journal of a Residence on a Georgian Plantation in 1838–9*, New York, 1863, pp. 25–26. This famous English actress who captured the hearts of Americans in the 1830s and married Pierce Butler, owner of a large rice plantation on the Altamaha River delta of coastal Georgia, delayed the publication of her journal at the request of her husband. Its publication after the outbreak of the Civil War was credited with preventing England from aiding the Confederacy.

2. John Donald Wade, *Augustus Baldwin Longstreet: A Study of the Development of Culture in the South*, New York, 1924, p. 57.

3. Mills Lane, *The People of Georgia*, Savannah, 1975, pp. 130–33.

4. George G. Smith Jr., *History of Methodism in Georgia and Florida*, Macon, 1877, p. 157.

5. William Peterfield Trent, "Dominant Forces in Southern Life," *Atlantic Monthly*, vol. 79, 1897, pp. 45–46.

6. Thomas E. Watson, *Bethany: A Story of the Old South*, New York, 1904, pp. 10–11.

7. Rebecca Latimer Felton, *Country Life in Georgia in the Days of My Youth*, Atlanta, 1919, p. 29.

8. Henry W. Grady, "The Farmer's Home," *Southern Literary Readings*, edited by Leonidas Warren Payne Jr., Chicago, 1913, p. 254.

9. Clement Eaton, *The Mind of the Old South*, Baton Rouge, 1964, p. 105.

10. John Donald Wade, *Longstreet*, op. cit., pp. 59–60.

11. Julia Collier Harris, *The Life and Letters of Joel Chandler Harris*, Boston and New York, 1918, pp. 8–9.

12. James Silk Buckingham, Esq., *The Slave States of America*, London, 1842, vol. 2, p. 62.

13. *Oglethorpe Echo*, February 2, 1900, as cited by E. Merton Coulter, *James Monroe Smith, Georgia Planter*, Athens, 1967, p. 167.

14. Lee Soltow and Aubrey C. Land, "Housing and Social Standing in Georgia, 1798," *Georgia Historical Quarterly*, vol. 64, 1980, pp. 448–58.

15. Emily P. Burke, *Reminiscences of Georgia (1840–41)*, Oberlin, 1850, pp. 39, 78.

16. Lucius Q. C. Lamar, *Compilation of Laws of State of Georgia 1810 to 1819*, Augusta, 1821, p. 533.

17. Oliver H. Prince, *Digest of the Laws of the State of Georgia, Second Edition*, Athens, 1837, pp. 613–14.

18. G. Robert Coatney and Robert G. Scholtens, *Bulletin of the National Association of Watch and Clock Collectors, Inc.*, vol. 17, 1975, pp. 454–77.

19. *Georgia Messenger*, Macon, July 11, 1826, p. 3, col. 5.

20. *Columbus Weekly Enquirer*, January 4, 1833.

21. *Columbus Enquirer*, March 1, 1834.

22. *The Southern Whig*, Athens, April 3, 1845.

23. *Empire State*, Griffin, August 27, 1856; *Atlanta Weekly Enquirer*, November 13, 1856.

24. All botanical names are taken from Wilbur H. Duncan and John T. Kartesz, *Vascular Flora of Georgia*, Athens, 1981.

25. *Macon Advertiser*, July 9, 1831.

26. *Georgia Messenger*, Macon, January 21, 1836.

27. *Columbus Enquirer*, August 3, 1847.

28. *Southern Miscellany*, Madison, May 28, 1842.

29. *Columbus Enquirer*, December 4, 1844.

30. *Georgia Literary and Temperance Crusader*, Atlanta, November 29, 1860, p. 4, col. 3.

31. George White, *Statistics of the State of Georgia*, Savannah, 1849, pp. 150, 178, 264.

32. Diary of David Thurman, 1850–51, Manuscript Collection of Wilbur Kurtz, Atlanta Historical Society.

33. Letter, Manuscript Collection of John Riley Hopkins, Atlanta Historical Society.

34. For photographs of four Simpson pieces, see Henry D. Green, *Furniture of the Georgia Piedmont before 1830*, High Museum of Art, Atlanta, 1976.

35. Letter of Mrs. Lucian C. Wilson, Washington, Georgia, January 26, 1982.

36. *Sketches from the Early History of Athens, Georgia, 1801–1825 by Doctor Henry Hull*, edited by Augustus Longstreet Hull, Athens, 1884.

37. *Georgia Express*, August 6, 1808, p. 4.

38. *Pioneer Citizens' History of Atlanta, 1833–1902*, Atlanta, 1902, p. 116.

39. *Cherokee Phoenix*, November 12, 1828.

40. *Georgia Messenger*, Macon, February 11, 1836, p. 3, col. 4.

41. *Albany Patriot*, July 23, 1857.

42. *Macon Telegraph*, December 19, 1826.

43. *Milledgeville Journal*, April 1, 1821.

44. Mrs. Anne Royall, *Mrs. Royall's Southern Tour or Second Series of the Black Book*, Washington, 1831, vol. 2, pp. 124–25.

45. *Georgia and Carolina Gazette*, Petersburg, Georgia, August 22, 1805.

46. John A. Chapman, *History of Edgefield County*, Newberry, South Carolina, 1897, pp. 192–93.

47. Franklin M. Garrett, *Atlanta and Environs*, 1954, vol. 1, pp. 541–42.

48. George R. Jones, *A History of Pythagoras Lodge No. 41, F & A M*, Decatur, Georgia, 1944, pp. 2–3.

49. *Transactions of the Southern Central Agricultural Society*, 1846 to 1851, Macon, 1852, p. 324.

50. Ibid., p. 345.

51. *Atlanta Daily Intelligencer and Examiner*, December 19, 1857.

52. *Rome Weekly Courier*, January 9, 1858.

53. Robert Eldridge Bouwman, *Traveler's Rest and the Tugaloo Crossroads*, Atlanta, 1980.

54. Rebecca Sproull Fouché, *Our Mother's Memories of That Other Beautiful World We Used to Live in before the War*, September 1912, typescript, original at Valley View, Cartersville, Georgia.

55. For example, *Southern Banner*, Athens, February 22, 1834, and January 21, 1842.

56. Augustus Longstreet Hull, *Annals of Athens, Georgia, 1801–1901*, Athens, 1906, p. 114 (written ca. 1879).

57. Ernest C. Hynds, *Antebellum Athens and Clarke County, Georgia*, Athens, 1974, p. 130.

58. Quillie Norman, *A Short History of the Norman-Maxwell Families*, Shady Nook, Hartwell, Hart County, Georgia, 1953, typescript copy at Atlanta Historical Society.

59. Chronicle of the Tiller-Moon Family, handwritten by Mrs. Royal Wilburn Johnson, February 27, 1930, Atlanta Historical Society; Ledger June 17, 1874, to July 25, 1879, Bird I. Moon, Atlanta Historical Society; Tombstone, Fork Creek Cemetery, Carlton, Georgia.

60. *Augusta Daily Chronicle and Sentinel*, December 2, 1851.

61. *The Soil of the South*, Columbus, November 1853.

62. *Augusta Daily Chronicle and Sentinel*, April 8, 1854.

63. *Augusta Daily Chronicle and Sentinel*, June 1, 1854.

64. *Augusta Weekly Constitutionalist*, September 17, 1857.

65. *Daily Constitutionalist, Augusta*, July 18, 1865.

66. *Augusta Evening News*, November 18, 1884.

67. *Atlanta Daily Herald*, January 4, 1873; May 1, 1873.

68. Bill Cotton, "Country Chairs," *Antique Finder*, Suffolk, England, October 1973, p. 21.

69. Anita B. Sams, *Wayfarers in Walton*, Monroe, Georgia, 1967; interviews 1982 and 1983 with Oscar Barton, Eunice Barton Guest, Eva Mae Barton, and Robert Barton.

Georgians at Home

Here is a random sampling of nineteenth-century Georgians and a few of their possessions—houses they lived in, furniture they used. These Georgians worked at various occupations and lived in various parts of the state. Nearly all, though engaged in one or more additional vocations, followed agricultural pursuits as well. Perhaps their furniture, their houses, their faces, and their bearing—and a little information about the lives they led—can convey a feeling, if not an understanding, of their Georgia.

Some Families

A FAMILY GROUP IN THE INTERIOR OF THE STATE OF GEORGIA.

Sir Basil Hall, British traveler and writer, discovered this group of Georgians at home on March 22, 1828, near the Yam Grandy Creek in the backwoods between Riceborough and Macon. Setting up his camera lucida, an early optical instrument that reflected an image on paper, he traced with pencil his unidentified host for the night and three of the man's sons, including in the picture their slat-back chairs and one small, high table. According to Hall:

All these Figures were sketched, by their own desire, at a house where we slept in the interior of the State of Georgia. The old gentleman . . . chose his own attitude. . . . [1]

Courtesy of Special Collections, Robert W. Woodruff Library, Emory University.

The next evening, after a memorable crossing of the swollen Yam Grandy Creek, Sir Basil reached another house in the Georgia forest. Of this house and its occupants he wrote:

…we reached a solitary house from which both the master and mistress were absent; but three pretty little girls, the eldest not more than twelve years of age, set to work instantly, in the most businesslike manner, to prepare supper for us. One of them brought a glass of milk, warm from the cow, … another set about cooking, and the third arranged the table; while everything about the establishment was neat, clean, and well ordered.

Almost all these forest houses in the interior of the State of Georgia consist of two divisions, separated by a wide, open passage, which extends from the front to the back of the building. They are generally made of logs, covered with a very steep roof, I suppose to carry off the heavy rains. The apartments, at the ends of these dwellings, are entered from the open passage which divides the house in two, the floor of which is raised generally two or three feet from the ground. This opening being generally ten or twelve feet wide, answers in that mild climate the purpose of a verandah, or sitting room during the day.[2]

A far cry from Basil Hall's subjects, though also posing in a slat-back chair, is Robert McAlpin Goodman (1820–1906), painted around mid-century in Marietta, Georgia, by an unknown artist. Robert Goodman went to work for a newspaper in Augusta at age twelve when his father died. He later went into the marble business, thereby earning enough money by 1842 to study law at Yale. He moved to Marietta in 1847, where he bought land and also published and edited a series of newspapers. Though a farmer and a slaveholder, he was staunchly opposed to secession, writing editorials in support of the Union. Before the Emancipation Proclamation, he freed his own slaves. He was the author of at least two books on philosophy and religion.

A slat-back highchair holds the doll of little Lily Blue (1874–1956) of Buena Vista, Georgia. A tintype records eight-year-old Lily (later to become Mrs. Charles Warren Lowe) and the chair she herself used at an earlier age. Courtesy of Mrs. Frank Tabor.

Notes

1. Captain Basil Hall, R.N., *Forty Etchings, From Sketches Made with the Camera Lucida, in North America, in 1827 and 1828*, London, 1829.

2. Captain Basil Hall, Royal Navy, *Travels in North America, in the Years 1827 and 1828*, Edinburgh, 1829, vol. 3, pp. 271–72.

Robert McAlpin Goodman, oil on canvas.

A Great Statesman

Alexander H. Stephens (1812–83) was a scholar, successful lawyer, United States Congressman for twenty-six years, vice president of the Confederacy, and later governor of Georgia. From about 1834 until his death, he lived at Liberty Hall in Crawfordville, Taliaferro County, in the eastern portion of the Georgia Piedmont. He was born in the log dwelling on his father's farm about two miles north of Liberty Hall. Although orphaned at age fourteen, Stephens was profoundly influenced by his father and later wrote of him:

He was industrious, systematic and frugal; not greedy of gain but proud of his independence. He looked upon labor as honorable and impressed this idea upon his children. . . . He loved his home. . . . here he ploughed, hoed, reaped, super-intended the building of all his houses, laying with his own hands the chimneys of stone or brick. He tanned his own leather, made his own lasts, and all the shoes for the family. He bought little or nothing, and came as near living within himself as any man I ever knew. . . . Whatever he turned his hand to he did, and did well. This was a maxim with him, which he used to enforce by quoting the lines from Pope:

"Honor and shame from no condition rise:
Act well your part, there all the honor lies."

Small of stature (he never weighed more than a hundred pounds), plagued with ill health all his life, and permanently crippled by an ac-cident in 1868, "Little Aleck" (southern pronunciation of Alex) chose never to marry. However, he had loyal servants and numerous friends and acquaintances, and the hospitality of Liberty Hall was extended to visitors from all walks of life. In 1921 Stephens's former slave, Eliza, then eighty-two years of age, said, "No one ever turned away hungry from Liberty Hall; no charge was ever made for meals or lodging."

Stephens owned thirty-one slaves in 1864 just prior to emancipation. Most of them remained with him after the war, including Harry and Eliza, who adopted the Stephens surname and who from 1850, when they married, had been his mainstays at Liberty Hall.

Harry and Eliza Stephens. Courtesy of the Georgia Department of Natural Resources.

In 1875 the simple two-story house, which Stephens had purchased in 1845, was rebuilt and enlarged, primarily for the accommodation of his many guests. The new house, though acclaimed to be stylish, was still plain with a hip roof instead of gable ends and a one-story veranda extending all the way across the front. The 1875 house has remained essentially unchanged until the present time and is open to the public as a state of Georgia historic site.

Liberty Hall, 1865. Taken about the time Union troops arrested Stephens in May of 1865; original in the National Archives, Washington, D.C.

Reference: Martha F. Norwood, *Liberty Hall: Taliaferro County, Georgia*, Georgia Department of Natural Resources, Atlanta, 1977.

1 Chair

Taliaferro County
1850–70
Attributed to Harry Stephens
H. 37½", S.H. 14½"; W. 19½"
Primary wood: Hickory
Seat: Oak splints

Description: The finials are cylinders surmounting an inverted pinched cone. The round posts are graduated, tapering as they reach the bottom. The top slat is pegged to the scored posts. The four slats are arched and bowed and are uniform in size. The arched portion of the top slat is broken off. Six rounds connect the base (one in front and back and two on each side). The seat is woven of oak splints. An old finish is on the chair.

History: According to oral tradition, Harry Stephens, Alexander Stephens's trusted slave and friend, made this chair. As with many Georgia chairs, the arch of the top slat has been split off, possibly because of the common practice of placing an ironing board between two chairs resting on the top slats.

2 Bench

Taliaferro County
1870–80
H. 28½"; S.H. 17¾";
W. 17½"; L. 74"
Primary wood: Yellow pine

Description: The seat is one solid pine board with side aprons which are attached by lap joints to the ends. The stretchers are attached to the ends in the same manner as the aprons, running through the outer edges of the center support member, which is nailed to the seat. The ends are cut at the top edge at a 45-degree angle with an applied rolled "crest." Cutouts in these ends then create handles for moving the piece about. The ends and the center supporting member are all cut at the bottom to form feet. The shape of the cut of these members resembles the top half of a heart (see Figure 82). The seat has been reinforced by L-irons. The bench has an old varnish finish.

History: This bench was probably made about 1875 when Liberty Hall was rebuilt and enlarged. In all likelihood it graced the large center hall to accommodate visitors waiting for an audience with the distinguished owner.

3 Windsor chair

Taliaferro County
1850–60
H. 28", S.H. 14½"; W. 20"
Primary woods: Tulip poplar
   and hickory

Description: The crest rail is formed in a double layered method, the top protruding beyond and curving over the lower section. The crest is then glued and nailed to the main arm section. The arms terminate in a modified knuckle shape, a form continuing from earlier Windsor chair designs. The supporting spindles are turned with a center flattened round, enter the plank seat and are glued. The ring-turned legs tenon into, but not through, the seat. They are connected by four plain stretchers, and the foot ends in a form that repeats the finial shape seen on the chair attributed to Harry Stephens (see Figure 1). A later black paint covers the chair surface.

History: This is the only surviving Windsor chair from a set owned by Stephens at Liberty Hall.

4 Table

Taliaferro County
1840–60
H. 28"; W. 36½" (with grain), 36¼"
    (against grain)
Primary wood: Yellow pine
Secondary wood: Yellow pine

Description: The round top sits on
a square base. The legs are tapered.
The drawer face appears to be the
same depth as the remaining apron
depths but is, in fact, shallower (see
Detail). The dovetail arrangement is
half-dovetail top and bottom with
two full ones between. The bottom is
beveled and slips into grooves in the
drawer sides. There is a scooped-out
area beneath the center of the drawer
front for opening the drawer. On the
inside beneath the drawer area are
double tiers of boards connecting the
front and back legs. These boards are
beveled on the ends and screwed into
the legs. The top tier may have housed
a shelf, as does the lower tier, but it
may also have been purely decorative.
The shelf, with cutout corners, rests on
the side members and is nailed.

History: This was Alex Stephens's
writing table. In 1866, Henry Cleve-
land, author of the first biography, the
manuscript of which was approved by
Stephens before publication, wrote:

The inner room is the sanctum sanctorum.
If the visitor comes in winter, a light tap
is given on the door, a quick but pleasant
voice says "Come in" and turning the door
knob of the door gives admittance. . . .
There is a little round top writing-table,
with eyelet press, and papers and scraps.
More papers and scraps are in the little
table drawer, and the mind of the owner is
the index to them all, if they are not dis-
turbed. That annoys him greatly. His old
office, and another library, are at the court
house, but he seldom goes to it.[1]

When Stephens rebuilt Liberty Hall
in 1875, he moved this table into his
bedroom, the front room on the right
of the downstairs center hall. Here
it has remained. About 1900, some
seventeen years after Stephens's death
and while the house was being used
as a boardinghouse, the table is again
described, this time in a newspaper
article:

. . . at the foot of the bed the little table
holding a few books and the gas lamp
with its quaint little green paper shade
awry, and looking curiously old-fashioned
and pathetic. How many nights sat he by
its flame, delving, delving! —how many
long, weary nights counted the hours on
that bed of suffering![2]

Notes
    1. Henry Cleveland, *Alexander H. Stephens
in Public and Private with Letters and Speeches
before, during and since the War* (Philadelphia:
1866, pp. 20–27).
    2. Newspaper article, "Vandalism, Neglect
. . . Effacing Piece . . . Every Hallowed Trace of
Alex Stephens" [title indistinct, some missing],
c. 1900. Copy in files of Georgia Department
of Natural Resources, Division of Parks and
Historic Sites, Atlanta.

A Wheelwright

At age ten, John Fitz Jarrell (1810–84) moved with his father, mother, and younger brothers and sisters to Jones County, Georgia, from North Carolina. His father, Blake Fitz Jarrell (1785–1856), a Virginian by birth, was married in North Carolina in 1809. An industrious and successful farmer, Blake had by the time of his death assembled holdings of approximately 3,300 acres in Jones County and owned twenty-five slaves.

John followed in his father's footsteps. By 1863, he owned in excess of six hundred acres of land and forty-two slaves. He was an expert wheelwright, a carpenter, a blacksmith, a mason, a weaver, and a tanner, as well as a good farmer. Among the products of his workshop, in addition to wheels and wagons, were furniture, coffins, and tools. John was the father

House built by John Fitz Jarrell, ca. 1847. His widow, Nancy Ann Jarrell, seated left, is surrounded by servants and family members. Her daughter, Nancy Ann (Annie), maker of the washstand on the porch, stands to her immediate right. (Photograph taken in 1899.) Courtesy of the Georgia Department of Natural Resources.

of fourteen children, seven by each of his two wives. From 1847 until his death he lived in the frame house pictured here. Fortunately, the house was spared by Sherman's forces in 1864. However, John's gin house was destroyed; all his livestock was confiscated; and the capital investment in his slaves, valued at $37,800 on the tax digest of 1863, was lost.

After John's death in 1884, one of his sons, Benjamin Richard Jarrell (1867–1958) continued to operate the farm. He, too, was a wheelwright with the mechanical and organizational skills of his father. He added a steam engine used to power a saw and planing mill, a grist mill, a cotton gin, and a syrup mill.

In 1973, all of John Fitz Jarrell's surviving descendants gave the plantation to the state of Georgia, and it is now operated as a historic site.

References: Victoria Reeves Gunn, *Jarrell Plantation: A History*, Typescript, Georgia Department of Natural Resources, Atlanta, 1974. Allene Jarrell Yeomans, *Mem'ry Motes*, Buford, Georgia, 1980. Interviews with Willie Lee Jarrell, John Milton Jarrell, and Allene Jarrell Yeomans, 1981, 1982.

John Fitz Jarrell. Courtesy of the Georgia Department of Natural Resources.

5 Chairs, Table, Benches

Chairs
Monroe County
1850–60
Attributed to John Fitz Jarrell
H. 35½"; S.H. 16"; W. 16½"
Primary wood: Hickory
Seat: Oak splints

Description: Flattened ball finials, with a ring-turning underneath and an elongated neck, top the graduated posts. The three slats are arched and bowed, the upper and lower ones being pegged into the posts. The legs are tapered at the bottom. There are seven rounds (two in the front and on the sides and one in the back). Traces of red paint remain. The seat is woven of oak splints.

Table
Monroe County
1850–60
H. 29"; W. 39½"; L. 86½"
Primary wood: Yellow pine
Secondary wood: Yellow pine

Description: The top of the table is made of four boards, which are nailed onto the body or aprons. The tapering legs and the aprons are joined by mortised-tenoned and pegged joints. There are three cross supports underneath the top, the center one of which mortises through to the outside. The apron and legs retain traces of the old red paint.

Benches
Monroe County
1850–60
H. 15¼"; W. 18"; L. 86¼"
Primary woods: Tulip poplar
and yellow pine

Description: The seating surface and the boot-jack ends are made of poplar. These ends are set in from the edges, tenon through the top of the seat, and are wedged. The sides are made of yellow pine and are nailed to the edges of the seat.

History: For meals, children were seated on the benches, the chairs being reserved for grown-ups. According to a Jarrell descendant, the chairs were probably made by John Fitz Jarrell. The splint bottoms are said to have been woven to replace the original cowhide bottoms in 1905 by George Calhoun, a black man who also made cotton baskets.

Detail a

Detail b

6 Slab

Monroe County
1850–60
Attributed to John Fitz Jarrell
H. 57" (overall), 48¾" (serving); W.
64"; D. 21¾"
Primary wood: Walnut
Secondary woods: Yellow pine and
tulip poplar

Description: The splashboard is
mortised and tenoned into the plinths
and the whole unit is then tenoned
into the top. The plinths have molded
tops. There is faint evidence of a green
painted line around the plinths and
splashboard, as seen on Figure 60. The
entire body is of mortise-and-tenon
construction with tiny pegs holding
the tenons in place. The drawers are
half-dovetailed top and bottom with
two full dovetails between. The drawer
bottoms are two horizontal boards
beveled and slipped into grooved
sides. The odd glass knob is original;
the others are later replacements.*

The cupboard doors are also mortised,
tenoned, and pegged by two small
pegs placed on the diagonal at each
joint. The center doors are recessed
flush with the rear of the center legs,
which are tenoned into the lower
drawer cross support. Some of the
door hinges are missing. Inside there
are walnut drawer runners with a continuous piece across the back, passing
through the drawer dividers. There is
also a full-length walnut support for
the top running across the back of the
case (see Detail a). In the cupboard
section there are full-height poplar
cupboard dividers, and the walnut top
support runs through these dividers.
The back legs are rabbeted on the back
surfaces from the top to the bottom
of the case to receive the yellow pine
backboard. This backboard is then
nailed into the legs, and across the top
and the bottom (see Detail b).

History: According to descendants
of John Fitz Jarrell, this piece was
referred to as the slab or sideboard.

Benjamin Richard Jarrell, John's son
who died in 1958, attributed its manufacture to his father. Within memory
of living descendants, the piece was
used in the dining room of the 1847
house to store whiskey for medicinal
purposes, ham, sidemeat or bacon, and
linens. Butter was kept on top of the
slab in a dish placed in a glazed stone-
ware bowl containing water to keep
out ants and to keep the butter cool.

---

* Very few pieces having glass knobs were found
through the survey (see Figures 56 and 105).

7 Washstand

Monroe County
1895–1900
Attributed to Nancy Ann Jarrell
H. 35¼"; W. 16½"; D. 17"
Primary wood: Tulip poplar

Description: The top and the three-sided splashboard are joined to each other and attached to the base. The top board runs front to back and the shaped sides are nailed to the sides of the top. The splashboard is pierced on all three sides, a heart motif in the backboard and an "X" in each side board. The legs and apron as well as the lower cross-members that support the shelf are joined by mortise-and-tenon joints and pegged. The shelf is nailed onto cross-members and notched at the corners to fit around the legs. About 3" below the shelf the legs begin to taper. Traces of red paint are detectable.

History: Made by Nancy Ann (Annie) Jarrell (1880–1930), daughter of John and Nancy Ann Jarrell. The washstand has stood since its completion on the front porch of the 1847 house.

A Planter

Left: James Caldwell Sproull, oil on canvas. Courtesy of Dr. and Mrs. Robert F. Norton.

Above: Eliza Marshall Sproull, oil on canvas. Courtesy of Dr. and Mrs. Robert F. Norton.

James Caldwell Sproull (1816–66), a planter, came with his wife and young children from the Abbeville District, south Carolina, to Cass County, Georgia, in the late 1840s. This was ten years after the removal of the Cherokee Indians from this part of Georgia to Oklahoma along the Trail of Tears. In 1842, James had married Eliza Margaret Marshall (1823–1906), herself the daughter of a South Carolina planter, and three of their four children were born in South Carolina before the move, the

third child being but a babe in arms when the journey was undertaken. In the fertile Etowah River Valley, James Sproull established a large plantation of between 2,000 and 3,000 acres. Here he built his striking brick classic revival home, which he called Valley View. In the words of his daughter, Rebecca Sproull Fouché (1844–1918):

Valley View, home built for Mr. and Mrs. James Caldwell Sproull, ca. 1850, near Cartersville, Georgia. Courtesy of Dr. and Mrs. Robert F. Norton. (Photograph by William Hull)

When Father built this house he had the trees cut from his own land, sawed at his own mill; the bricks were made by his own Negroes from his own dirt; the lime was burnt from his own rocks; the carpenters were waited on by his own servants. The walnut trees (they were numerous and large then) that some of the furniture was made of grew on his plantation. He was a magnificent organizer, a successful planter, a "gentleman of the old school," cultured, loyal and true—his judgment was the highest court of appeals in this neighborhood. His office of ruling elder in the Presbyterian Church was to him a sacred trust and a high honor.[1]

The German cabinetmaker, Vitenger, who was brought to Valley View by James Sproull to make furniture, is thought to have crafted the staircase, the wood-grained paneling, and other millwork in the house. (For additional information on Vitenger, see introductory essay.)

During the Civil War, Valley View lay in the line of attack of Federal troops as they fought their way from Tennessee to Atlanta. During most of this fierce fighting, Sproull and his family took refuge in Alabama. Though the plantation was raided by Yankee soldiers prior to the departure of the Sproull family to Alabama and occupied by Yankee troops for three months thereafter, the house was spared and the Sproulls returned home following the cessation of hostilities. James Caldwell Sproull, long an invalid, died in 1866, but Valley View to this day continues to be owned by his descendants.

Note

1. Rebecca Sproull Fouché, *Our Mother's Memories of That Other Beautiful World We Used to Live in before the War*, September 1912, typescript, original at Valley View, Cartersville, Georgia.

8 Candlestand

Bartow (formerly Cass) County
1850–60
Attributed to "Witey" Vitenger
H. 29 ½"; W. 16 ¼"; D. 14"
Primary woods: Walnut and
  rosewood veneer
Secondary wood: White pine

Description: The top is one piece of walnut rounded off on the corners and edges and nailed to a beveled cross-member, which is nailed and screwed into the shaft. The shaft is octagonal in shape and graduates in size from the top to the bottom. It enters the base section, which forms two of the four shaped feet. The other section, forming the other two feet, is notched in the center joining a matching notch in the first section. The joinery of the base sections is concealed by rosewood veneer. Rather than the typical construction of nailing or screwing the base to the shaft, a metal pin projects into the shaft to serve as its support.

History: Descended to the present owner from James Caldwell Sproull. According to family tradition, the candlestand was made by a German cabinetmaker, "Witey" Vitenger. See introduction under cabinetmakers for information on Vitenger.

9 Crib

Bartow (formerly Cass) County
1850–60
Attributed to "Witey" Vitenger
H. 31"; W. 48"; D. 26½"
Primary wood: Walnut
Secondary wood: Yellow pine

Description: The round-cornered posts extend to form the feet, which are turned to elongated bulbous shapes with wide rings and tapering terminations. Inside the crib, the interior edges of the posts are grooved. Below the crib section, the grooved edges are chamfered to diminish the heavy appearance of the posts. Small turn-buckles release the fall side, which is hinged on the lower edge (see Detail). The spindles taper from the center toward the top and bottom and are doweled into the rails. A supporting board inside the crib is notched to receive the slats. The ends and stationary side are joined by mortise-and-tenon joints.

History: Descended to the present owner from James Caldwell Sproull. According to family tradition, the crib was made by a German cabinetmaker, "Witey" Vitenger. See introduction under cabinetmakers for information on Vitenger.

10 Washstand

Bartow (formerly Cass) County
1850–60
Attributed to "Witey" Vitenger
H. 29¾"; W. 31¾"; D. 17"
Marble top: 1⅛" thick
Primary wood: Walnut
Secondary wood: Yellow pine
Marble

Description: The marble top and splashboard have rounded edges. The top rests on the case. The ogee shape of the drawer is repeated on the upper corner of the case. The drawer is cut from solid wood, not veneered as is usually seen on pieces of this type. The sides, front, and back are joined with single large flat dovetails on the top surfaces of the case. The doors, of tongue-and-groove construction, are paneled and have an applied half-round molding forming the closure. The sides are paneled in the same manner. The front corners of the stiles, apron, and feet are rounded. Below the apron, the front feet are shaped into simple brackets and nailed onto the case. The back feet are continua-tions of the back stiles. Two beveled backboards slip into the grooved stiles and are nailed, forming the back of the case. There is a medial shelf inside the case. The hinges are original, but the lock mechanism is replaced.

History: Descended to the present owner from James Caldwell Sproull. According to family tradition, the washstand was made by a German cabinetmaker, "Witey" Vitenger. See introduction under cabinetmakers for information on Vitenger.

A Cabinetmaker

Elijah Mixon (1795–1873) was born in Beaufort County, North Carolina, and moved to Georgia in the early 1820s. He married Charlotte Aughtry of Hancock County in 1823. An account by Atticus G. Haygood, Methodist Bishop and longtime president of Emory College, gives a vivid picture of the arrival and early days of Elijah and Charlotte in Newton County, where they spent the rest of their lives.

Soon after their marriage, traveling in an old fashioned gig, a feather bed tied on behind it, and a few changes of apparel, their all of earthly goods, they moved to what is now Newton County, then almost an unbroken wilderness. There, on a lot of land drawn in one of the land distributions by the State of Georgia to her citizens in that day, they struck camp, cleared a patch, and built a log cabin with a dirt floor. In this cabin—converted by and by into a blacksmith shop (for in a year or two they had a comfortable dwelling), the eldest son, the Rev. Asbury C. Mixon, was born. They did not have a chair to sit upon. Brother Mixon has often told me how he "scored" two blocks of wood from a pine log to make stools, one for himself and one for his wife.

. . . Poor as they were they were church going people. They went and went regularly. I have often heard Mrs. Mixon, in telling of their early struggles, say she used to go barefoot to the neighborhood of the Church, with her shoes and stockings tied up in a bundle. She would then put them on till after meeting. Returning, she would adopt the same method of saving her shoes.[1]

Elijah worked hard all his life and did well as a carpenter, a carriage maker, and a cabinetmaker. He and his wife had eight children. In order that their children receive the best possible education, they moved in

Facing page: Elijah and Charlotte Mixon, ca. 1870.

Home on the original Elijah Mixon land in Newton County. After graduating from Emory College in 1845, the Rev. Asbury Coke Mixon, Elijah's son, lived here until his death in 1919 at age 95. (Photographs by William Hull)

1838 to the new town of Oxford, where the Methodist Church had just established Emory College. In Oxford Elijah built some of the town's earliest houses and operated a cabinet shop. Writing in 1877, in a tribute to the Mixons following Charlotte's death, Bishop Haygood remembered the shop:

Twenty years ago, when a schoolboy, I passed every day their humble cottage, the work shop opening on the sidewalk. . . .[2]

Descendants say pine table in surviving outbuilding was built by Elijah Mixon. (Photograph by William Hull)

Notes

1. Atticus G. Haygood, "Their Sphere Filled Full," *St. Louis Christian Advocate*, February 4, 1877.
   2. Ibid.

11 Folding table

Newton County
1840–60
Attributed to Elijah Mixon
H. 28¼"; W. 16½" (leaves dropped),
    42½" (open); D. 33¾"
Primary wood: Cherry
Secondary woods: Yellow pine
    and cherry

Description: The two-board table top is screwed onto the apron and the body. Beneath the drop-leaves, the body is yellow pine and the leaf supports are cherry. The leaves are hinged and drop from ruled joints. The tapering legs are joined to the apron by mortise-and-tenon joints and are pegged. Several pegs extrude on the inside of the apron area.

History: Descended in the family of Elijah Mixon. In the 1873 inventory of his estate, this table was listed as a folding table and valued at $5.00.

12 Sideboard

Newton County
1840–60
Attributed to Elijah Mixon
H. 53¼" (overall), 45⅞"
 (serving);W. 57¼"; D. 20¼"
Primary wood: Cherry
Secondary woods: Yellow pine
   and cherry

Description: The top is a solid board with cleated ends. The undercut molding is then applied to these cleats and around the front edge. Doweled to the top is the splashboard. It is made of two boards beveled on the back side, which fit into the outer framing and medial divider. Both the drawers and the doors below have ivory escutcheons, and the drawers retain the original wooden knobs. The drawers are joined by full dovetails. The backs of the drawers slip into grooves cut in the drawer sides. The drawer bottoms extend beyond the drawer sides to act as stops.

The doors are paneled, a shorter panel above a longer one, and set into frames. The upper panel grain is placed horizontally and the lower one vertically. The sides of the case are constructed in the same manner. The feet are continuations of the stiles, and are supported on the reverse side by heavy blocks. The spurred foot-brack-ets are thin boards, set into grooves cut into the feet and nailed to a yellow pine frame underneath. The interior of the sideboard has two shelves in each compartment.

The back of the case is made of two horizontal, beveled yellow pine panels, which slip into the sides of the case and are separated by a full medial cherry divider. The upper and lower framing boards of the back dividers mortise into the main structure of the back stiles.

History: Descended in the family of Elijah Mixon. In the 1873 inventory of Elijah Mixon, this sideboard was valued at $10.00.

An Innkeeper

Devereaux Jarrett (1785–1852) was reared and educated in Oconee County, South Carolina. About 1807, he married his first cousin, Sarah Patton. Shortly thereafter he began to purchase property in Franklin County, Georgia, just across the Tugaloo River from Oconee County. By 1818, Devereaux and Sarah lived in a large log cabin on Toccoa Creek and owned twenty-one slaves and almost 2,000 acres. He farmed, owned a commissary, and engaged in money lending.

By 1833, Devereaux Jarrett was able to purchase from his friend and neighbor, James R. Wyly, a 2,276-acre plantation containing the residence inn that he later named Traveler's Rest. Here he operated the inn and numerous other enterprises including a commissary, a tanyard, a post office, a smithy, mills, and a toll bridge across the Tugaloo River. By 1850, Devereaux Jarrett was a wealthy man, owning 14,400 acres and sixty-eight slaves.

Devereaux Jarrett, proprietor of Traveler's Rest. Photograph (date unknown) obtained from Jarrett descendants. Courtesy of the Georgia Department of Natural Resources.

Traveler's Rest under Jarrett's proprietorship became a famous stagecoach stop. Both George W. Featherstonhaugh and James Silk Buckingham, English travelers in America in the 1830s, stopped at Jarrett's inn. Featherstonhaugh, who came to the inn in 1836 following a visit to Toccoa Falls, published the following account:

We now proceeded for eight miles at a rapid pace down the steep southern slope of the mountains, through beautiful woods and dales, to Jarrett's, on the Tugaloo, a main branch of the Savannah. Here I got an excellent breakfast of coffee, ham, chicken, good bread, butter, honey, and plenty of good new milk for a quarter of a dollar. The landlord cultivated an extensive farm, and there was a fine bottom of good land near the house; he was a quiet, intelligent, well-behaved man, a great admirer of Mr. C —— [Calhoun], and seemed anxious to do what was obliging and proper, more from good feeling than for the poor return he chose to take for his good fare.[1]

Three years later, in 1839, James Silk Buckingham with his family spent a night at Traveler's Rest. He wrote:

Leaving Tukoa [Toccoa Falls], we proceeded by an excellent road—which seemed, indeed, by contrast with the one we had just passed over, to be perfection—and after a smooth and luxurious drive of eight miles, we arrived before sunset at a large farm-house and inn united, kept by a Mr. Jerritt [sic]: the

directions by which we were enabled to distinguish it from other houses in the neighbourhood was this — that twas "the only house with glass windows in it on the road."[2]

Traveler's Rest, south view, 1977. Courtesy of the Georgia Department of Natural Resources.

With the passing of the stagecoach as a mode of travel, the popularity of Traveler's Rest gradually declined. Although one of Devereaux Jarrett's sons continued to operate the tavern after his father's death in 1852, by the time a railroad to Toccoa, the county seat, was completed in 1873, Traveler's Rest as a stagecoach inn had seen its day.

Descendants of Devereaux Jarrett continued to live at Traveler's Rest until its purchase by the state of Georgia in 1955. It is presently operated as a historic site by Georgia's Department of Natural Resources.

Notes

1. George W. Featherstonhaugh, *A Canoe Voyage*, vol. 2, London, 1847, p. 264.
2. James Silk Buckingham, *The Slave States of America*, vol. 1, London, 1842, p. 162.

Reference: Robert Eldridge, *Traveler's Rest and the Tugaloo Crossroads*, Atlanta, 1980.

13 Corner cupboard

Stephens County
1840–60
Attributed to Caleb Shaw
H. 94¾"; W. 39¾"; D. 22¼"
Primary woods: Walnut with maple
  escutcheons
Secondary wood: Yellow pine

Description: The cornice is comprised of four parts. The top board is nailed to a flaring step-out. The latter board is attached to a capped and rounded molding. This molding is nailed to a deeply coved and beveled molding, which attaches to the facia board and case sides. Just below the cornice, a 1⅛" grooved projecting molding is also attached to the facia board and acts as a cap for the doors. The doors are paneled, the upper ones having a third section in which the panels are placed with the grain running horizontally. The door frames are joined by tongue-and-groove joints and glued. The knobs, hinges, and maple escutcheons appear to be original. Down the back edge of the two sides is a cove molding that runs vertically between the grooved molding above the doors and the base (see Figures 14 and 67). The front stiles are capped at the corners by rounded and reeded columns, which meet at the medial section of the case in a 5"-wide projecting form of the same reeding. These two 5"-wide sections are joined by a heavy, raised, modified gadroon-carving which continues around the sides of the case. At the bottom, the base is made of a deep projecting 10" board into which the turned feet are doweled. The apron is then comprised of five reeded vertical sections capped by a matching baseboard, which forms the inside bottom of the cupboard. The backboards are planed and are of tongue-and-groove nailed construction. The backboards and the shelves are made of yellow pine.

History: This piece is attributed to Caleb T. Shaw, who made furniture in the 1840s and 1850s for Devereaux Jarrett. (For further information concerning Shaw, see introduction under cabinetmakers).

Another Planter

Augustus Dozier (1807–1902) was born in Columbia County in the eastern Piedmont of Georgia. At about age twenty-one, he settled in nearby Oglethorpe County, five miles east of Lexington, where he remained for the rest of his life. He married Martha Howard of Oglethorpe County, whose forebears had migrated to Georgia from Maryland, and by 1850 they had seven children. Gus, though primarily a farmer, was also a surveyor. By 1859, he had accumulated 750 acres of land and owned eighteen slaves.

No written accounts chronicle Augustus Dozier's life, but tales about him have been passed from generation to generation within his family.

Augustus Dozier and three of his children in front of their home at White Oak Plantation, Oglethorpe County. In the 1850 census, Augustus was 43, William A. was age 2, Victoria E. (left rear in picture) was 11, and Sara P. (right in picture) was unborn. (Photographer, date unknown.) Courtesy of Mr. and Mrs. Ben Lancaster.

George P. Dozier, son of Augustus Dozier, who, according to the Dozier family Bible, was "killed in the Battle of Sharpsburg, September 17, 1862, 19 years." Ambrotype from collection of the Kenan Research Center at the Atlanta History Center.

He is said to have been small of stature, never weighing more than 140 pounds, but possessed of a fiery temper. A great-grandson recalls that he always wore long hair to cover a missing ear, which had been bitten off by an adversary in a fight. The same great-grandson related that on one occasion Governor Wilson Lumpkin rode up on horseback while Gus was talking with one of his hands at the edge of a cornfield. The ex-governor had complaints about the quality of a wagon load of corn he had purchased from Dozier—too many nubbins. Without saying a word Dozier took the hoe from his slave's hands and knocked his distinguished visitor out of the saddle. A great-granddaughter related a family story concerning a late-nineteenth-century trip into Lexington to see and use the newly invented telephone. Gus was at that time nearly deaf and, of course, could not hear what was said to him over the telephone receiver. His only remark was: "I knew this thing would never work."

14 Corner cupboard

Oglethorpe County
1845–55
H. 86¾"; W. 44"; D. 24"
Primary wood: Yellow pine
Secondary wood: Yellow pine

Description: The three-section cornice is nailed to the facia board and case sides. The molded framing along the back edges of the cupboard (see Figures 13 and 67) continues around the sides and the front at the top, appearing to be an added section of the cornice. A flat molding separates the upper and lower cupboard sections. The paneled doors are mortised, tenoned, and pegged. One upper door has an added ½" strip as it butts against the other door. The base is cut to form front feet and is nailed to the case. The molded framing described above fits along the top of the base.

The wide, rough-sawn vertical backboards are nailed to the case and to each of the three interior shelves. The backboards are cut at the bottom in the shape of the front base section, the joining of which forms the back center foot.

The surface is painted and grained in red and black. The panels are bordered by a darker tone. Outlining these painted borders is an ochre line, simulating inlay.

The locks and hinges are original. Small areas of paint flaking have been restored.

History: This corner cupboard was among the early furnishings of the dwelling built, circa 1840, by Augustus Dozier at White Oak Plantation in Oglethorpe County. The cupboard remained in the same house and in the same family ownership until 1979.

15 Sideboard

Oglethorpe County
1840–60
H. 53¾" (overall), 42¼" (serving);
  W. 56½"; D. 20¼"
Primary woods: Birch with
  walnut knobs
Secondary wood: Yellow pine

Description: The splashboard consists of end plinths with nailed molded cornices connected by a top beveled board that is tenoned and nailed into the plinths. The splashboard is joined to the top of the sideboard by large dowels that pass through the top. The top is pegged to the case. Front and back stiles, turned at the bottom to form feet, hold the paneled sides.

There are two upper drawers and three center graduated drawers, which are flanked by paneled-door cupboard sections. The drawers are joined by half-dovetails top and bottom with smaller dovetails between. The drawer bottoms are beveled, slipped into grooves in the drawer sides, and nailed across the back. A wide center drawer runner serves both the upper drawers. Solid board dividers, separating the center drawers from the cupboard sections, tenon through the bottom of the case. The door rails tenon all the way through the door stiles. The case bottom is nailed flush with the sides, front and back.

The horizontal backboards slip into grooves cut in the back stiles and are nailed to the vertical drawer and cupboard dividers. The brass hinges, some of the iron locks, and the escutcheons, one of which is upside down, are original. The walnut knobs also appear to be original.

History: This birch sideboard was among the early furnishings of the dwelling built, circa 1840, by Augustus Dozier at White Oak Plantation in Oglethorpe County. The sideboard remained in the same house and in the same family ownership until 1979.

16 High chair

Oglethorpe County
1835–55
H. 39", S.H. 23"; W. 13¼"
Primary wood: Hickory
Seat: Oak splints

Description: Below the bulbous elongated finial tops are double ring-turnings separated by pinched necks. The posts then graduate in diameter, terminating with deep scribes above suppressed-ball feet. The chair has two bowed slats, which are arched across the top and bottom. On the bottoms they rake inward from the scribed posts, joining the arches. The top slat is pegged to the posts.

The splayed front posts graduate in diameter as they descend, with scribed marks around the top, at the seat entrance, around the two middle pinched sections, and above the suppressed-ball feet. The posts are connected by double-box rounds, the higher front one serving as a footrest. The seat, woven of oak splints, is torn on one side.

Traces of a later white paint are on the surface.

History: This high chair was among the early furnishings of the dwelling built, circa 1840, by Augustus Dozier at White Oak Plantation in Oglethorpe County. The high chair remained in the same house and in the same family ownership until 1979.

A Country Editor

Joseph Addison Turner

Joseph Addison Turner (1826–68) was a newspaper editor, a lawyer, and a planter in Putnam County, in the heart of the plantation belt of middle Georgia. He was the son of William Turner, who settled permanently in Putnam County shortly after its organization in 1807, and the grandson of Joseph Turner Jr., of the southeastern Virginia county of Dinwiddie, who had migrated to Georgia in the late eighteenth century. William Turner assembled a large tract of land that he named "Turnwold." It was situated several miles from Eatonton, the county seat. Here he operated a successful plantation. His son, Joseph Addison, became a lawyer and a politician, and in 1850 married Louisa Dennis of Eatonton. Soon thereafter, he purchased a 1,000-acre plantation adjoining his father's land and moved with his wife into a plain-style house that had been built much

earlier in the century on this tract. Here they grew cotton and corn, operated a tannery, and even ran a hat factory. They eventually appropriated the name "Turnwold" for their plantation. The plantation house stands today, but most of the outbuildings no longer exist.

Among the structures at Joseph Addison Turner's "Turnwold" was a print shop. Here he edited and published *The Countryman*, a weekly journal containing news, poetry, and essays on agriculture, politics, philosophy, and humor. It was molded after Joseph Addison's *The Tatler* and other eighteenth-century English literary newspapers. Publication commenced in 1862. The paper was immediately successful and was soon circulated in every state of the Confederacy. Joel Chandler Harris, author of the "Uncle Remus" stories, got his literary start at age fifteen as an apprentice typesetter in the print shop of *The Countryman*. Shortly after the close of the war, Turner was arrested by Federal military authorities for editorial comment considered disloyal to the United States. Restrictions were imposed that he considered violative of freedom of the press. His spirit broken by these restrictions and by his own financial ruin resulting from the demise of the plantation system, he permanently suspended

Turnwold, the home of Joseph Addison Turner. Courtesy of Special Collections, Robert W. Woodruff Library, Emory University.

THE COUNTRYMAN.

BY J. A. TURNER. —"BREVITY IS THE SOUL OF WIT"— $2 A YEAR.

VOL. V. TURNWOLD (NEAR EATONTON) GA., TUESDAY, APRIL 7, 1863. NO. 1.

A Northern Opinion of Southern Society.

"Among the most striking episodes in the proceedings of the Unitarian Autumnal Convention, which opened its session in New York last week, is the feeling excited by the remarks of Rev. Dr. Bellows, in an eulogy of Southern social life, and the influences proceeding from it. The opinion so frankly expressed by the reverend gentleman has elicited the most bitter comment among the members of the convention :

No candid mind will deny the peculiar charm of Southern young men at college, or Southern young women in society. How far race and climate, independent of servile institutions, may have produced the Southern chivalric spirit and manner, I will not consider. But one might as well deny the small feet and hands of that people, as deny a certain inbred habit of command ; a contempt of life in defence of honor or class ; a talent for political life, and an easy control of inferiors. Nor is this merely an external and flashy heroism. It is real. It showed itself in congress, early and always, by the courage, eloquence, skill, an success with which it controlled majorities. It showed itself in the social life of Washington, by the grace, fascination, and ease, the free and charming hospitality by which it governed society. It now shows itself in England and France, by the success with which it manages the courts and the circles of literature and fashion, in both countries. It shows itself in this war, in the orders and proclamations of its Generals, in the messages of the rebel congress, and in the essential good breeding and humanity (contrary to a diligently encouraged public impression) with which it now divides its medical stores, and gives our sick and wounded as favorable care as it is able to extend to its own. It exceeds us, at this moment, in the possession of an ambulance corps.

I think the war must have increased the respect felt by the North for the South. Its miraculous resources, the bravery of its troops, their patience under hardships, their unshrinking firmness in the desperate position they have assumed, the wonderful success with which they have extemporized manufactures, and munitions of war, and kept themselves in relation with the world, in spite of our magnificent blockade ; the elasticity with which they have risen from defeat, and the courage they have shown in threatening again and again our capital, and even our interior, cannot fail to extort an unwilling admiration and respect. Well is General McClellan reported to have said (privately) as he watched their obstinate fighting at Antietam, and saw them retiring in perfect order, in the midst of the most frightful carnage, 'What terrific neighbors these would be! We must conquer them, or they will conquer us!' "

Woman.

"Women do not transgress the bounds of decorum so often as men, but, when they do, they go greater lengths. For with reason somewhat weaker, they have to contend with passions somewhat stronger. Besides, a female by one transgression forfeits her place in society forever. If once she falls, it is the fall of Lucifer. It is hard, indeed, that the law of opinion should be most severe on that sex which is least able to bear it ; but so it is, and if the sentence be harsh, the sufferers should be reminded that it was passed by their peers. Therefore, if once a woman breaks through the barriers of decency, her case is desperate ; and if she goes greater lengths than the men, and leaves the pale of propriety farther behind her, it is because she is aware that all return is prohibited, and by none so strongly as her own sex. We may also add, that as modesty is the richest ornament of a woman, the want of it is her greatest deformity ; for the better the thing, the worse will ever be its perversion, and if an angel falls, the transition must be to a demon.'

An Honest Man.

"The Bank of England Directors had a terrible fright two or three weeks ago—not on account of the loss of their water-marked paper, but from a summary invasion of the bullion of the bank. A correspondent of the Birmingham Post, tells the story thus :

The directors received an anonymous letter, stating that the writer had the means of access to their bullion room. They treated the matter as a hoax, and took no notice of the letter. Another more urgent and specific letter failed to rouse them. At length, the writer offered to meet them in the bullion room, at any hour they pleased to name.—They then communicated with their correspondent through the channel he indicated, appointing 'some dark and midnight hour' for the rendezvous.

A deputation from the Board, lantern in hand, repaired to the bullion room, locked themselves in, and awaited the arrival of the mysterious correspondent. Punctual to the hour, a noise was heard below, some boards in the floor were, without much trouble, displaced, and the Guy Fawkes of the bank stood in the midst of the astonished directors. His story was very simple and straight-forward. An old drain runs under the bullion room, the existence of which became known to him, and by means of which, he might have carried away enormous sums. Inquiry was made. Nothing had been abstracted, and the directors rewarded the honesty and ingenuity of the anonymous correspondent—a working man, who had been employed in repairing the sewers—by a present of £800."

Avarice.

"After hypocrites, the greatest dupes the devil has, are those who exhaust an anxious existence in the disappointments and vexations of business, and live miserably and meanly, only to die magnificently and rich. For, like the hypocrites, the only *disinterested* action these men can accuse themselves of, is that of serving the devil without receiving his wages ; for the assumed formality of the one is not a more effectual bar to enjoyment than the real avarice of the other. He that stands every day of his life behind a counter, until he drops from it into the grave, may negotiate many very profitable bargains ; but he has made a single bad one, so bad, indeed, that it counterbalances all the rest. For the empty foolery of dying rich, he has paid down his health, his happiness, and his integrity, since a very old author observes, that 'as mortar sticketh between the stones, so sticketh fraud between buying and selling.' Such a worldling may be compared to a merchant who should put a rich cargo into a vessel, embark with it himself, and encounter all the perils and privations of the sea, although he was thoroughly convinced beforehand that he was only providing for a shipwreck, at the end of a troublesome and tedious voyage."

COMPANY.—"Those who have resources within themselves, who can dare to live alone, want friends the least, but, at the same time, know how to prize them the most. No company is far preferable to bad, because we are more apt to catch the vices of others than their virtues, as disease is far more contagious than health."

---

publication of *The Countryman* on May 8, 1866. In the last issue he editorialized with resignation in an article entitled "Adieu":

[*The Countryman* was] a representative of independent country life, and home of the planter. These are gone and *The Countryman* goes with them.

He moved from his beloved "Turnwold" to the town of Eatonton. Within two years he was dead, at the age of forty-two.

References: Paul M. Cousins, *Joel Chandler Harris*, Baton Rouge, La., 1968. Julia Collier Harris, *The Life and Letters of Joel Chandler Harris*, Boston and New York, 1918. Louis T. Griffith, "Three Writers in Middle Georgia and Their Influence on Southern Culture," *New Directions in Preservation, Georgians Research Georgia*, Georgia Trust for Historic Preservation, Madison, Ga., 1974, pp. 42–51.

17 Windsor chair

Putnam County
1810–30
H. 33 ¼", S.H. 16 ¾"; W. 16 ¾"
Primary woods: Tulip poplar
and hickory

Description: The crest rail is simply turned, deeply scribed at each spindle entrance, and extends beyond the outer spindles. These end spindles are bamboo-turned and scribed, as are the seven smaller ones between. The dished seat is rounded in form, and the splayed legs repeat the form of the spindles. The legs are tenoned through the seat, and are flush with the seat surface. The medial stretcher has an extra bamboo turning.* A later varnish finish is on the chair.

History: From Turnwold Plantation, the home of Joseph Addison Turner, editor and publisher of *The Country-man*, a newspaper published during the Civil War. As a boy, Joel Chandler Harris was employed by Turner and lived at Turnwold. Harris adopted this rural setting for much of his later writing.

* Similar Windsor chairs have been traced to Putnam County ownership (see Figures 175 and 176, *Furniture of the Georgia Piedmont before 1830* by Henry D. Green [Atlanta: High Museum of Art, 1976]).

A Baptist Preacher

Jesse Mercer (1769–1841) was born in Halifax County in northeastern North Carolina, the son of a Baptist preacher, Silas Mercer. As a lad Jesse moved with his family to Georgia, was baptized at age seventeen in the Kiokee Church near Augusta, and was ordained a Baptist minister at age twenty. He served as pastor for many years at four churches that his father had founded in eastern Georgia. Jesse's hymnbook, known as Mercer's *Cluster*, went through seven editions from 1813 to 1835 and included a few songs of his own composition. He was largely instrumental in the establishment of the Georgia Baptist Convention (of which he was president from the date of its founding in 1822 until his death nineteen years later), Mercer University, founded in 1833, and *The Christian Index*, a religious newspaper that he owned, published, and edited.

As one of the most prominent clergymen of the most popular denomination among nineteenth-century Georgians, Jesse Mercer was memorialized by many writers of his own day. Pertinent to his domestic and public life are excerpts from a biography by his lifelong friend, the Reverend C. D. Mallary:

On the 31st of January, 1788, being then in his nineteenth year, he was united in marriage to Miss Sabrina Chivers, daughter of Mr. Joel Chivers, and at the time of their marriage, step-daughter of Mr. Oftnial Weaver, of Wilkes county. She was a pious and orderly member of the Phillips' Mill church, having been baptized about the same time that Mr. Mercer became a member. . . . Miss Chivers was a poor orphan girl, bringing to her husband upon their marriage, a no larger portion of worldly goods than a feather bed; yet she possessed what was far more essential than mere earthly treasures, piety, prudence, industrious habits, and a heart devoted to the comfort and usefulness of her companion. . . . She was indeed a *help-meet* for her husband; for, beside her ordinary domestic duties, she spun and wove with her own hands, all the cloth he wore, and gained not a little renown through the country, for the neatness and beauty of her manufacture. . . . She submitted with great fortitude to the lonely life that she led in his absence, which was relieved only by the company of one of her maiden sisters, (of whom she had several,) who usually staid with her. . . . If there was a probability of his detention by high waters and inclement weather, she could hardly be drawn off to talk of any thing else; and accustomed to his punctuality, she would be constantly peering through a little chink, (she had one opening towards each end of the road,) looking with the liveliest interest for his return. As soon as he appeared, she would cry out "yonder he comes! poor thing!" and dropping every thing would run out to meet him with the greatest joy.[1]

[After the death of his first wife]

On the 11th of December, 1827, Mr. Mercer was united in marriage to Mrs. Nancy Simons, widow of Captain A. Simons, deceased, and then residing in Washington. His last marriage brought a considerable increase to his worldly possessions, and that he might not be needlessly encumbered by secular cares, most of this property was sold, and the proceeds thrown into such investments, as would yield him a reasonable income, with the least possible inconvenience and anxiety to himself.

Mr. Mercer considered himself truly fortunate in his last marriage. His second companion was no less devoted to his wishes and happiness than the first; possessing a spirit of unbounded liberality, she entered heartily into all his

The home of Jesse and Nancy Simons Mercer in Washington, Wilkes County, Georgia, during the 1830s and 1840s. Now demolished. Courtesy of Mercer University.

benevolent plans for the advancement of the Redeemer's kingdom, and was entirely willing that the avails of her large estate should be consecrated to pious purposes.[2]

The personal appearance of Mr. Mercer was peculiarly interesting, well calculated to arrest the attention of the beholder, and fix a lasting impression on his mind. None who had once seen him would be very likely to forget him.... In height he rose somewhat above the ordinary standard; in his younger days, as has already been noticed, he was spare, but in his advanced years, when his health was good, he was moderately corpulent. Time had gradually removed the greater portion of his hair, leaving at last but a few, thin straight locks on the sides and back part of his head, which still retained, however, their original dark brown color. His extreme baldness revealed to all the exact size and conformation of the citadel of his noble mind. This conformation was very remarkable. The horizontal length of his head from his eyebrows back, was very great, whilst his forehead seemed to rise upward with a greatly receding slope even to the very crown, exhibiting a most striking development of what phrenologists term the organs of benevolence, veneration and firmness.[3]

Jesse Mercer's watch cabinet, dated 1811.

Commenting on his dedication to learning and mental agility, George White records:

Such was his thirst for knowledge, that after his marriage and ordination, he went to school two years, to the Rev. Mr. Springer, a Presbyterian clergyman, under whom he made considerable proficiency in the learned languages.

In 1798, Mr. Mercer was a member of the Convention which was appointed to amend the State Constitution. His services in that body were highly valuable. A lawyer moved that ministers of the Gospel be ineligible to the office of legislator, which was warmly advocated by both doctors and lawyers. Mr. Mercer offered an amendment, to the effect that both these professions be included in the contemplated act. The motion was speedily withdrawn.[4]

Notes

1. C. D. Mallary, *Memoirs of Elder Jesse Mercer*, New York, 1844, pp. 27–29.
2. Ibid., pp. 108–9.
3. Ibid., p. 395.
4. George White, *Historical Collections of Georgia*, New York, 1854, pp. 684–85.

18 Desk and bookcase

Possibly Wilkes County
1810–30
Upper case: H. 50"; W. 39⅝"; D. 12⅝"
Lower case: H. 44½"; W. 41⅝"; D. 22"
Primary woods: Walnut and light
   wood inlay
Secondary wood: Yellow pine

Description: The cornice of the bookcase section is made in three parts. A
cove molding is nailed to the outside
of a narrow, flat, beaded board, which
is mounted onto a similar board and
attached to the case. The framing of
the two doors is of mortise-and-tenon
construction double pegged on the diagonal (see Figures 6, 54, and 68). The
eight panes of each door are divided
by raised molded mullions. There is an
inlaid keyhole escutcheon in one door,
above which is a small brass knob and
below an inset brass sliding latch. The
doors are hinged directly to the sides
of the case. Molding surrounds the
lower edge of the upper case and is
nailed to it. Inside there are four fixed
shelves, the two lower of which have
medial dividers.

   In the desk section, the slant-top
and four graduated drawers are inlaid
with cut-cornered inlay. In addition,
the slant-top is inlaid with the initials
"J" and "M" divided by a diamond
shape, above which is an inlaid
escutcheon. The original brasses with
beehive motif are inscribed, "Nothing without labor" (see Detail a). The
sides of the case continue to the floor
to form the blocking, or support, for
the applied base. The case is then cut
away in the center sections to allow
for the scrolled shaping of the base
(see Detail b). The base is in the form
of bracket feet dovetailed at each
corner. The drawers are dovetailed
with half dovetails top and bottom
and two central full ones. The bottoms
of the drawers are beveled, slipped
into grooves cut into the heavy sides,
and nailed across the backs. There is a
full dustboard between the second and

Detail a

Detail b

Detail c

third drawers. On either side of the top drawer are slides to support the molded-edge slant-top when in writing position. Inside, the center prospect door is made of crotch-grained walnut bordered by applied molding. This door is flanked on either side by four small drawers below four pigeon holes, which have scalloped valances (see Detail c).

The back edges of the upper and lower case sides have been rabbeted out to receive the vertical pine backboards. These are then nailed in place.

History: This desk belonged to Jesse Mercer. At the public sale of his personal effects it was purchased by Col. David Butler of Madison, the lawyer who drew Mercer's will. The desk descended to Miss Bessie Butler, from whom Mercer University later acquired it.

A Schoolmaster

Joseph Walker (1808–89) was the son of Joseph and Elizabeth Walker, natives of South Carolina, who settled in Wilkes County, Georgia. In the 1820s, Joseph (the son), on reaching maturity, moved to Dekalb County. In 1828 he married a widow, Jane Murphey Towers, who was seven years his senior. They built a frame house, which was modified in the course of years by additions. In 1879, Walker refers in his will to this house as his "family mansion." He named it "Mount Pleasant" after the town near Charleston, South Carolina, from whence his mother had come. Unfortunately no nineteenth-century photographs or drawings depict the house. A portion of the original house remains under layers of outer and inner sheathing. Joseph Walker was one of the last persons to attempt to raise silk commercially in Georgia. Original plantings of the white mulberry (*Morus alba* L.), a Chinese species imported for the culture of silkworms, survived on the grounds at least until 1952, and seedling trees of the white mulberry are still found there.

For many years a schoolmaster, Walker taught in three schools in Dekalb County: Panthersville, Ingleside, and a Clarkston district school, the "Walker School," named for him. Sometime before Walker's death in 1889, Decatur's earliest historian, Levi Willard, wrote in a series of letters published posthumously:

. . . but the old patriarch of school teachers is the venerable Joseph Walker, and besides a music teacher.[1]

In addition to being a schoolmaster, Walker was a planter and a prominent lay Baptist. He was one of the organizers of Indian Creek Baptist Church in 1839 and later of the Clarkston Baptist Church. When Sherman's forces burned Indian Springs Church in 1864, Joseph Walker wrote to a friend in the North, who immediately sent $325, a sum sufficient to rebuild the church. Walker was concerned about the welfare of the freed blacks after the Civil War. He donated land for the Mount Pleasant Church for black Baptists and that church's cemetery, adjoining his home place. He also gave land to Dekalb County for the county home for indigents.

Note

1. Levi Willard, "Early History of Decatur Written Many Years Ago," *DeKalb New Era*, December 2, 1920, p. 1.

Reference: *The Collections of the DeKalb Historical Society*, ed. Elizabeth Austin Ford and Austin McNeill Ford, vol. 1, Decatur, Georgia, 1952.

Facing page: A recent photograph of a remaining portion of the Joseph Walker homeplace, Mount Pleasant. (Photograph by William Hull)

19 Frame

Dekalb County
1835–50
Attributed to Joseph and
 L. S. Morgan
H. 46½", W. 53¾"
Primary wood: Walnut

Description: The frame is chamfered
from the inside to a flat 1½" area.
Bordering this is a raised beveled
outer section, mitered at the corners,
glued, and nailed.

History: According to family tradition, wood from a walnut tree cut on
the grounds of Joseph Walker's home
was used by Joseph and Lawrence
Sterne Morgan to fashion this frame
in their cabinet shop in Decatur. Lawrence Sterne Morgan was the father of
Henry Browning Morgan, who married Juliann Walker, Joseph Walker's
daughter. For further information on
the Morgan brothers' cabinet shop, see
introductory essay.

*The oil portrait on canvas (artist
unknown) of Joseph Walker and his
wife, Jane Murphey Towers Walker, was
painted sometime after their marriage in
1828. The date April 22, 1828, appears
on the page under Joseph Walker's quill
pen. On the wall in the background is
a portrait of Elizabeth Walker, Joseph's
mother.*

20 Bureau

Dekalb County
1835–50
Attributed to Joseph and
    L. S. Morgan
H. 37¼"; W. 42⅛"; D. 21½" (upper
    body), 19⅞" (lower body)
Primary wood: Walnut
Secondary woods: Yellow pine and
    tulip poplar

Description: The two-board top is pegged to the case. The deep facia board tenons into the stiles. The upper two-drawer section overhangs the lower three drawers by 1⅝". The upper stiles with half-turned tapering drops are applied to the main stiles. The stiles are cut away to receive the lower frames of the side panels and terminate in ball-turned feet.

The drawers have half-dovetail construction top and bottom with narrow dovetail joints between. The bottoms of the drawers are beveled, slipped into grooves in the sides, and nailed across the back. There are no dustboards.

The horizontal backboards are yellow pine and tulip poplar and nailed to the case.

Two of the drawer locks are missing, and some knobs have been replaced.

History: This bureau descended in the family of Joseph Walker. According to family tradition, it was made in the shop of Joseph and Lawrence Sterne Morgan in Decatur. The present owner is a descendant of both Lawrence Sterne Morgan and Joseph Walker.

Explanations to the Catalog

In the introductions to the various furniture categories are general statements which apply to the different forms that follow. In addition, certain specific technical characteristics peculiar to forms within the given group are discussed.

Some terms and characteristics apply to all six categories and others to certain forms within one or more groups.

In all cases, common names for woods, both primary and secondary, have been used.

Where original paint is intact, this has been noted in the descriptions. No attempt has been made in the catalog to assign original finishes to hardwood pieces unless there is positive evidence of such. Often chairs were left with no finish, though some were painted or varnished.

Nineteenth-century nomenclature for the forms has been used except for "three-cornered cupboards." These are referred to in the catalog as corner cupboards. Additionally, for clarity, chair bottoms are called seats. The parts of slat-back chairs are referred to as posts and rounds (see introduction to Furniture for Sitting); the same parts of Windsor chairs are respectively called stiles and stretchers. Seats of most of the slat-back chairs in the exhibition have sagged through use. The seat height given each chair in the catalog is an approximation between the highest and lowest point of the present seat.

Many of the tables found in the survey are finished on all four sides, indicating that they were meant to be used in such a way that all sides could be visible. No attempt has been made to define the use of most of these tables by assigning any object name other than "Table."

In the few incidences where rose-head nails were found, these were mentioned (see Detail, Figure 68). Other nails included both wrought and cut with square, T-shaped, or rectangular heads. Original wire nails were seen in a few pieces of very late date.

In all cases the term "escutcheon" refers to keyhole escutcheons, either inset or applied, made of iron, brass, wood, or ivory.

A V-shaped cutout is found on the tops of some desk legs as well as on those of tables, slabs, and other case pieces (see Detail a, Figure 107). The cut extends one to two inches deep on the interior corners of the legs or stiles. This cut was made after the leg (or stile) was attached to the apron (or side) and cut flush.

According to some present-day woodworkers, the purpose of this V-cut was to eliminate "high spots" when such occurred.

The doors of most bookcase sections of desks seen in the survey were hinged directly to the sides of the case and not to a front stile. This construction feature holds true for all seven of the bookcases with doors illustrated in the catalog.

A construction feature seen on several slabs is a horizontal board supporting the top along the back, inside the case. This board, approximately two inches thick and three inches front to back, spans the entire interior width of the slab and is attached to the back by either nails or screws (see Figure 6, Detail a).

Many bureaus and desks seen in the survey have one or more back supports for the drawer runners. The side runners join these back supports by tongue-and-groove or mortise-and-tenon joints. Sometimes the runners tenon into the supports and sometimes the reverse is the case. In most of the pieces, the drawers were heavy, being constructed of thick yellow pine or poplar boards, and this fact may account for the provision of extra support (see Figure 94, Detail b and Figure 109, Detail).

Measurements have generally been stated as height, width, and depth. In some cases these have been given for overall dimensions and for body dimensions to indicate the degree of overhang for the top or cornice.

In each furniture category, when possible, pieces were selected to illustrate a range of sophistication within the concept of "plain style."

Furniture for Sleeping

Sleeping furniture in nineteenth-century Georgia ranged in all aspects from crude and rude to sublime. The most elemental form was a pole rack, built into the side of a log house and covered with a straw mattress. Across the South, as far as Texas, this was known as the "Georgia horse,"[1] perhaps because of the rough ride it gave. Weary travelers passing through, as well as Georgians who later moved westward, carried with them memories of uncomfortable sleeping on these pole racks. At the other end of the scale was the extremely tall four-post bedstead with cords or slats to support a feather bed of goose down. Sleeping furniture was essentially the same in every part of the United States, though perhaps the post height of deep South bedsteads was greater, on the average, than their northern counterparts. Emily Burke, nineteenth-century visitor to Georgia, commented on the height of the bed in her guest room at a plantation house near Savannah in the 1840s:

This had very high posts and was covered with a spread so small that it gave the bed the appearance of standing on stilts![2]

Nineteenth-century inventories referred to beds as "bedsteads," and mattresses as "beds." "Bed furniture" consisted of sheets, counterpanes, quilts, coverlets (sometimes called "coverlids"), pillows, mat, rope, and rope key—all that went with a bedstead and its bed, including tester rack and hangings if present. Bed hangings sometimes included netting, either hung from the tester rack or simply draped over the bedposts. Regarding one item of bed furniture encountered in Georgia, a British traveler, Mrs. Basil Hall, commented from the vicinity of Dublin, Georgia, on March 25, 1828:

As to the sheets being of check, blue cotton, we have got quite used to that, and are not to be daunted by such trifles.[3]

In general "bedsteads and furniture" were accorded relatively high values on inventories and were frequently the subject of special bequests in wills. This is due more to the value of the textiles included in the "bed furniture" than to the value of the bedstead itself.

The corded bedstead was a mainstay in Georgia, especially in the early part of the century. A long rope was stretched through holes or around knobs from one side rail to the other and then woven over and under from the head rail to the foot rail. To hold the bed firmly together the rope was tightened frequently with a rope key. A mat woven of white-oak splints or other material was usually placed directly on the ropes, and on the mat rested a bed mattress of hair, straw, corn shucks, or Spanish moss. A feather bed was the uppermost layer, if one were available or desired. In Hancock County one Georgia farmer's wife, Mrs. Joel Hight, made a goose-down feather bed as a wedding present for each of her eight daughters, the first of whom was married in 1885.

Slatted bedsteads and bedsteads bottomed with solid boards were also common in Georgia, particularly as the century progressed and metal hardware, used to hold the bed together, became available. Trundle beds, cribs, and cradles were made throughout the century.

Notes

1. Lonn Taylor and David B. Warren, *Texas Furniture*, Austin and London, 1975, p. 41.
2. Emily P. Burke, *Reminiscences of Georgia (1840–41)*, Oberlin, 1850.
3. *The Aristocratic Journey, Being the Outspoken Letters of Mrs. Basil Hall Written during a Fourteen Month's Sojourn in America 1827–1828*, edited by Una Pope-Hennessy, New York and London, 1931, p. 236.

21 Under-eaves bedstead

Unknown county (north Georgia
  mountains)
1830–80
H. 32" (front legs), 22 ⅝" (back legs);
  W. 26 ¼"; L. 70"
Primary wood: Yellow pine
Secondary wood: Yellow pine
Callaway Plantation, Washington, Ga.

Description: The four legs taper above
and below the center in the same
manner with a slight bevel down each
corner. The tops are cut flush across.
Diagonal boards, which serve as head-
and footboards, are nailed to the front
and back legs. One is original, but the
other appears to be an early replacement. The side rails are beveled in
the same manner as the legs. Holes
bored in the sides receive the rope,
which holds the bed taut and acts as
a bottom to support the bedding. No
vestige of paint is apparent.

22 Bedstead

Hart County
1840–60
H. 47½"; W. 55"; L. 77"
Primary woods: Walnut and
    tulip poplar
Secondary wood: Yellow pine

Description: The mushroom-topped walnut posts are ring-turned. A lamb's-tongue shape is carved on all four posts where the lower edges of the head- and footboards enter. Below the pine rails the posts are turned to tapering feet.

The poplar head- and footboards differ greatly in pattern. The headboard is cut in a center-pointed crest flanked by graduating half-circles. The cutouts in the sides of the headboard are half-circles. The footboard is cut in four pointed crests with triangular side cutouts. The head- and footboards tenon into the posts and are nailed to them. The pine rails tenon into the posts and are held taut by rope.

History: Descended in the family of Will Crittendon, Gold Mine Community, Hart County. Similar turnings on bed posts of other Hart County beds are extant.

23 Bedstead

Burke County
1830–50
H. 88¾"; W. 58⅛"; L. 79½"
Primary woods: Maple and
  yellow pine
Secondary wood: Yellow pine

Description: The tall maple posts are all turned in the same manner. Below the rails, the posts relate closely in shape to those of Figure 25. The headboard is made of yellow pine and is scrolled across the top. It slips into slots cut into the inside of the head posts. Evidently the headboard was broken at one time and a 1½" portion is missing. The rails are notched out in 1" and 4" cuts to receive slats. The cut-out areas are numbered from 1 to 10 in numerals. The bed is held together by bed bolts, secured with the original iron wrench (see Detail). The quilt is from Sandersville, Georgia, and was a wedding present to the current owner's grandmother in 1867.

History: This bedstead was purchased by the current owner's mother in Burke County in the 1930s. At the time of that purchase another bedstead, almost identical, was bought from the same household. The beds had no finish but were "scrubbed white."

24 Bedstead

Randolph County
1840–60
H. 88"; W. 56"; L. 86"
Primary wood: Tulip poplar
Secondary wood: Yellow pine
Westville Village, Lumpkin, Ga.

Description: The posts are boldly turned with shallow, flat ring-turnings interspersed with deeper projecting ones of varying shapes and combinations. The scrolled headboard is deeply cut and the footboard shape is a repeat of the plainer lower section of the headboard. The headboard and footboard join the posts by mortised, tenoned, and glued joints. The pine rails tenon into the posts and are held taut by roping. A dark varnish finish is on the surface.

25 Child's bedstead

Stewart County
1850–70
H. 60"; W. 51½"; L. 61"
Primary wood: Walnut
Secondary woods: Yellow pine
    and tulip poplar
Bedingfield Inn, Lumpkin, Ga.,
    Stewart County Historical Society

Description: The posts are turned with mushroom-capped tops, above a bulbous form. Ring-turnings are in-terspersed along plain-turned sections. Holes in the tops of the posts suggest use of either a tester or extensions for supports to hold bed drapings. The posts are squared where the upper and lower rails enter. The foot termination relates to Figure 23. The molded arched headboard has deep circles cutting in at the lower edges of the arch, and then curving down to join the head posts. Spindles, echoing the turnings of the posts, are placed beneath the headboard and between the upper and lower rails. One side is hinged for lowering. The bolts, seen from the outside, secure the notched slat supports.*

History: Bed descended in the Singer family of Lumpkin, Stewart County. It is believed by the family to have been made for the children of Johan Singer, an early settler in Stewart County from Stuttgart, Germany.

* This bed relates to Figure 181 in the catalog *Furniture of the Georgia Piedmont before 1830* by Henry D. Green (Atlanta: High Museum of Art, 1976).

26 Crib

Unknown south Georgia county
1850–70
H. 23"; W. 30"; L. 47⅜"
Primary wood: White pine

Description: The body of the bed is joined by mortise-and-tenon joints and pegged into the posts, which are rounded at the top and chamfered on all edges. The posts are rounded again at the bottom. Holes drilled into the bottom edges of the sides receive the rope for supporting the bedding. The crib retains traces of the original red paint.

27 Child's bedstead*

Heard County
1830–80
H. 27¾"; L. 47¾"; D. 21⅞"
Primary woods: Yellow pine
   and hickory
Secondary wood: Ash

Description: The top rail is rounded.
The spindles are square and turned
into dowels where they enter the top
rail and the kerf-sawn seat. Each
spindle is held tight by a wedge set
into the top surface. A thick 3" ash
board is nailed to the two-board
pine seat. The legs, which are roughly
shaved and chamfered, pass through
this board and through the seat and
are wedged.

History: Descended in the Cook
family of Cooksville community,
Heard County.

* It has been suggested that this piece might
have been a bench rather than a bedstead.

Furniture for Sitting

Inventories from throughout Georgia confirm the fact that the turned, slat-back chair was by far the most common form of seating furniture in Georgia homes throughout the nineteenth century. In only a few instances was the term "slat-back" used in the inventories to describe this chair. "Common," "plain," "sitting," "setting," and "split-bottom" were the usual descriptive terms. Chair was pronounced "cheer" by many, and this pronunciation still survives in rural Georgia. The material used for the seat was a favored means of identification, and the following materials, preceding the word "bottom," appeared in chair entries in Georgia inventories: reed, rush, flag, straw, hay, shuck, split, splat [*sic*], hide, rawhide, leather, lather [*sic*], willow, and bark. Undoubtedly many of the numerous entries of chairs without further description referred to these slat-back chairs.

Inventories from twenty-two sample counties in all sections of the state contribute additional facts about Georgia seating forms. Windsor chairs, made in Georgia and in the North, were common in the state through the 1830s but their numbers declined thereafter. Fancy chairs appeared on inventories only from the 1820s through the 1840s, and even then they were rare. Some rocking chairs appeared as early as the first decade of the nineteenth century, but the form became noticeably more common after midcentury. Easy chairs, sofas, and settees were rare throughout the first half of the century, and only a slightly larger number were listed in inventories in the last half. Two corner chairs were included in first-decade inventories in Hancock County, but none thereafter. Cottage chairs and parlor chairs showed up in the 1840s and were common from the 1850s through century's end. However, not one was found through the survey. In later decades of the century, entries of lounge chairs, reading chairs, lamp chairs, cushioned chairs, stuffed chairs, stick chairs, and tête-à-tête chairs, among others, are found. Stools and benches appeared infrequently in the inventories; however, it is probable that these simple seating forms were more common in modest households that were not usually the subject of inventory or administration on the death of the owner.

In the hill country of north Georgia, a slat-back chair known today as the mule-ear chair was produced in the last three quarters of the century. The back "posts" of these mule-ears had no turned finials. Their front surfaces were shaved flat. Then the turned posts were soaked, and, while wet, bent backward to mimic the stiles of fancy chairs. Mule-ears were later made in all sections of the state, but they predominated only in the northern part of Georgia. In Piedmont Georgia and southward, the predominant slat-backs had straight back posts topped with turned knobs or finials of differing, distinctive shapes. Each chairmaker developed a favorite finial, which he adopted as his trademark. These finial-tipped slat-backs were derived from English prototypes and were made throughout the eastern United States. Hickory and ash were favored woods for slat-back chairs.

Contemporary nomenclature of the parts of all slat-back chairs made in Georgia was invariably as follows: the upright members or stiles were "posts"; the stretchers were "rounds"; the seat was the "bottom"; and the two to four flat horizontal rails that tenoned into the back posts above the bottom were "slats." In most chairs only the top slat was pegged or nailed to the posts.

Solid, stretched cowhide bottoms are frequently found on chairs in middle and south Georgia. The use of the hide bottom in America may have begun in this state or in South Carolina in the eighteenth century, possibly from African antecedents. The hide-bottomed chair spread westward to Texas and is usually considered a deep southern form. Woven leather seats were used elsewhere, particularly in Canada.

The common slat-back was made into children's chairs, high chairs, arm chairs, side chairs, and rocking chairs. Being relatively lightweight and portable, it was used both in and out of doors. Fortunately many have survived. Most show damage, but these signs of wear tell tales. Surfaces worn flat on the turned back posts of a child's chair tell of children learning to walk by pushing the chair across the floor on its back. Rounded feet on the back posts and worn back surfaces of finials on a "settin' chair" bespeak the common practice of tipping back against a wall. A broken or worn top slat tells that it helped support an ironing board. Foot-worn rounds, multiple pocketknife nicks, and whittled or scratched initials also tell stories never written.

28 Puncheon bench

Laurens County
1820–60
H. 15½"; W. 9½"; L. 62"
Primary woods: Yellow pine
   and white cedar

Description: A portion of a pine log
has been cut so that the flat surface
serves as a seat. The four white cedar
legs were roughed out and placed at
angles through the seat. They dowel
all the way through the surface and
are close together, splaying outward to
the floor.

29 Stool

Elbert County
1820–60
H. 5¾"; W. 8½"; L. 13½"
Primary woods: Walnut and hickory

Description: The legs are made of
either tree branches or small saplings
from which the bark was removed. No
attempt was made to turn them. Two
are hickory and the third is walnut.
The three legs tenon through the
beveled walnut seat and are wedged in
the centers.

30 Windsor chair

Oconee County
1810–30
H. 35"; S.H. 16½"; W. 16⅜"
Primary woods: Ash, tulip poplar,
    and hickory

Description: The bowed hickory back
is deeply scribed and the seven spindles are bamboo-turned. The poplar
seat is thick but not deeply saddled in
the center. The bamboo shape of the
seven spindles is repeated in heavier
form in the four splayed legs. The ash
legs are joined by three turned stretchers in the form of an "H" and are
tenoned through the seat. The center
stretcher conforms to the shape of the
legs. A later varnish finish is on the
chair surface.

History: This Windsor chair, one
of a set, descended in the family of
Augustus Pope Cochran of Gresh-
amville community, Oconee County.
According to family tradition, the set
was made on the plantation.

31 Windsor chair

Jones County
1835–55
H. 32½", S.H. 16"; W. 15⅛"
Primary woods: Hickory and
   tulip poplar

Description: The crest rail, or upper slat, is joined to the uprights by
mortise-and-tenon joints and is held
in place from the back by sprigs. The
medial slat receives the four ar-
row-shaped spindles. Beginning just
below the medial slat, the uprights
are shaved to the top. The seat is
basically square in shape, rounded on
the front corners and scooped out in
the center. The bamboo-turned legs
tenon into the seat bottom but do not
come through the top surface. Four
stretchers connect the legs, the front
one being bamboo-turned but worn
on the top surface. The seat and slats
are poplar, and the legs, uprights, and
spindles are hickory. It was probably
painted.

History: This chair, along with three
matching chairs and a long matching Windsor settee, descended in the
William Griswold Morgan family of
Clinton, Jones County.

32 Windsor chair

Clarke County
1835–55
H. 32⅛", S.H. 17"; W. 15"
Primary woods: Cucumber magnolia
   and tulip poplar

Description: The slightly arched crest
rail, or upper slat, mortises into the
uprights, which are shaved off upward
from midsection. The middle rail is
straight and receives the four turned
spindles. The back posts are decorated
with four score marks, which form
shallow rings just below the joining of the middle rail. The seat rakes
from back to front, tapering on the
front edge. The legs are splayed. The
front legs have shallow ring turnings, as does the front stretcher. The
legs tenon into the seat but do not
come through to the top surface. The
remaining three stretchers are plain-
turned.

33 Chair

Warren County
1850–70
Attributed to John Reynolds
H. 34½", S.H. 14"; W. 19¼"
Primary woods: Soft maple
   and hickory
Seat: Cowhide

Description: Ball finials on each post
top two ring-turnings, which are
divided by a short pinched neck. The
posts graduate in diameter almost to
the bottom at which point they taper
slightly. The three slats are angular in
shape and the top one is pegged from
the front. The turned front posts are
rounded on top and tapered at the
bottom. There are seven rounds (two
in the front and on each side, and
one in the back). The hide seat is
notched in the front corners to fit over
the top of the front posts and is pulled
taut underneath.

History: See introduction under
cabinetmakers for information on
John Reynolds.

34 Chair

Pierce County
1840–70
H. 36 ¼", S.H. 9 ½"; W. 16 ½"
Primary wood: Hickory
Seat: Cowhide

Description: The finials are whittled from the graduating posts. The three slats are equally spaced between the tops of the posts and the seat level. The hide seat is notched to fit around the posts and pulled taut underneath. The posts are connected by seven rounds (two in the front and on each side, one in the back). One of the front posts has been repaired on the bottom.

History: Descended in the family of first owner, Jane Albritton Jones (1833–1912), of Effingham and Pierce counties in the lower coastal plain of southeast Georgia.

35 Chair

Wilkinson County
1880–90
Attributed to Alfred J. Pierce
H. 36½", S.H. 18½"; W. 17"
Primary wood: Oak
Seat: Cowhide

Description: The finials are ball-turned with elongated necks above a heavier flattened ball-turning. The back posts graduate in diameter until just below the bottom round, where they taper to form feet. The three slats are arched and bowed. The front posts are boldly turned and scribed above bulbous and tapered feet. The front rounds are modified balaster-turned and those on the sides and the back are plain-turned. The hide seat is notched out at the front, passes over the top of the front posts, and is pulled taut underneath.

History: See introduction under cabinetmakers for information on A. J. Pierce.

36 Chair

Baldwin County
1890–1910
Attributed to Ben Dismuke
H. 35¼", S.H. 15"; W. 19"
Primary wood: Hickory
Seat: Cowhide

Description: The finials are simple, bulbous forms with a long neck taper-ing to the posts. The posts graduate in diameter almost to the bottom where they form tapered feet. The posts are scored for placement of the three slightly arched slats. The top slat is pegged from the front side. The scored posts are connected by seven rounds (two in the front and on each side, and one in the back). The hide seat is notched to fit over the top of the front posts and tied taut underneath (see Detail).

History: See introduction under cabinetmakers for information on Ben Dismuke.

37 Chair

Walton County
1835–55
Attributed to Billy Barton
H. 36", S.H. 14"; W. 18"
Primary wood: Maple
Seat: Oak splints

Description: The finials are modified acorn shapes. The posts are tapered from top to bottom. Ring turnings are evenly spaced down each post until just below the seat level. The posts are then plain until they terminate in ringed feet. The four bowed, undulating slats, dipping in the center of each upper edge, are most unusual. The top slat is pegged to the posts. The front posts, double-turned between the seat and first round, are connected by two plain rounds. There are two rounds on each side and one connecting the back posts. The seat is made of oak splints.

History: See introduction under cabinetmakers for information on Billy Barton.

38 Chair

Stewart County
1830–50
H. 36¼", S.H. 15"; W. 18¾"
Primary wood: Hickory
Seat: Oak splints
Westville Village, Lumpkin, Ga.

Description: The pointed-round finials are double pinched below the tops.
The sausage-turned back posts, scored
for placement of the slats, graduate
in diameter until they reach the seat
level, at which point the turnings
discontinue and the posts remain the
same diameter to the bottom. The
three slats are angular in shape. The
front posts are also sausage-turned
and terminate in pad-type feet. The
posts are scored for placement of the
eight boxed rounds. The seat is woven
of oak splints.

History: This chair descended in the
family of William H. House, who
married Mary Jane Gromberry in
Stewart County on July 31, 1834.
According to family members, the
chair was originally bottomed with
woven corn shucks.

39 Chair

Putnam County
1860–90
H. 36", S.H. 14"; W. 18¼"
Primary woods: Maple and hickory
Seat: Oak splints
Uncle Remus Museum, Inc.,
    Eatonton, Ga.

Description: Elongated scored finials with long pinched necks top the plain-turned graduating posts. The three bowed slats are arched across the tops and the top one is pegged to the posts. The front posts are plain-turned. The posts are joined by seven rounds (two in the front and on each side, and one in the back). The seat is woven of oak splints.

40 Chair

Stewart County
1856
Attributed to Perry Spencer
H. 35¼", S.H. 15½"; W. 18¼"
Primary wood: Hickory
Seat: Hickory splints
Westville Village, Lumpkin, Ga.

Description: The pointed finials on short shaped necks have score marks at the widest point and are again scored just beneath the necks. The posts graduate slightly until the foot is formed by a deep scoring and beveled taper. The three slats are angular in shape. The posts are scored to mark the slat and stretcher entrances, and a deep scribe delineates the tapered feet (see Figures 42 and 43). The posts are connected by seven rounds (two in the front and on each side and one in the back). The loosely woven seat is made of hickory splints.

History: This is one of a set of chairs made for the Chattahoochee County courthouse in Cusseta built in 1854. The Inferior Court of Chattahoochee County entered the following order on May 7, 1855:

Ordered by the Court that the County Treasurer be authorized to purchase fire dogs and setting chairs for the use of the Courthouse and one chair for the judge's stand, and further ordered that he have one table made for each Jury room and a sufficient number of tables for the Bar all to be round tables.

On May 2, 1856, the same court entered the following order:

Ordered by the Court that the County Treasurer pay Perry Spencer the sum of sixty-one dollars and forty cents for account of chairs for the use of the Courthouse.

41 Chair

Cobb County
1850–70
H. 30½", S.H. 12"; W. 17"
Primary woods: Hickory and
    soft maple
Seat: Oak splints

Description: The back posts with "mule-ear" terminations are shaved down the front surface. Just above the seat level the posts are ring-turned, continuing as plain turnings to the bottom. The three slats are arched, and the top one is pegged. The plain front posts are connected to each other and to the back posts by seven rounds (two in the front and on each side and one in the back). The bottom is woven of oak splints.

History: This chair descended in the Adams family of Kennesaw, Cobb County, Georgia.

42 Chair

Walton County
1870–80
Attributed to Billy Barton
H. 33½", S.H. 15½"; W. 17¾"
Primary wood: Soft maple
  and hickory
Seat: Oak splints

Description: The posts have no finials but are shaved on the front surfaces in "mule-ear" terminations. This chair is most unusual in that the shaved back posts are incised in a trailing vine design. There are three straight slats, all of which are nailed in place by tiny brads. Ring turnings decorate the front posts and the lower section of the back ones. The eight boxed rounds are turned with central rings and the front two are both ring- and flattened-ball-turned. The tapered terminations of the posts echo those of Figures 36, 40, and 43. The seat is woven of oak splints.

History: See introduction under cabinetmakers for information on Billy Barton.

43 Chair

Douglas County
1840–60
H. 41⅞", S.H. 16"; W. 22¼"
Primary wood: Hickory
Seat: Oak splints

Description: The descending graduated posts have flattened-ball finials that are scored around the middle. Additional score marks along the posts for the slat and round entrances are interspersed with ring-turnings and a pinched area below the seat. The slats, stepped in shape across the top, have vertical score marks to define small arched areas on the lower edges. The upper two slats are pegged to the posts.

The arms tenon into the back posts, flaring to handrests as they pass over the tops of the front posts. The front posts tenon into the handrests, and like the lower part of the back stiles, are ring-turned with pinched areas between. The posts terminate in tapered feet (see Figures 36 and 42). The posts are joined by double-box rounds.

The oak-splint seat is a replacement. Traces of green paint can be seen in the ring-turnings and under the handrests.

44 Rocking chair

Clarke County
1840–60
H. 46", S.H. 17½"; W. 24¾"
Primary wood: Unknown
Seat: Oak splints

Description: A slight swell tops the graduating back posts. The front posts are cut away just beneath the arms in an elongated turning. The center of these turnings is double scored to add to the decorative aspect of this detail. Each of the four uniform, arched slats is rounded across the top and is pegged into the posts. The flat, scrolled arms tenon into the front of the back posts and onto the top of the front posts. There are six rounds (one in the front, two on each side, and one in the back). The rockers fit into the rabbeted posts and are nailed to them. The green paint has oxidized to a dark color. The seat is woven of oak splints.

History: This chair was specially made for Wilson Lumpkin (1783–1870), Governor of Georgia from 1831 to 1835. He was the father of Martha Lumpkin, for whom Marthasville, later to become Atlanta, was named. The chair was probably made in Athens after 1842, when he built his home "Rock Hill." In his later years he was very portly.

45 Rocking chair

Wilkinson County
1900–1910
Attributed to Jesse Pierce
H. 38½", S.H. 14½"; W. 18⅝"
Primary woods: Hard maple,
    hickory, and oak
Seat: Cowhide

Description: The finial is a modified
urn shape with a short neck and a
half-ring turning beneath. The maple
posts graduate in diameter as they descend. The posts taper on entering the
oak rockers and are nailed to them.
The top slat is angular in shape; the
other three are slightly arched. Score
marks for placement of the maple slats
are evident. The posts are connected
by seven hickory rounds (two in the
front and on each side and one in the
back). The hide seat, a recent replacement, is notched to fit over the front
posts and pulled taut underneath.

History: See introduction under
cabinetmakers for information on
Jesse Pierce.

46a Child's chair

Wilkinson County
1890–1900
Attributed to Alfred J. Pierce
H. 20½", S.H. 9"; W. 13¼"
Primary wood: Hickory
Seat: Cowhide

Description: The round finials are scored around the middle. The neck pinches in with a score mark at the base. As the finial becomes the post, there is another score mark. The back posts then graduate in diameter to the bottom. The two slats are slightly arched. The club- or bat-shaped arms repeat the scoring close to the front. The front posts enter and support the arms from the underneath side. The posts are turned to cone shapes at the arm juncture, graduating to the same diameter as the back posts. Plain boxed rounds secure the base. The hide seat loops around the front posts (broken away on one) and is pulled taut underneath. The posts are cut away on the lower outside surface to allow the blade rockers to fit flush with the posts to which they are bolted. The chair retains its original brown paint.

46b Child's chair

Wilkinson County
1900–1920
Attributed to Jesse Pierce
H. 17½", S.H. 7"; W. 13¼"
Primary wood: Hickory
Seat: Cowhide

Description: The flattened finials with short necks swell to flattened ring-turnings. The posts graduate in diameter to the rockers. The two slats are arched across the top. The club-shaped arms have double score marks just before the entrance of the front posts and are flat across the front. The front posts have a 1"-round turning and an elongated neck before being plain-turned to the rockers. There are four rounds in a boxed arrangement. The hide seat, which was notched out and placed over the front posts before the arms were attached, is pulled taut from underneath. The posts are turned to dowels at the bottom and glued into the blunt-end rockers.

History: See introduction under cabinetmakers for information on Alfred J. and Jesse Pierce.

47 Child's chair

Putnam County
1835–45
Attributed to John Harmon
H. 18¼", S.H. 6"; W. 13½"
Primary wood: Hickory
Seat: Oak splints
Uncle Remus Museum, Inc., Eaton-
    ton, Ga.

Description: The finials are flattened
balls with elongated necks. The posts
graduate in diameter from top to
bottom with rings formed by incis-
ing on the lower part of the posts.
Score marks for placement of the
two arched slats are on the posts. The
arms are simple rounds that connect
to the inside of the front posts with
the handrests extending above the
arm connections. Single boxed rounds
secure the base. Traces of blue-green
paint are evident. The seat is made of
oak splints.

History: John Harmon is thought to
have made this chair in Hall County
for his granddaughter, Ella Nora
Harmon, born April 8, 1835. The chair,
having descended in the family to the
present day, has a detailed history of
use by family members from 1835 to
1967 with one or more sojourns in
each of the following counties: Hall,
Jackson, Franklin, Dodge, Putnam,
Colquit, and Lowndes. The present
owner in Putnam County has placed
the chair on loan to the Uncle Remus
Museum in Eatonton, Georgia.

48 High chair

Elbert County
1810
H. 38½", S.H. 21½"; W. 12½"
Primary wood: Hickory
Seat: Rush

Description: Ball finials with a short pinched neck are part of the graduating back posts. The three bowed slats are slightly arched across the top. The arms are plain-turned and connect the back and front posts. The front posts extend above the arms with a deep score mark and rounded handrest. Between the handrest and the seat is an elongated pinched area before the front posts begin graduating in diameter to the floor. Double boxed rounds connect the posts. The top front round is heavily worn from being used as a footrest. The seat is made of rush. The finish is worn.

History: This chair was made on the Elbert County plantation owned by Robert Jones and his wife Susannah Grant Allen Jones for their daughter Alice Narcissa, born September 25, 1809. It has descended through six generations of the same family to the present owner.

49 High chair

Wilkinson County
1890–1900
Attributed to Alfred J. Pierce
H. 31½", S.H. 18½"; W. 15¼"
Primary woods: Ash and hickory
Seat: Cowhide

Description: The finials are flattened ball turnings with pinched necks. The flared back posts graduate in diameter until just below the lower rounds, where they taper to the bottom. The upper angular-shaped slat and the lower arched one are secured by pegs. Score marks for the placement of the slats and rounds are clearly evident. The arms taper to a dowel and enter the back posts. They extend over the front posts, which dowel into the underside of the arms. The front posts have a slight bulbous appearance and half-ring turnings as they descend, tapering below the bottom round. There are five rounds (two in the front, one on each side, and one in the back). The higher front one no doubt served as a footrest. The hide bottom is cut out at the corners and pulled taut underneath the seat.

History: Descended to the present owner from his grandfather, Alfred J. Pierce, chairmaker. See introduction under cabinetmakers for further information on A. J. Pierce.

Furniture Related to Food and Drink

Four forms generally considered to be peculiarly southern fall into this category: the slab, or huntboard as it is now called; the liquor stand, or cellarette; the sugar box, or sugar chest; and the turn-top table, or lazy Susan. Other pieces of furniture used in the preparation, storage, or serving of food or drink include sideboards, cupboards, safes, eating tables, biscuit tables, and water tables.

Slabs were tall, long-legged, shallow-cased sideboards or tables, some standing as high as fifty inches. No two identical slabs have been located, although several have been found that appear to have been made by the same craftsman. Some slabs had turned legs, but most had square tapered legs, tapering on the inside surfaces. Some slabs had no drawers or cupboard sections. Some had a small central door opening into one large cupboard space. Others had single or multiple drawers of various sizes and configurations — with or without cupboard sections. In the survey it was noted that the tops of many slabs were made of two boards, the front board being considerably wider than the back board.

The question of how the slab developed and how it was used has not been answered. A clue is provided in the following excerpts from an account of the wedding of William Benson Jefferson Norman and Julia Ann Maxwell on July 9, 1871, in Hart County, Georgia:

The rain had ceased by now and the wedding party was relieved of the ordeal of going to the kitchen, where the wedding supper was to be served, in a drenching rain. The only difficulty now was to keep the long skirts from sweeping the wet flag stones between the house and kitchen. The kitchen was a short distance from the residence and was used for many purposes, besides cooking and eating. On special occasions, it was made to look quite festive.

They always had a high table for their weddings and the people stood up to eat. The bride and groom stood at one end at [*sic*] the preacher at the other. . . . The table was beautifully decorated with home-made artistry. The candlesticks were dressed up with pendants of curled paper and the candle light threw a soft glow over the artistically prepared food. . . . There were many cakes decorated with "flat cedar" and boxwood leaves in fancy designs on the white icing. Some of these were on high crystal cake-stands and some on low ones. These were placed on the table so as to give the proper high and low accent and the remaining spate was filled in with other things. Such as hand molded butter, sheep in pens made of stick candy and bowls of red apples, if the late apples would last that long. Chinkapins and chestnuts in small containers were pretty and gave the suggestion that the thriftiness of squirrels might be followed by newlyweds, too.

The wedding supper consisted of three famous Southern meats, ham, steak, and chicken; the three famous Southern indispensables, bread, butter and gravy; the three famous Southern pies, potato, apple and egg custard, and topped off with boiled custard and cake.

The infare, the next day was an important event, too, with the wedding party and close relatives and friends attending. The infare was a feast prepared by the groom's people and held at his home. . . . There were not as many guests as were at the wedding and sometimes the guests were seated for the infare dinner. But usually they stood at a high table decorated with fancy food similar to the wedding table.[1]

Slabs were made throughout the nineteenth century. After the 1830s, sideboards with deep cases developed as a form, continuing like slabs to be made throughout the century.

Of the forms generally considered characteristically southern, liquor stands and sugar boxes were the rarest in Georgia. There were few inventory entries and there are very few surviving examples. Perhaps their small size and portability accounts for the disappearance of some that were listed on nineteenth-century inventories. Undoubtedly some were destroyed or removed during and immediately following the Civil War. On Friday, December 16, 1864, in Liberty County in coastal Georgia, Mrs. Mary S. Mallard wrote:

They [forty or fifty Union soldiers] broke open Grandfather's old liquor case and carried off two of the large square gallon bottles, and drank up all the blackberry wine and vinegar which was in the case.[2]

No entries of "lazy Susans" were found in nineteenth-century Georgia inventories. Old-timers familiar with the form know it as a "turn-top table." Numerous "round tables" appear in nineteenth-century inventories and some of these entries probably refer to this form. John Muir, the famous naturalist, native of Wisconsin, wrote on October 2, 1867, at the home of Dr. Perkins near the Savannah River between Augusta and Savannah:

The family table was unlike any I ever saw before. It was circular, and the central part of it revolved. When any one wished to be helped, he placed his plate on the revolving part which was whirled around to the host, and then whirled back with its new load. Thus every plate was revolved into place, without the assistance of any of the family.[3]

Ulrich Bonnell Phillips recalled a lazy Susan table used in Troup County during his boyhood in the nineteenth century. The table was the same type as the one described by John Muir, but the method of serving food thereon varied:

The round dining table had above it, as a device for diminishing the need of attendance, a disk which might be revolved to bring to hand any dish desired. [4]

All the cupboards found in the survey, both three-cornered and flat-back, were made in one piece and most had solid doors, plain or paneled. A few three-cornered cupboards with glazed doors were found. The flat-backed cupboards located had solid doors or, occasionally, were made without upper doors, having open shelves in the upper section. The cupboards were made of pine and/or poplar, usually painted, as well as of hardwoods such as walnut. Hinges were usually butt type of iron or brass, sometimes applied to the outside surface of the piece rather than being recessed.

Safes were flat-backed cupboards, usually with panels of loosely woven cloth, tin, or screen wire to protect the food while providing ventilation, as well as protection from insects. A few safes contained solid wooden panels. The safes were generally made of pine and usually painted. Many were elevated on long tapered legs.

Water tables held buckets of water to fill pitchers for washstands and supply water for other household and kitchen uses. Biscuit tables, used in kitchens, were fitted with thick wooden blocks or marble slabs on which dough was rolled.

Notes

1. Quillie Norman, *A Short History of the Norman-Maxwell Families*, Shady Nook, Hartwell, Hart County, Georgia, 1953, pp. 205–8.
2. *The Children of Pride*, edited by Robert Manson Myers, New Haven and London, 1972, p. 1227.
3. John Muir, *A Thousand-Mile Walk to the Gulf*, Boston, 1916, p. 59.
4. U. B. Phillips, *Life and Labor in the Old South*, Boston, 1929, p. 337.

50 Slab

Hart County
1810–30
H. 40½"; W. 49" (body), 52" (top);
    D. 17" (body), 19⅛" (top)
Primary wood: Yellow pine
Secondary wood: Yellow pine

Description: The one-board top overhangs the back of the case. It is nailed to the body. The case and the slender tapered legs are joined by mortise-and-tenon joints and pegged. The two deep drawer fronts and backs are joined to the drawer sides by half-dovetails on the top edge and full dovetails for the remaining depth. The drawer bottoms are beveled, slipped into grooves in the sides, and nailed across the back. The interior drawer divider is solid from the top to the bottom and nailed to the top and bottom with T-head nails. The upper and lower sections of the divider mortise all the way through the backboard and are wedged (see Detail, Figure 54). There is a solid dustboard that serves as the runner for the drawers.

The keyholes are cut on the horizontal, obviously to fit the locks the maker had. The locks are actually cupboard door locks and are placed on their sides inside the drawer fronts. Parts of the original bail handles are still intact. On the side of one drawer is the name "E. V. White." The original paint has oxidized to a dark green.

51 Slab

Richmond County
1800–1830
H. 40"; W. 48½" (body), 53¾" (top);
   D. 18"
Primary wood: Walnut
Secondary wood: Yellow pine

Description: The one-board top is pegged to the case. The edge of the top is rabbeted, giving the appearance of a molding. The case is joined to the tapered legs by mortised, tenoned, and pegged construction. Before the top was attached, the three sections forming the front were slipped from the top of the legs into grooves cut in the sides of each leg and then pegged. The center section, with a high arch cutout, is spurred on the lower edges. These spurs, once part of the middle board, have cracked as a result of shrinkage. The sides of the case are cut in the same design as the center

front section. To hide the drawer sides, free-floating panels are rabbeted on their inside surfaces and catch on the drawer runners (see Detail). One of these panels is original; the other panel is replaced.

The overlapping molded-edged drawer fronts are joined to the drawer sides by half-dovetails top and bottom with large dovetails between. The back of the drawer repeats this construction. The drawer bottoms are beveled on the front edges, slipped into grooves in the drawer sides, and nailed across the backs. Nailed to the back of each deep drawer bottom is a 1" x 7" horizontal strip which serves as a drawer stop to keep it from falling out. The two deep drawers were compartmentalized for bottles, although the dividers in one are now missing. The locks with brass escutcheons are original, but the bail handle brasses are replacements installed in original holes. Evidence of later knobs can

be seen on all drawers. In the center drawer, flanking the brass bail handles, are the inlaid initials "J.B." The drawer runners tenon all the way through the horizontal backboards. The backboards are pegged to the case.

52 Slab

Chatham County
1820–40
H. 45"; W. 50" (body), 61⅞" (top);
   D. 22" (body), 24⅞" (top)
Primary wood: Yellow pine

Description: The thin top with wide overhang repeats the crispness of the entire piece. The back edge of the top is placed flush with the back apron and the top is nailed on. The tapered legs and the apron are joined by mortise-and-tenon joints and pegged. There is no evidence of early paint.

History: Descended in the family of the owners of Grove Point Plantation, Chatham County.

53 Slab

Elbert County
1810–30
H. 49 ⅞"; W. 43 ¾"; D. 19 ¼"
Primary wood: Yellow pine
Secondary wood: Yellow pine

Description: This slab is the tallest one found in the survey. The solid board top is attached to the case by 1/2" diameter pegs, or dowels. The sides, apron, and legs are joined by mortise-and-tenon joints and are pegged. The vertical drawer divider is cut with two tenons, which pass through the top and are visible from above. Long pegs then are placed through the top edge and pass through the tenons to secure them (see Detail).* There is no facia board above the drawer tops, but below them is an unusually deep apron. The drawers are joined by exceptionally wide (2 ¼") dovetail joints (see Figure 96). The edges of the drawer fronts cant slightly inward as they join the sides. The sides of the drawers are rabbeted across the back edge to receive the drawer backs. The sides continue past this joint and act as drawer stops. The drawer bottoms drop into the drawer frames and are nailed all around. The runners tenon into, but not through, the case back and the front apron. Drawer guides are nailed to the case sides. The tapered legs are cut with a "V" cutout at the top (see Detail a, Figure 107, and Figures 101 and 119). The backboard is one board set into the legs and pegged (see Detail b, Figure 6). The original Spanish brown paint remains on the surface. The knobs are not original.

History: Descended in the Dillishaw family of Elbert County, Georgia.

* The same construction feature is seen on Figure 56.

54 Slab

Carroll County
1837
Attributed to James Clayton
H. 39¾"; W. 59⅜" (body), 62¾" (top);
    D. 18⅝" (body), 20⅜" (top)
Primary wood: Yellow pine
Secondary wood: Yellow pine

Description: The solid board top is nailed to the case. A flat beaded molding is applied to the case directly beneath the top. The case is joined by mortise-and-tenon joints and is pegged. The front four legs are reeded the full depth of the case. The rest of the leg surfaces remain plain. The reeding is repeated on the divider between the small center drawers. The arrangement of the drawers, two shallow over two deeper ones, with two small drawers side by side above a central cupboard section, conforms more to sideboard configuration than do most slabs. The drawers are scribed around the edges. They are joined with half-dovetail joints top and bottom and full ones between. The drawer bottoms are beveled, slipped into grooves in the drawer sides, and nailed across the back.

The two-panel door, hinged on one side, is mortised, tenoned, and double-pegged on the diagonal (see Figures 6, 18, and 68). A quarter-round molding delineates each panel.

The two small center drawers slide on one wide medial runner behind the reeded drawer divider. This runner, pegged from the front, tenons all the way through the backboard. Beneath the case and behind the two center legs are braces, which, like the above runner, are pegged from the front reeded section and tenon all the way through the backboard (see Detail and Figure 55). The single board backboard fits flush between the back legs and is joined to them by mortised, tenoned, and pegged construction.

The knobs are replacements. Traces

of orange-red paint on top surfaces of some of the drawer fronts suggest that the slab was originally painted.

History: Descended in the family of James Clayton. Glued inside the top left drawer is an undated, unsigned paper, upon which is written by hand: "This sideboard was made about 1837 by James Clayton for his daughter Harriet Asbury Clayton Harper. She gave it to her granddaughter, Eulalia Harper Hughie, the oldest daughter of George W. Harper, who died in 1945 at the age of 100 years, one month and 14 days."

55 Slab

Oglethorpe County
1820–40
H. 47½"; W. 57½" (body), 60½" (top);
   D. 22" (body), 23¼" (top)
Primary woods: Birch and light
   wood escutcheons
Secondary wood: Yellow pine

Description: The 1"-thick two-board top is screwed from underneath to the case. The case is joined to the tapered legs by mortise-and-tenon joints and is pegged. The two beaded drawers have inlaid light wood escutcheons.

The locks are original. The drawer fronts are joined by half-dovetail joints top and bottom with narrow ones between. The back of the drawer has full dovetails only. The two-board drawer bottoms are beveled, slipped into grooves in the sides, and nailed across the back. Halfway up the case, medial drawer guides are nailed to the sides.

The beaded doors of the cupboard section are hinged and close with a lapped closure. An inlaid light wood escutcheon fronts an original lock on one door. The boards, which comprise the interior cupboard sides and sepa-

rate it from the drawers, extend below the case bottom, serving as a surface on which to nail the drawer runners.

The upper and lower edges and the middle section of the cupboard dividers tenon vertically all the way through the backboard. They extend beyond the backboard in the manner of the horizontal board of Figure 54, Detail. The backboard is set in flush with the legs and joined to them by mortised, tenoned, and pegged construction.

The brass knobs are replacements and one drawer front has a patch.

56 Slab

Harris County
1830–45
H. 49" (overall), 46½" (serving);
 W. 53½"; D. 20½"
Primary wood: Yellow pine
Secondary wood: Yellow pine

Description: The shaped splashboard is nailed to the back edge of the two-board top. The top is nailed to the case. The apron and the tapered legs are joined by mortise-and-tenon joints and are pegged. The vertical drawer dividers are cut with tenons, which pass all the way through the top and are visible from above. Long pins are then placed through the edge of the top and pass through the tenons to secure them (see Detail, Figure 53).

The center cupboard section is flanked by two drawers. The overlapping beveled fronts are rabbeted to receive the sides and are nailed to them. The backs of the drawers are also nailed in place as are the flush drawer bottoms. The glass knobs are Sandwich-type and appear to be original (see Figure 6). The surface retains much of the original ochre paint. The sapwood has caused the paint to separate, emphasizing the grain of the pine (see Figure 113).

57 Slab

Franklin County
1830–50
H. 48" (overall), 42" (serving);
  W. 48½"; D. 19"
Primary wood: Birch
Secondary wood: Yellow pine

Description: The splashboard is flat across the center 6" top section, then flows downward and upward, ending in delicate scrolls. It is screwed to the back edge of the one-board top. The top is nailed to the case. The sides and tapered legs are joined by mortise-and-tenon joints and are pegged. The medial drawer divider repeats this joinery and is double pegged. The drawers have half-dovetail construction top and bottom with full dovetails between. The drawer bottoms are beveled, slipped into grooves in the sides, and nailed across the back. The drawer runners mortise into, but not through, the front apron and the back.

The legs are boldly tapered from the inside just below the case level. The backboard is one board set flush with the legs and pegged. One drawer lock is still intact. The brass escutcheons are original but the knobs are replacements.

History: The slab descended directly from Seaborn Tate of Franklin County.

58 Slab

Franklin County
1870–80
Attributed to William Bennett
H. 44"; W. 60⅝" (body), 64½" (top);
   D. 18¼" (body), 21⅜" (top)
Primary wood: Yellow pine
Secondary wood: Yellow pine

Description: The two-board top (one 17⅛"deep, the other 3½"deep) is nailed onto the body. The tapered legs are joined by mortise-and-tenon joints and are pegged. The drawer front is beveled on the sides and the bottom, and overhangs the cutout in the apron. The heavy flush drawer bottom is nailed in place. An unusual method of locking the drawer is the placement of a nail through a small hole in the top and into an aligned hole on the top edge of the drawer. Original red paint is intact. The knobs appear to be original.

History: This slab descended in the family of William Bennett, of Franklin County, who according to family tradition was the maker.

59 Child's slab

Habersham County
1870–80
H. 24½"; W. 36" (body), 42" (top); D.
    12" (body), 14⅜" (top)
Primary wood: Yellow pine
Secondary wood: Yellow pine

Description: The two-board top (one 13¼"deep, the other 1⅛"deep) is nailed with square-head nails to the apron. The tapered legs are joined to the apron by mortise-and-tenon joints and are pegged. The drawer front overlaps the cutout in the apron. The drawer front is rabbeted and the sides are nailed on with T-head nails. The drawer bottom is flush and slips into grooves cut into the drawer sides. The back of the drawer is cut with mitered corners and nailed in place to hold the bottom. The drawer runners tenon into, but not through, the back apron.

60 Slab

Clarke or Madison County
1870–80
H. 47½" (overall), 44" (serving); W. 46"; D. 21"
Primary woods: Yellow pine and birch
Secondary wood: Yellow pine

Description: The splashboard is shaped at the ends and nailed to the top. The top is made of two boards (one 17¼"deep, the other 5¼"deep) joined by a tongue-and-groove joint.

There is a deep molding strip nailed to the case just beneath the top. The applied beaded molding that frames the side panels and three sides of each drawer opening in the case is nailed on. A matching bead is cut on each side of the center drawer divider, giving the illusion of applied beading. The center divider tenons into the case framing and is pegged. The drawers, with original cast-iron pulls, are rabbeted to a very thin front (about 1/8" thick) and the sides nailed in. The flush bottom is nailed from the

sides and the back. There is a wide center runner with a medial drawer guide, which is nailed to the front apron. A board is placed all the way across the inside of the back to serve as a drawer stop. The legs are tapered from the inside in such a manner that they almost appear to be splayed. The body is painted Spanish brown (now oxidized) and accented by green decoration in the form of outlines, slashes, and stars.

61 Sideboard

Oconee County
1840–60
H. 54" (overall), 43" (serving); W.
  60 ¼"; D. 22 ¼"
Primary woods: Walnut and mahogany veneer
Secondary woods: Yellow pine and
  tulip poplar

Description: A wide center plinth and
two vertical end plinths are connected
by horizontal banded sections to form
the splashboard. The splashboard is
doweled onto the top, and, like the
convex drawer fronts, is made of
mahogany veneer on poplar. The two-
board drawer bottoms are chamfered,
slipped into grooves in the sides, and
nailed across the back. The center
graduated drawers and flanking doors,
as well as the top, are mahogany veneer on yellow pine. The walnut knobs
and brass keyhole escutcheons appear
to be original. Surmounting the
rope-turned and acanthus-leaf-carved
columns on the case is a banded vertical section which repeats the design of
the plinths. The walnut front feet are
doweled into the columns; the back
feet are cut with two 2" tenons, which
mortise into the rear stiles. The back
feet are smaller and more delicately
turned than the front feet.

The walnut sides of the case are
paneled. The interior shelves are
poplar. The back is made of three long
horizontal boards, which are held in
place by the mortised, tenoned, and
pegged stiles.

History: This sideboard descended
in the family of James Madison
Willoughby (1820–84) of the Antioch
community of Oconee County.

62 Cupboard

Webster County
1850–60
H. 54½" (overall), 46" (serving);
 W. 43¼"; D. 18¼"
Primary wood: Yellow pine
Secondary wood: Yellow pine
Bedingfield Inn, Lumpkin, Ga.,
 Stewart County Historical Society

Description: The pitched splashboard is set into pointed end plinths and nailed to the top. A flat molding is applied to the top of the arch. Undercut decorative bracket returns stabilize the splashboard. The beaded ogee drawer front is applied to the drawer face and overlaps the fronts of the stiles. There is a scooped-out area under the center front edge of the drawer facing, which serves as a handle or pull. The drawer sides are joined to the front and the back by half dovetails top and bottom and one center full one. The drawer bottom slips into grooves cut in the sides and is nailed across the back edge. The tongue-and-groove joints of the door frames are glued. Decorative Gothic arch cutouts are glued to the front surface of the paneled doors and repeat the cutout design of the feet on the sides. One front bracket return is missing. The four tongue-and-groove backboards are nailed to the case. Under the front apron, 2" blocks support the bottom boards. Inside, there is a medial shelf. Traces of the original ochre paint are evident.

63 Cupboard

Gilmer County
1830–50
Attributed to Wesley Davis
H. 63¾"; W. 32"; D. 8½" (upper
   body), 12⅝" (lower body)
Primary wood: Yellow pine
Secondary wood: Yellow pine

Description: The top is nailed to the sides. The scalloped cornice fits into a cutout in the sides and is nailed in place. Below the cornice, the sides rake toward the back, and descend in a straight line almost to the lower shelf level, where they rake forward to form the deeper lower cupboard section. The sides terminate in boot-jack ends which act as feet. Three shelves are nailed in place, and a dish rail tenons through the sides. Applied to the front edges of the sides are chamfered 2" strips to hide the shelf joints. The lower front section is made of three vertical boards, the center one of which serves as the door. These boards do not extend to the floor, but instead leave a "toe opening" at the bottom. Iron hinges secure the door, and a turn-buckle keeps it closed. Inside is one shelf. The vertical rough-sawn backboards are nailed to the case. The original green paint is intact. The lower part of one scallop has been replaced.

History: This cupboard, a rare form in Georgia, was purchased from the great-granddaughter of Wesley Davis, who made it in Gilmer County, Georgia, between 1830 and 1850. He supposedly made four such cupboards, one for each of his children, but this is the only one extant.

64 Safe

Taylor County
1835–50
H. 82⅝"; W. 43½" (body),
    48¼" (cornice); D. 19¾" (body),
    22" (cornice)
Primary wood: Yellow pine
Secondary wood: Yellow pine

Description: The cornice is made of four composite boards. Attached to the body of the case is a carved dentil molding with drilled holes above the dentils. On top of and projecting from this board is another, which is nailed onto the dentil board. Again on top of and projecting from this second board is a thicker one. Finally the board forming the top of the case extends beyond all this as the top of the cornice. The upper section of the one-piece safe has two doors. Nail holes indicate that fabric or some other protective covering was applied to the doors and the sides. A turn-buckle holds the doors closed and butt hinges join them to the front stiles. The door frames are joined by tongue-and-groove joints and two drawers divide the upper and lower cupboard sections. The stiles continue to form raked feet.

Inside, there are loose shelves, which were at one time nailed in place. The drawer runners are flat boards. Unbeveled bottoms are set into grooves in the drawer sides and nailed in place. The sides of the shallow drawers are very thick and extend 3½" beyond the drawer backs to act as stops. The horizontal backboards are neatly chamfered and cut in a ship-lap method. On either side of each board, a flange or flat dovetail-type joint connects the boards (see Detail, Figure 101). These boards are all set within the framework of the body. The knobs appear to be original.

The main body color is blue. The safe is decorated on the drawers, lower doors, and sides with cut-cornered panels consisting of a white background sponged and dotted with blue, green, and rust paint.

65 Safe

Stewart County
1830–50
H. 66"; W. 46"; D. 24⅝"
Primary wood: Yellow pine
Secondary wood: Yellow pine

Description: The two-board top is joined by a tongue-and-groove joint and nailed onto the body. The body is joined by mortise-and-tenon joints, and is pegged. The panels are bordered by molding applied around the outer edges. The door is hinged with butt hinges. The back is made of tongue-and-groove boards, which are set into the rabbeted edges of the tapered back stiles and nailed (see Detail b, Figure 6). The outside edges of the tapered stiles, or legs, and the bottom edge of the body are beaded. Inside, there are two shelves and a solid bottom. The oxidized original red-brown paint remains intact. The knob for the door is missing.

History: Descended in the Dowd family of Stewart County from the former owner, John Barry Brazier.

66 Safe

Laurens County
1840–60
H. 70"; W. 40⅜"; D. 17½"
Primary wood: Yellow pine
Secondary wood: Yellow pine
Tin

Description: The cornice is made in three parts. The 1" x 2" beaded strip is nailed to the top of a deep cove molding. This molding is nailed to the case. A small round molding is nailed to the case beneath the cove, completing the cornice. The case is joined by mortise-and-tenon joints and is pegged, as are the doors. The stiles begin to taper below the cupboard section, forming tall tapered legs. The 9" x 13" punched-tin panels are held in place by mitered strips around each tin. There are three tins in each side and in each lapped door. An old turn-buckle holds the doors closed. A repair of an earlier closure can be seen on the upper part of the doors. The iron hinges are original. Inside the safe, strips nailed to the stiles form slots for the two shelves to slip into. The bottom is recessed. The edges of the rough-sawn horizontal backboards have been beveled and are nailed with T-head nails to the outside of the stiles. This backboard placement relates to Figure 101. The surface retains its original Spanish brown paint.

67 Safe

Greene County
1840–60
H. 58⅝"; W. 41⅛"; D. 16½"
Primary wood: Yellow pine
Secondary wood: Yellow pine
Callaway Plantation, Washington, Ga.

Description: The coved molding is nailed onto the front and sides of the case with the top resting on this molding and nailed. The molded strip down the back edge of the side is similar to that found on other cupboards (see Figures 13 and 14). At the base, this molding is sharply cut inward as a termination.

The doors are held on by original iron butt hinges. The six panels of tin have been punch- or slash-decorated from the inside out to represent the Georgia arch in the Great Seal (see Detail).* The wooden knob and brass keyhole escutcheon are original. The sides continue down to form boot-jack feet, which scallop up toward the center. The backboards are roughly planed and are nailed with square-head nails. Inside are two shelves. The original red paint is still intact over most of the surface.

* A number of safes from the same general area with similar construction details have pierced tin panels depicting, with slight variations, the Georgia arch.

68 Corner cupboard

Greene County
1810–30
H. 90"; W. 49½"; D. 20½"
Primary wood: Yellow pine
Secondary wood: Yellow pine

Description: The cornice is made in two sections. The cove molding is nailed to a flat beaded molding. This lower molding is nailed to the case. The cupboard top is unusual in that it is placed flush with the top of the cornice. Canted and fluted stile facings, forming pilasters, are applied to inner stiles and nailed to them. A medial molding makes the cupboard appear to be made in two parts. The bracket feet are nailed to the inner stiles. The stiles are shaped to conform to the feet and serve as the foot blocking. The bottom molding is nailed on the front. The eight-paned doors are mortise-and-tenon joined and double pegged on the diagonal (see Figures 6, 18, and 54). The door framing and the medial mullions of the upper doors tenon all the way through. These medial mullions are single pegged. All the mullions are raised and molded. Inside are three shelves.

The lower doors have raised beaded panels. The doors have lapped closures and original iron surface-mounted hinges. Inside is one shelf.

Three wide planed backboards are vertically placed running the full height of the cupboard. The center one continues to the floor, forming the supporting back foot. The backboards are held in place by rose-head nails (see Detail). The brass knobs are not original. The cupboard was probably painted and has been refinished.

69 Corner cupboard

Habersham County
1850–60
H. 93"; W. 48½"; D. 19½"
Primary wood: Walnut
Secondary woods: Yellow pine
   and tulip poplar

Description: The arched broken
pediment has turned finials on each
of the three plinths. This pediment is
attached to the facia board with an
applied molding. The cupboard top is
recessed beneath the pediment. Both
the framing and the doors are joined
by mortise-and-tenon joints and
pegged. The outside edges of the front
stiles are double-beaded, continuing
down to form the spurred feet. Shaped
corner blocks support the feet.

   The two eight-paned upper doors
are beaded and have raised arched
mullions. The lower doors are paneled
with the beveled surface on the outside. The brass hinges on the doors are
original. A molding strip finishes the
lower edge of the case. The backboards
are circular-sawn, the center one continuing to the floor to form the back
foot support.

   Inside, there are three shelves. Two
of the finials, one upper edge of the
pediment, and the knobs have been
replaced. Dark crazed varnish has
been removed.

History: Descended in the Lambert
family of Habersham County near
Clarkesville, entering the Meaders
family of White County when John
Milton Meaders married Mattie
Lambert circa 1873–74. Their children
included Cheever and L. Q. Meaders,
potters of the Mossy Creek District.

70 Corner cupboard

Franklin County
1845–55
H. 90½"; W. 48"; D. 21¼"
Primary wood: Yellow pine
Secondary wood: Yellow pine

Description: The cornice is comprised of two sections. The upper board is 5" deep and rounded on the front edges. It is nailed to a reeded, flared molding which is nailed to the cupboard sides and the facia board. On the back edges, reeding 1½" wide extends the full height of the cupboard. This reeding is repeated where the case front joins the sides. A ¼" strip is added to the left side of the upper cupboard opening just outside the hinges. The case is joined by mortised, tenoned, and pegged construction, as is the door-panel framing. The four reeded panels of the two doors of the upper cupboard section are separated by plain dividers. These dividers form elongated crosses in each door. A small patch on the lower right stile of the left-hand door repairs a hinge cut, apparently a mistake of the cabinet-maker. The paneled lower doors are separated from the upper doors and from the floor by cross-members, on the upper of which turn-buckles are screwed to hold the doors closed. The iron hinges and locks are original. One keyhole is cut on its side rather than vertically. On the back of the cupboard, one wide pine board on each side angles into a narrow center backboard. These backboards are nailed to the case sides, to the two shelves in the upper section, and to the single shelf in the lower section. The oxidized blue paint is original.

History: Descended in the Thornton family of Franklin County.

71 Corner cupboard

Fannin County
1840–60
H. 88"; W. 38⅛"; D. 24⅜"
Primary wood: Walnut
Secondary wood: Yellow pine

Description: The cornice is made of a double tier of boards, the top one nailed to the lower one and this one to the facia board and sides of the case. Two 5"-wide stiles are nailed at the outside edges to 3¾"-wide side returns. The stiles and side returns continue to form the front feet. The side returns are nailed to the bottom of the case. The four doors open to a center divider and are hinged to the stiles. The brass hinges of the lower section are original and the iron ones are replacements. The upper doors are comprised of two boards each, held in place by butterfly joints. Turn-buckles, pivoting on large wrought nails, hold the doors closed. Original hand-forged iron handles are attached in cotter-pin fashion. The lower doors are solid. The right one split at some point, and this split is secured by butterfly joints. The three-lobed apron is joined to each stile by a large, wide dovetail. The lower door divider dovetails into the center of the apron. The butt-joined backboards were shaved with a carpenter's hatchet (see Detail). The interior shelves are nailed to the stiles in front and to the backboards with square-head nails.

72 Corner cupboard

Banks or White County
1875–95
H. 95"; W. 50"; D. 24"
Primary wood: Yellow pine
Secondary wood: Yellow pine

Description: The cornice sits within
the front stiles and is shaped from
the sides to the center in the forms of
a scallop, a half-round, and a central
keystone. The stiles are chamfered
on the sides and joined to the side
returns. The paneled doors are joined
by mortise-and-tenon joints held with
tiny pegs. Six of the cast-iron strap
hinges appear to be original. The scalloped apron almost touches the floor
at the deepest points of the scallops.
Both apron and cornice are nailed in
place. Four shelves are in the upper
section and one in the lower. The
vertical backboards are rough-sawn
and nailed to the shelves and the body.
There is no evidence of early paint.

History: Descended in the Meaders
family, potters in the Mossy Creek
District of White County.

73 Turn-top table

Sumter County
1840–60
H. 28"; W. 54" (with grain),
    53" (against grain); turn-top:
    W. 33¾" (with grain), 33¼"
    (against grain)
Primary wood: Yellow pine
Secondary wood: Yellow pine

Description: The two-board turn-top section is secured by two 2"-wide, 31½"-long iron cleats, which cross in the center and are screwed to the turn-top on the underside. Two battens further secure the boards. The iron turning rod is tapered at the tip. This rod passes through a 1½" x 3" batten, which mortises through the side apron and is visible from the outside. The rod then rests on another cross-member running in the opposite direction and is nailed to the bottom of the apron with rose-head nails. The overhanging top is nailed to the body with T-head nails. The apron and legs are joined by mortise-and-tenon joints and pegged.

History: This table was found in the old Mitchell home in Sumter County, in southwest Georgia. The owner, who would have been a child in the 1870s, said that as children she and her brothers and sisters used to climb on top of the table and turn one another around whenever their parents would go to town for provisions.

74 Turn-top table

Oglethorpe County
1850–70
Attributed to Jim Harrison
H. 29½"; W. 61" (table),
    40" (turn-top)
Primary wood: Yellow pine
Secondary wood: Yellow pine

Description: The turn-top section is made of three tongue-and-groove boards, slightly beveled along the under edges and held together by two narrow braces that are screwed across the underneath side. A flush cross, beveled and rounded on the ends, further supports the top and forms the base for the iron turn-top mechanism (see Detail).

The tabletop boards are joined by tongue-and-groove joints and are nailed to the aprons. Underneath, a cross-member, strengthened by small side braces, receives the post of the turn-top. The turned legs have short

lamb's-tongue-type carvings at the apron level. The feet are tapered bulbous forms.

The top is scrubbed and the base retains its original Spanish brown painted surface.

History: Jim Harrison, who lived in the Philomath-Rayle section of Oglethorpe County, is said to have made this table for Pete Dalton from the Little River section of the same county.

75 Turn-top table

Gordon County
1880–1900
James B. Henson
H. 30"; W. 61" (with grain), 59¾"
 (against grain); turn-top: W. 36"
 (with grain), 35½" (against grain)
Primary wood: Yellow pine
Secondary wood: Yellow pine

Description: The turn-top boards are
secured by a beveled batten that runs
across the underneath side. A 5"-thick
pine block, beveled on the ends from
the top to the table, is screwed onto
the batten, establishing the height of
the turn-top section. A hand-forged
iron wagon-wheel axle serves as the
mechanism upon which the turn-top
rotates (see Detail).

Underneath the table top a 2" x 4"
batten is screwed all the way across
the table and a square hole is cut
through the center of it to receive the
turning rod of the turn-top. The
top, made of circular-sawn boards, is
screwed to the body. The tapered legs
are cut away at the top to receive the
apron, which is screwed to the legs.
On the inside of the apron are thick
reinforcing boards screwed to it from
the outside.

History: Made by James B. Henson
(born in 1856), a blacksmith living on
a farm in Gordon County in northwest Georgia. The present owner is
the granddaughter of the maker.

76 Banquet table

Putnam County
1815–30
H. 28½"; W. 48⅛"; L. 112 ¾"
Primary wood: Walnut
Secondary woods: Yellow pine
    and tulip poplar

Description: The three-part table (center drop-leaf and two D-end sections) has a solid walnut top. The leaves drop from a ruled joint that is hinged in three places across the table. The aprons of the D-ends are made of walnut veneer applied to poplar frames. The center-section aprons are veneered on yellow pine. The swing gates are yellow pine and the interior beveled corner blocks are poplar. A double-beaded molding finishes the bottom edges of the aprons. The flat-reeded panels of the upper legs (see Detail)* are attached to the apron frames by screws entering from the inside. The legs are then pinched and ring-turned before being reeded and tapered. The feet terminations consist of bulbous turnings and tapered extensions. The finish is untouched, and evidence of water bleaching, probably from mopping the floors, is seen on the feet.

History: This table descended to the present owner from her great-great-grandmother, Charity Jane Lawrence Jenkins Reed of Putnam County.

* Flat-reeded panels of this type appear in Philadelphia furniture.

77 Folding table

Oconee County
1840–60
H. 28¾"; W. 41⅞"; L. 57"
Primary wood: Mahogany
Secondary wood: Yellow pine

Description: The leaves are attached to the top by hinges on ruled joints. The top is screwed to the apron from underneath. The table has six legs, two of which swing out to support the leaves. The gates are made of yellow pine. The aprons are plain and join the top of the legs, which form panels of a flatly carved flower and leaf motif. Below the apron level, the legs are turned with flattened rings before the main body becomes a spiraled acanthus-leaf carving. Above the feet, the ring-turnings are repeated, the tapered legs terminating in brass castors. Beveled yellow pine corner blocks strengthen the apron.

History: Descended directly to the present owner from Barton Thrasher, on whose plantation between Watkinsville and Farmington in Oconee County the table was made.

78 Liquor stand

Upson County
1810–30
H. 41"; W. 24¾" (case), 25¼" (stand);
 D. 14⅛" (case), 14⅞" (stand)
Primary woods: Walnut and light
 wood inlay and escutcheons
Secondary woods: Yellow pine
 and walnut

Description: The liquor case and the stand are two separate parts. The one-board top of the case is set between cleated ends and is pegged. The molding surrounding the top is double-beaded along both edges. The case is dovetailed front and back and the bottom is nailed to the case. A light wood diamond-shaped escutcheon fronts an original lock. At the lower edge of the back there is a small gouge on either side where, originally, screws passed through the case, holding it to the stand. The case has never had interior bottle dividers.

A cove molding is nailed to the top of the stand. The lower edge and the apron and the tapered legs are beaded, and are joined to each other by mortised, tenoned, and pegged construction. The mixing board, which slides into the stand, is made of a horizontal pine board with walnut pegged cleats and a walnut front facing. The facing is banded with light wood stringing. Inside the stand, double 1" pine strips, running front to back along the stand sides, form slots into which the mixing board slides. The drawer, also bordered with light wood stringing, has a diamond-shaped inlaid escutcheon repeating the one in the case. The lock has been replaced. One original brass knob remains on the drawer; the other knob is broken off, and those on the mixing board are replacements.

The drawer front is joined by half-dovetails top and bottom with full ones between; the drawer back has three full dovetails. The planed and beveled drawer bottom slips into grooves in the drawer sides and is nailed across the back. Horizontal blocking further secures the bottom. The piece retains the oxidized original finish.

History: Descended in the family of James Means, a pioneer settler in Upson County. In 1977, when the piece was moved for the first time in this century, Confederate currency was still strapped to the bottom of the case.

79 Water table

Oglethorpe County
1840–60
H. 34"; W. 33¼"; D. 24"
Primary wood: Yellow pine

Description: The two-board top is nailed to the apron. The joining of the apron and legs is unusual in that the joints are not mortised and tenoned. Instead, the front surfaces of the legs are notched out; the apron is mitered on all corners, placed against the notched-out legs, and nailed. The legs, double chamfered in a decorative manner, pass behind the lower shelf apron with the same construction features as the upper apron and taper to form the feet. The lower two-board shelf is notched out to fit around the legs and nailed to the lower apron. A rounded molding strip conceals the joining of the shelf to the apron. Oxidized Spanish brown paint is still intact.

History: This table descended in the family of G. H. Arthur of Maxeys, Oglethorpe County, whose forebears settled in that county in the eighteenth century. It was sold in 1980 at the auction of Mr. Arthur's estate.

80 Biscuit table

Jenkins County
1840–60
H. 31⅞"; W. 30" (body), 36⅛" (top);
  D. 18" (body), 20⅜" (top)
Primary woods: Yellow pine and oak
Secondary woods: Yellow pine and
  tulip poplar

Description: The two-board top has applied molding around the edges (missing at front and one side). It is pegged through the top of the upper apron. The upper apron is made by four boards butted against each other. Around the bottom of this section is a beaded molding strip, mitered at the corners and nailed on. This forms a recessed area under the top to allow it to fold down over the thick poplar slab inside (see Detail). This slab serves as the work surface. The tapered legs and the beaded apron are joined by mortised, tenoned, and pegged construction. The drawer is missing molding on the sides and part of the lower edge. One large dovetail connects the drawer front to the sides. The drawer bottom is beveled, slipped into grooves on the two sides, and nailed.

History: Descended in a family who, since the colonial era, has owned a plantation in that part of Jenkins County formed out of the original county of Burke. Probably made in the years prior to the Civil War, the table continued in use into this century for biscuit making three times a day. The top was closed over the rolled biscuits to encourage them to rise before baking. Once a year the block was scrubbed and put out to sun.

81 Sugar box

Upson County
1840–60
H. 29½"; W. 29½"; D. 19¾"
Primary woods: Tulip poplar
    and walnut
Secondary woods: Yellow pine
    and tulip poplar

Description: The two boards of the beveled poplar top are set between cleated ends and glued. The walnut stiles are joined to the case framing by mortise-and-tenon joints and are pegged. Below the case the stiles are tapered to form feet. Raised poplar panels are on all four sides. The yellow pine bottom is cut out to fit around the stiles and is nailed to the case. A brass escutcheon covers the keyhole for the original lock.

The hinged top lifts, revealing a two-section interior (see Detail). The yellow pine and poplar divider is offset, fits into grooves in the panel framing, and is braced. The inside corners of the stiles have been chamfered to the case bottom and are pegged to the framing.

On the surface of all four sides, the poplar boards are stained to blend with the walnut legs.

Furniture for Textile Storage

Furniture for storing clothing, linens, and other textiles includes chests, bureaus, wardrobes, and linen presses.

Chests, now generally called blanket chests, held all kinds of textiles, including clothing. More chests were found in the survey than any furniture form other than slat-back chairs. There was a great range in size. Most were six-board chests, though a number were paneled. A few rested on stands, but most were supported on bracket or turned feet attached directly to the case. Some had drawers beneath the well section, but most had a single compartment, either dovetailed or nailed at the corners. Many contained a till box affixed to one side just under the top. The tops of the chests were hinged to the backs with iron strap or butt hinges, the latter being more common. A few chests were of walnut, birch, or other hardwood; a few had inlay; but most were of pine or poplar and were painted. Very few with graining or with painted and decorated motifs were located in the survey.

Bureaus were generally heavy and solidly constructed, often being made of thick boards. They stood on bracket or turned feet or on feet made from extensions of the stiles. The bureau fronts were straight. Wooden knobs were the most commonly used drawer pulls though, as with tables and slabs, a few bureaus were fitted with brass or glass pulls. By the 1840s, bureaus and other types of furniture were produced in the larger towns in shops by craftsmen utilizing various machines but also doing skilled handwork.

Wardrobes were common because most homes had no closets. It is therefore hard to explain the rarity of linen presses, which were cupboards with shelves for holding linens. Very few were found in the survey or in nineteenth-century inventories. The wardrobes, when made of pine or poplar, were frequently painted. A number with painted or wood-grained surfaces survive.

82 Chest

Walton County
1820–30
H. 28"; W. 43¼"; D. 14½"
Primary wood: Yellow pine
Secondary wood: Yellow pine

Description: The one-board top is bordered by a double-beaded molding. The case is of nailed construction. The case sides are cut to form feet in the shape of a heart top (see Figure 2). Scalloped corner brackets are nailed to the front feet and to the bottom frame.

One of the two thumb-molded drawers retains its original oval brass pull. The letters "W. J." are stamped on the underside of the bail of this pull. The drawers are joined by full square dovetails front and back. The drawer bottoms are set flush with the drawer sides and nailed. The drawer divider tenons through and is nailed to the case bottom. The drawer runners tenon into the frame bottom front and back.

The back of the chest repeats the configuration of the front except for the corner brackets and the drawers. In place of drawers, there are flush pine panels.

The hinges of the top are replaced, and the lock is missing. The original blue paint is intact.

83 Chest

DeKalb or Cobb County
1830–50
H. 22¼"; W. 44¾" (overall), 43¼"
(body); D. 17"
Primary woods: Walnut with
light wood inlay
Secondary wood: Yellow pine

Description: The top of the chest, with applied molding, rests on the top corners of the beaded legs.* The case is basically a dovetailed box with applied legs and molding. The beaded legs conceal the dovetail construction. Below the case the beading of the legs is terminated by an inward rake, forming the feet. Molding frames the lower edges of the case, and with the applied legs forms a paneled appearance. Strap hinges hold the top to the case. The inside of the top has been routed out to receive battens, placed there to prevent warpage. One batten is still intact; the other is missing. The lock is nailed rather than screwed in place. Inlaid in the front of the chest within a horizontal and pointed cartouche are the initials "H.P."

History: Descended in the family of Hardy Pace (1785–1864), who was born in North Carolina and came in the 1820s from Putnam County to that part of DeKalb County which was cut off to form Fulton in 1853. In the 1830s, Hardy Pace established a ferry across the Chattahoochee River, the road to the ferry being called Pace's Ferry Road, a street name persisting in Atlanta to this day. Shortly before 1840, Pace moved across the Chattahoochee River into Cobb County and founded the settlement now known as Vinings, later operating a tavern there. (Franklin M. Garrett, *Atlanta and Environs*, vol. 1, Athens, 1969, p. 108).

* Lining the top of the chest are pages from newspapers and books of earlier dates than the chest appears to be. Unidentifiable as to name or place of publication, one newspaper page contains an announcement, dated July 5, 1814, that David W. Crawford, Collector of Revenue, would be "in Warrenton in the county of Warren on Monday, Sparta in the county of Hancock on Wednesday, and Greensboro in the county of Greene on Friday." These counties are all located near Putnam County in middle Georgia.

84 Chest

Glascock County
1830–50
H. 24½" (front), 23" (back); W. 46½";
　D. 18"
Primary wood: Yellow pine
Secondary wood: Yellow pine

Description: The top is most unusual in that the sides extend beyond the case and are rabbeted on the lower edge to receive the molding. On the front edge, a rabbeted one-inch strip is added to form the same overhang as the sides, and the lower molding is then applied to this strip. On all three sides this molding is nailed onto the rabbeted area, creating the appearance of a typical full-box molding. The case is dovetailed front and back.

Although the base molding appears to be a separate piece, it is, instead, part of the base section (see Figures 85, 86, and 87). In this section, the sides dovetail into the front. The front base section is cut to form bracket feet and deep scallops which project toward the center. The base is nailed onto the lower edge of the case. Inside the chest are original strap hinges, a till with secret drawer, and a double iron lock. The piece retains the original blue painted surface.

85 Chest

Upson County
1830–50
H. 23"; W. 48"; D. 17½"
Primary wood: Yellow pine
Secondary wood: Yellow pine

Description: The top is one board bordered by a double-beaded molding. The case is joined by dovetails on each corner, and the feet continue the same joinery on the front. The base is made from one board on each side, cut out to form feet. The upper edges of these boards are beaded to appear as if a molding strip were around the base (see Figures 84, 86, and 87). The front is cut in a deep double scallop. Wedged corner blocks strengthen the feet. The bottom of the chest drops inside the case and is nailed. The base is nailed to the outside of the case. The original till and hinges are intact.

The lock is missing and one back foot support has been replaced. The chest retains its original red paint.

History: This chest was originally a part of the furnishings of the Shattles house, built in the early 1830s between Barnesville and Yatesville. The house, now demolished, was a plantation plain-style house of two stories with English Carpenter locks, cross-and-Bible doors, and Federal-style mantels.

86 Chest

Madison County
1830–50
H. 21¾"; W. 44½"; D. 18¼"
Primary wood: Yellow pine
Secondary wood: Yellow pine

Description: The beaded molding is nailed to the edges of the top. The body is joined by dovetails both front and back, as are the feet. At each corner of the case, a peg is placed through the upper edge of the case down into the top dovetail.* Although the base molding appears to be a separate piece, it is, instead, part of the base sections (see Figures 84, 85, and 87). Inside, there is evidence of a wide till, now missing. An off-center divider separates the chest into two sections. The original strap hinges and green paint are intact.

* This is a construction feature of chests made by Germans in the Shenandoah Valley of Virginia.

87 Chest

Franklin County
1830–50
H. 24½"; W. 42"; D. 16⅛" (body),
17¾" (base)
Primary wood: Yellow pine
Secondary wood: Yellow pine

Description: The solid board top is bordered by a butt-joined molding. The case and the base are both joined by dovetails front and back. Although the base molding appears to be a separate piece, it is, instead, part of the base sections (see Figures 84, 85, and 86). The front is cut into bracket feet with scored scrolls. The back base is unusual in that it repeats the shape of the front base without the scrolls. The side base sections are notched in a pyramid shape;* a wide till is inside

the case. The unusual apple green paint is original. The hinges have been replaced.

History: Papers dating from the 1950s found in the chest at time of purchase suggest use in the Winn family of Royston, Franklin County (see Figure 92).

* Several other pieces from northeast Georgia have been seen with this notched foot design.

88 Chest

Walton County
1861
H. 23½"; W. 42½"; D. 18¾"
Primary wood: Tulip poplar
Secondary wood: Tulip poplar

Description: The molding surrounding the edges of the top is double beaded and nailed on. Two butt hinges hold the top to the case. The case is nailed together, and the bottom is nailed to the sides. The base is comprised of applied molding and feet.

The feet, which are nailed to the chest, are formed from one piece across each side and the sides butt against the front. The back foot supports are long, arched extensions which are nailed into the bottom and sides of the base section.

The body retains its original painted and decorated surface. The background color is blue-green. Flowing from the bottom edges of a red and mustard circle and hex-sign motif are graduating ribbon designs. On each side of this central motif are horizontal red teardrops with a mustard dot at the tips. On the far right and left sides of the front are modified hex designs with mustard pointed ovals on the top and sides and another graduated ribbon flowing to the base. Across the bottom of the case are the initials and date: "MA TH 1861 CL TIT." On the sides of the case is a slightly different hex sign with a circle connected to line capitals by an elongated pointed oval. The original lock is intact.

History: Purchased from the estate of a descendant of the Clegg family, pioneer settlers in Walton County.

89 Chest

Polk County
1840–50
H. 21"; W. 40¾"; D. 17½"
Primary wood: Yellow pine
Secondary wood: Yellow pine

Description: The solid board top is bordered by a double beaded molding. The case is nailed together, the sides being slipped in between the front and back. The scrolled bracket feet are nailed to the bottom of the case. A heavy molding frames the joining of the case and the feet. The original lock is intact. The painted surface is an oxidized deep blue. On the top an ochre elongated diamond motif is emphasized by white flourishes on all four corners. The front is outlined in ogee form by the same ochre color

and bordered by a white line. Traces of ochre and white hatching are on the molding. The name "D. BROWN" is written in white across the front and on one end. Above the name on the end panel is an H-shaped motif with flourishes on either side. Intertwining lines decorate the outside edges of the sides (see Detail). The feet are outlined in the ochre color.

History: This chest was found near Cedartown, Polk County, in northwest Georgia. Oral tradition in the black family from whom the chest was obtained indicated that it had descended in their family since shortly after the Civil War. It was a gift from the former owner of their slave ancestors, a planter named Brown of Polk County, whose surname they adopted upon emancipation.

90 Chest

Jackson County
1840–60
H. 23"; W. 48"; D. 17½"
Primary woods: Yellow pine with
 birch or maple escutcheons
Secondary woods: Yellow pine
 and tulip poplar

Description: The top is one board bordered by a molded strip which is nailed on. The body is paneled and the frames for the panels are joined by mortised, tenoned, and pegged joints. On the sides, the lower panels correspond to the two front drawers. A molding strip surrounds the lower edge of the case. The stiles continue down to form the turned feet. The drawer fronts are rabbeted to receive poplar sides, which are nailed in. The drawer bottoms are beveled on all four sides, slipped into grooves in the sides of the drawer, and nailed across the back. A wide drawer runner with a medial guide separates the two drawers. The side runners are also unusually wide. The backboard is beveled in the same manner as the drawer bottoms and is set between the stiles and the apron. The panels and drawer fronts are painted red and the body green. The paint has oxidized to a dark color. Birch or maple diamond-shaped escutcheons are unpainted. The knobs appear to be original.

91 Chest

Sumter County
1845–65
Attributed to Micajah Buchanan
H. 36 ¾"; W. 40 ¾"; D. 18"
Primary wood: Birch
Secondary wood: Yellow pine

Description: The upper case and the drawer section are two separate pieces, creating a chest-on-frame. The top, or lid, is not original. The front of the case has twelve full dovetail joints on each side. The back sides of the case are rabbeted out to receive the thick backboards which are nailed flush with the sides. The projecting division between the upper and lower cases is actually the bottom of the upper case. The drawer is dovetailed with three full dovetail joints, the top one beginning about ½" from the top in the manner of the front of the upper case. The bottom boards of the drawer are flush with the sides and nailed to the bottom of the sides. The drawer runners are square until they approach the backboards. They are then cut into a peg shape, and this peg mortises through the back of the case. The pegs are wedged in the center to keep them tight. Boards above and below the drawer are mortised, tenoned, and pegged. The legs are cut in a lamb's-tongue shape as they leave the case and then are ring-turned. They terminate in a tapered bulbous form. The wooden keyhole escutcheons are applied. The drawer lock is intact.

History: Descended directly to the present owner from Micajah Buchanan, who made the chest for his daughter, Caroline. Born in South Carolina in 1804, Buchanan moved to Jasper County, Georgia, and then to Sumter County about 1820. He died in Sumter County in 1868.

92 Chest

Franklin County
1850–70
H. 24"; W. 38"; D. 17½"
Primary wood: Yellow pine
Secondary wood: Yellow pine

Description: The solid board top is bordered by a beaded mitered molding. The case is joined by dovetail joints, both front and back, to within 1½" of the top. At this point, T-head nails secure the front to the sides. Underneath the case two narrow boards running front to back at each end have been nailed to the chest bottom (see Detail).* The turned feet are doweled through these boards and through the bottom of the chest. The feet are then pegged from the outside front and back through the case. A second peg passes through the sup-

porting board from the sides and into the feet, thereby securing the feet both to the added board and to the case. Both the iron hinges and the wide till are original.

The surface is painted with an ochre background and then both rubbed and dotted with an umber color. On the sides, top, and front, there are red carrot-shaped designs with three featherlike projections emanating from the top and two others lower on the design. On the top and front the

carrot shapes are interspersed with green circles surrounded by the same elongated ovals suggesting sunburst designs. The feet repeat the ochre, red, and green coloration. Inside the lid are the following inscriptions in old flourished writing:

SAB
  Susan M. Winn
  Susan A. Burden
     S M Winn   her chist
                        1870

History: Bought in the Royston area, Franklin County, at the Holbrook family estate sale.

---

* Two other blanket chests and one bureau (Figure 99), found through the survey, have the same added-board construction. However, this chest is the only one in which the feet dowel all the way through the bottom of the case.

93 Chest

Hall County
1830–50
H. 23 ⅞"; W. 48"; D. 16"
Primary woods: Walnut with maple
   and cherry inlay
Secondary wood: Yellow pine

Description: The top is bordered by a flat double-beaded molding mitered at the corners. The two boards comprising the top are joined in an unusual manner. Three 2"-wide splints are set into mortises cut into the adjoining edges of the boards and are quadruple pegged. The case is paneled, the framing being joined by mortise-and-tenon joints that are double pegged.

There is a medial front panel divider. The stiles continue below the case level where they are turned to form feet. The upper and lower frames of the front are inlaid in the corners with stylized tulip designs. On the lower frame an inlaid diamond repeats the shape of the escutcheon in the upper frame. The medial frame section has an inlaid compass-star with dots at the ends of each point and corner serpentine designs. The panels are inlaid in motifs of half-sunbursts over isosceles triangles. These motifs relate to the painted designs of Figure 92.* The backboards and the bottom of the chest are yellow pine. The lock is intact.

History: Descended in the Whelchel family of Hall County. It entered the Meaders family of White County early in this century when Hattie Mae Whelchel married L. Q. Meaders, brother of Cheever Meaders, both potters of the Mossy Creek District.

* The chest also relates to an inlaid miniature blanket chest, Figure 93, in the catalog *Furniture of the Georgia Piedmont before 1830* by Henry D. Green (Atlanta: High Museum of Art, 1976).

94 Bureau

Rabun County
1820–40
Attributed to William Cathey
H. 48"; W. 36⅞"; D. 20⅜"
Primary wood: Walnut
Secondary wood: Yellow pine

Description: The solid-board top is pegged to the case and a beaded molding is nailed directly beneath the top. The case is joined by mortised, tenoned, and pegged construction. The front and side pieces of the base section, with double-molded top edge, are joined by dovetail joints. The base is nailed to the case. The design of the side apron, more elaborate than seen on most bureaus in the survey, establishes the design of the front apron, which is now missing the carved spurs along the bracket feet (see Detail a).

The overlapping drawer fronts are molded and scribed and have never had pulls. The drawer fronts and backs are joined to the sides by three full dovetails on each joint. The drawer bottoms are made of tongue-and-groove boards that run front to back. They are beveled on the front edges, slipped into grooves cut in the drawer sides, and nailed across the back. The side runners are nailed to the case and join the drawer dividers and back runner supports by tongue-and-groove joints (see Detail b). There are runner supports for each drawer as well as an under framing for the top. The material used in the construction of the chest, including the drawer dividers, is unusually thick. There is no bottom dustboard.

The vertical backboards extend to the floor and are nailed top and bottom to the case and to each of the drawer runner supports with square-head nails.

History: Descended in the family of William Cathey of Rabun County in the mountains of extreme northeast Georgia. According to family tradition, William Cathey was the maker.

Detail a

Detail b

95 Bureau

DeKalb County
1830–50
Attributed to Alex Chesnut
H. 44"; W. 37½"; D. 19½"
Primary wood: Walnut
Secondary wood: Yellow pine

Description: The dovetailed solid board top is finished with a reeded molding. The drawers are cock-beaded and half-dovetailed top and bottom with full dovetails between. There are two full dovetails on the back of the drawers. The drawer bottoms are beveled, slipped into grooves in the drawer sides, and nailed across the back. The runners of the two upper drawers join a continuous horizontal back runner by tongue-and-groove construction (see Figure 94).

The spurred bracket feet are dovetailed front and back. Vertical blocks and flankers, which are cut to conform to the shape of the feet, act as supports. The separate apron is double-cyma shaped and attaches to the underneath side of the bottom dustboard. Horizontal blocking stabilizes the apron.

The case sides are rabbeted to receive the three-planed, horizontal backboards, which are nailed to the case. On the top backboard, written in script with a pencil, is the signature: "A. Chesnut, Decatur, Ga.," under which is written: "Alex Chesnut."

The brasses are replacements. The drawer locks are intact.

History: Descended and still remains in the family of Alexander Chesnut (1809–81), who married Mary Ann McDill (1810–81) in DeKalb County and lived the remainder of his life in that county. His parents emigrated from South Carolina to Newton County, Georgia, in 1804. It is a family tradition that the bureau was made by him from timbers felled on the Chesnut land in DeKalb County.

96 Bureau

Madison County
1835–45
H. 36"; W. 32"; D. 18"
Primary wood: Walnut
Secondary wood: Yellow pine

Description: The two-board top is nailed onto the body. The stiles act as the outer framing of the side panels and continue down to form slightly tapered feet. The panels are held in place by upper and lower cross-members, which are mortised, tenoned, and pegged into the stiles. The front, back, and sides of the graduated drawers are joined together by one unusually wide (2"–2½") dovetail (see Figure 53). The bottoms of the drawers are beveled, slipped into grooves in the sides, and nailed across the back. Inside the case, vertical 1" x 2" boards are placed against the drawer runners from the top of the case to the bottom. These pieces serve as stops for the drawers. There is a solid bottom dustboard. The flat wooden knobs are original. The back is made of two tongue-and-groove pine boards nailed horizontally across the case.

97 Bureau

Stephens County
1835–55
H. 41½"; W. 34⅝" (body), 38⅝" (top);
   D. 19¾" (body), 20¼" (top)
Primary woods: Birch with light
   wood escutcheons
Secondary wood: Yellow pine

Description: The thin overhanging top is held in place by T-head nails. The top three drawers are all the same depth and dimension. The half-width bottom drawers are deeper than those above. Each of the drawers, with an original lock, has inlaid light wood escutcheons. The brass knobs are replacements in existing holes. Each side is composed of two thick panels, deeply beveled and evenly spaced between three 4" crosspieces. As the stiles extend below the case to form the feet, they are chamfered on all four edges and turned in a simple round. The drawers have evenly placed deep dovetails, both front and back. The drawer bottoms are beveled, slipped into grooves in the sides of the drawer, and nailed with T-head nails. The drawer dividers are mortised, tenoned, and pegged. The thick pine backboards are horizontally placed and repeat the construction of the side panels (see Figure 90). Dark crazed varnish was removed from the chest surface.

98 Bureau

Walton County
1840–50
H. 45⅛"; W. 45⅞"; D. 21" (upper),
   19⅜" (lower)
Primary woods: Yellow pine, birch,
   cherry, tulip poplar, with light wood
   escutcheons
Secondary woods: Yellow pine and
   tulip poplar

Description: The yellow pine one-board top is nailed to the case. One side of the case is made of poplar and the other of cherry. The stiles and the drawers are made of birch.

The stile facings that flank the two top drawers, and the center drawer divider, are made of cherry. Below the divided drawers are three graduated drawers, each of which has two original wooden knobs and an inlaid light wood escutcheon fronting an original lock. The drawer fronts are rabbeted and nailed to the sides. The drawer backs are dropped inside the drawer sides and nailed to them. The drawer bottoms are beveled, slipped into grooves in the drawer sides, and nailed across the back. A deep drawer divider separates the two top drawers and the second drawer. A matching board is placed across each back, and these serve as the drawer runners for

the two upper drawers. The rest of the drawers have a back runner support (see Detail, Figure 109) onto which the side runners are nailed.

The birch front feet and the yellow pine back feet are nailed to the chest bottom. A flat molding conceals these joints. The scalloped-apron shape is repeated on the case sides.

Two horizontal backboards, one of poplar and one of yellow pine, slip into grooves cut in the case sides and are nailed to the runner supports.

History: Descended in the Stephens family in the Split Silk community of Walton County.

99 Bureau

Madison County
1860–75
Attributed to W. B. Cooper
H. 48½" (overall), 45" (top); W. 36½";
  D. 17⅞"
Primary woods: Walnut and light
  wood escutcheons
Secondary wood: Yellow pine

Description: The splashboard is screwed to the top, which consists predominantly of a single walnut board. This board, however, was slightly shallow on one side so that a long narrow wedge had to be placed across three-quarters of the back edge, a feature quite common in rural furniture. The top is screwed to the case both from the top side and from underneath.

The front and back stiles are nailed to the case sides. The entire case rests on a 3½"-wide board running front to back to which it is nailed. Turned feet dowel into, but not through, this board (see Detail, Figure 92).

The dividers between the three small top drawers are tenoned and pegged into the facia board and the first horizontal drawer divider. The 1⅛"-thick horizontal dividers between the graduating drawers tenon into the stiles and are pegged. Each drawer has an inlaid light wood escutcheon fronting an original lock. The wooden knobs are also original. The 1⅛"-thick drawer fronts are joined to the drawer sides by 1"-deep dovetails top and bottom with slightly narrower ones between. Each dovetail joint is nailed. The drawer bottoms are beveled, slipped into grooves cut in the sides, and nailed across the back. The wide drawer side runners are joined to back runner supports by tongue-and-groove joints (see Detail b, Figure 94). This runner construction is used for all the drawers except the bottom one, where there is a solid dustboard. The vertical backboards are joined to

each other and to the back stiles by tongue-and-groove joints. They are nailed horizontally to each of the back drawer-runner supports.

On the side of one of the small drawers is penciled the name "W. B. Cooper."

History: Descended in the Mc-Whirter family of Comer, Madison County. William Cooper, the probable maker, is listed in the 1860 census of Burke County as a carpenter, age 27, from Burke County, born in South Carolina.

100 Bureau

Madison County
1870–80
Attributed to Bird Isaac Moon
H. 39"; W. 40⅛"; D. 18"
Primary woods: Tulip poplar
    and yellow pine
Secondary wood: Yellow pine

Description: A narrow splashboard with rounded corners is screwed onto the back side of the pine and poplar top. The drawer fronts and columns are poplar. The sides, drawer bottoms, drawer sides, and backboards are pine. The three drawers are ungraduated and retain several original flat wooden knobs. The top is nailed on. Heavy stiles continue to the floor, acting as a backing for the applied half-round ringed columns. Across each drawer divider a half-round molding is applied; the scrolled bracket of the front foot section attaches to the lowest round. The sides are cut in a boot-jack style to form the side feet. The drawer runners tenon into a back runner support and the backboards are then nailed to these supports (see Detail, Figure 109). The chest was probably painted.

History: This bureau descended in the family of the maker's brother, James P. Moon. See introductory essay for information on maker.

101 Linen press

Upson County
1830–50
H. 73¼"; W. 44" (body), 50" (top);
    D. 18"
Primary wood: Yellow pine
Secondary wood: Yellow pine

Description: The top is made of two boards with flat overlapping joints (see Detail). The top is an inch thick, beveled to a thin 1/4" edge from the underneath side and nailed on. The stiles continue to the floor and are tapered to form feet. The case is joined by mortise-and-tenon joints and pegged. The frames of the doors have the same joinery and hold the raised panels. The upper and lower doors, which are butt-hinged, are flanked by front side panels. Inside, the press is divided into two sections. There are three shelves in the top section and one in the lower. The top of each stile is cut with a deep "V" cutout (see Detail a, Figure 107, and Figures 53 and 119). The tongue-and-groove backboards are nailed to the outside surface of the back stiles instead of being placed flush with the sides (see Figure 66). On the outside edges the boards are chamfered within 5" of the top and bottom. The red buttermilk undercoat is richly colored with umber graining. The undercoat continues around the back on the chamfered edges of the backboards. The knobs appear to be original, as do the locks.

102 Wardrobe

Stewart County
1840–60
Attributed to Churchwell Patrick
H. 79"; W. 53⅛" (body), 59¾" (cornice); D. 18⅜" (body), 22" (cornice)
Primary woods: Yellow pine and tulip poplar
Secondary wood: Yellow pine
Westville Village, Lumpkin, Ga.

Description: The flaring cornice rests on a flat molding surrounding the top. Two full-length double-paneled doors are butt-hinged and set within stiles that rake at the bottom to form the front feet. The sides of the case and backboards are cut in the same manner to complete the feet. The frames for the panels of the doors are of tongue-and-groove construction. The body retains its original Spanish brown painted surface. The inset panels, beveled on the insides, are richly swirl-grained in red and black. In the top panels the graining pattern resembles a knot that radiates from the center. The interior is shelved only on one side to allow space for the hanging of clothes. The vertical pine backboards are nailed to the case side. The lock is missing.

History: This piece descended in the family of the present owner. A strong oral tradition has existed within the family that it was made by Churchwell Patrick, an early settler of Stewart County.

Furniture Related to Reading, Writing, and Record Keeping

Georgians entered the nineteenth century with respect for books. Even before the Revolutionary War, William Gerard De Brahm, surveyor general to George III for the Southern District of North America, commented in his report on the Colony of Georgia in the early 1770s:

There is scarcely a House in the Cities, Towns, or Plantations, but what have [*sic*] some Choice Authors, if not Libraries of Religious, Phylosophical [*sic*], and Political Writers. Booksellers endeavor to import the newest Editions, and take Care to commission the best, well knowing they will not incumber their Shops long, but soon find Admirers and Purchasers.[1]

A very respectable twenty-one Georgians from a total of approximately 400 persons throughout the United States and Europe were listed as subscribers to Alexander Wilson's pioneering nine-volume set of books illustrating in color the birds of America published in Philadelphia from 1809 to 1814.[2] By 1850 Georgia led all deep southern states by far in the number of copies printed annually of literary, miscellaneous, and scientific newspapers and periodicals, exceeded only by Pennsylvania, New York, Maryland, Massachusetts, and Ohio.[3]

This is not to say that nineteenth-century Georgians were bookworms. Indeed most were not, but books and furniture to store them in were a part of many households. For example, in Greene County in middle Georgia, roughly a third of the inventories recorded in the Ordinary's office from 1800 to 1870 contained desks, bookcases, or books.

The furniture related to reading, writing, and record keeping in nineteenth-century Georgia displays great variety. In the library at "Woodlands," the 1847–50 home of George Jones Kollock in the northeast Georgia county of Habersham, master builder and cabinetmaker Jarvis Van Buren installed built-in bookcases in a Gothic style befitting the design of the house.[4] Such built-in bookcases were exceptional, however. Some libraries were stored in freestanding bookcases with or without doors. Usually all the family books could be stored in a bookcase mounted on a desk or table, which was listed in inventories as a secretary, a secretary-bookcase, a desk and bookcase, or a desk and table. Thus storage for books, as well as for letters, documents, ledgers, pen, ink, and paper was contained in a single piece of furniture that also provided a convenient reading and writing surface. The bookcases were open or had paneled or glazed doors. Many contained pigeonholes for documents and account books. The desk section usually contained drawers, pigeonholes, or wells for additional storage.

Writing surfaces ranged from a flat tabletop preferred by Alexander H. Stephens at Liberty Hall to a rather elaborate drawer front that pulled out and fell or folded down, on the Empire secretary attributed to Tucker McDade of Putnam County, Georgia. The sloping writing surface of a lift top was a Georgia favorite, judging by the number of surviving examples found. The lift top covered a well in which a variety of items could be stored. The form is now generally referred to as a schoolmaster's desk or, when accompanied by a bookcase, as a plantation desk. The slant-front lid of a bureau desk became a writing surface when opened. Flanking the top drawer were two slides, which pulled out to support the lid. This was a common desk form in eighteenth-century America and continued to be made in Georgia well into the nineteenth century.

Probably no furniture form can give us a better reading of the owner's mind than the furniture used for reading, writing, and record keeping.

Notes

1. *De Brahm's Report of the General Survey in the Southern District of North America*, edited by Louis De Vorsey Jr., Columbia, S.C., 1971, p. 144.

2. Alexander Wilson, *American Ornithology*, vol. 9, Philadelphia, 1814.

3. J. D. B. De Bow, *Statistical View of the United States*, Washington, 1854, p. 157.

4. *The Architecture of Georgia*, edited by Mills Lane, Savannah, 1976, pp. 390–93.

103 Desk

Walton County
1800–1830
H. 42 ⅞"; W. 41 ⅞"; D. 21"
Primary wood: Walnut
Secondary woods: Yellow pine
   and tulip poplar

Description: The top of the case is dovetailed to the sides. The slant-top has cleated ends, which are cut to a 45-degree angle. The cleats are joined to the main body of the slant-top by mortise-and-tenon joints and are mitered at the corners. Behind the center prospect door are three gradu-ated drawers. Flanking the prospect door are four simple pigeonholes with divided drawer and a full-width drawer above. These small drawers are dovetailed together.

Below the slant-top are four gradu-ated drawers, the top one of which is narrower to allow space for the slant-top supports. The double-scalloped apron is cut into the front feet facings and bordered by an applied molding strip. The case sides are scalloped at the bottom and join the front feet facings. The main structure of the feet is tulip poplar, and under the apron, pine blocks reinforce the joining of the apron to the case bottom (see Detail). The drawers have half-dove-tail joints top and bottom with narrow ones between. The drawer bottoms are beveled, slipped into grooves cut in the drawer sides, and nailed across the back. Each of the drawer runners joins back runner supports by tongue-and-groove joints (see Detail b, Figure 94). The vertical backboards are beveled, and nailed across the top and bottom of the case as well as to each of the drawer runner supports.

The locks, brass escutcheons, and small drawer knobs are original. The brasses are not original but are placed in existing holes.

History: Purchased in the late 1930s in Walton County, near Social Circle, by the father of the present owner.

104 Desk

Warren County
1850–70
H. 3l"; W. 34½" (top), 32¾" (body);
 D. 19"
Primary wood: Yellow pine
Secondary wood: Yellow pine

Description: The top is nailed to the body, and the slanted writing lid, which covers a simple well, is held to the top by butt hinges. The sides of the case are joined to the slightly tapered legs by mortise-and-tenon joints and pegged. The lock is original. An applied molding on the front of the lid serves as a pen-stop. On the inside of the slant lid arc written the names "O C" and "W H Jewell." All the boards are deeply planed. The desk was painted red and has been varnished.

History: Descended in the family of D. A. Jewell (1822–96), who came from Winchester, New Hampshire. In 1856, Mr. Jewell and two other men purchased a textile mill built in the early nineteenth century by William Shivers. W. H. Jewell (dates unknown) and O. C. Jewell (1851–81), whose names appear on the desk, were sons of D. A. Jewell.

105 Desk and bookcase

Toombs County
1830–50
Bookcase: H. 48"; W. 35"; D. 11⅜"
Desk: H. 34½"; W. 36½"; D. 26⅞"
Primary wood: Yellow pine
Secondary wood: Yellow pine

Description: The cornice molding of the bookcase extends above the recessed top and is nailed to the facia board and the sides. The double-paneled door frames are hinged on the case sides and are joined by mortised, tenoned, and pegged construction. The horizontal framing of the panels tenons all the way through the frame sides. The boards in the top panels run horizontally and those of the lower panels are vertical. A brass escutcheon fronts the original lock. The knobs are missing. Inside the bookcase are three fixed shelves set into grooves cut into the sides. The shelves are held in place by tiny pegs in the case sides. The deep drawer retains its original glass knobs and brass escutcheon. It is joined by half-dovetails top and bottom with full ones between. The drawer bottom is planed and beveled and slips into grooves cut in the drawer sides. It is nailed across the back. The drawer slides on the bookcase bottom. Vertical backboards are nailed flush with the sides.

The body of the separate desk section is joined to the tapered legs by mortise-and-tenon joints and is pegged. The slant lid is bordered on the front edge by an applied molding that acts as a pen-stop. Inside the desk is a simple well. The three-board bottom is rough-sawn and nailed flush to the rabbeted sides. The backboard is set flush with the back legs and nailed in.

Traces of the original red paint are evident.

106 Desk and bookcase

Stewart County
1840–60
Attributed to Thomas W. Simpson
H. 54⅛"; W. 28⅛" (upper case), 30⅞"
     (mid-case), 28⅛" (lower case);
     D. 10¾" (upper case), 20⅜" (mid-
     case), 19⅜" (lower case)
Primary wood: Tulip poplar
Secondary wood: Yellow pine

Description: The desk is made in three sections. The upper section contains ledger slots and pigeonholes (see Detail). A molding is placed at the top edge of the upper case and nailed on. A flat board rests along this molding to finish the top. The panels of the hinged doors are set within a tongue-and-groove frame.

The middle section contains a double well and an area designed to hold pens. The fall front is hinged and folds out against the deeper well. This well section is joined by dovetail joints.

The lower section is the desk base and contains a single full-width drawer. The drawer front is joined with half-dovetail joints top and bottom and one full middle one. The back of the drawer is joined by two full dovetail joints. The drawer bottom slips into grooves in the sides and is nailed across the back. The legs are turned with a series of ring turnings between varying bulbous areas and tapered at the bottom to form feet. The circular-sawn backboards are yellow pine and are nailed onto the case. A dark varnish surface serves as a finish.

History: This piece descended in the family of the present owner. A strong oral tradition has existed within the family that it was made by Thomas W. Simpson, a pioneer settler in Lumpkin, Stewart County. Simpson was born near Nashville, Tennessee, on June 20, 1796, served in the South Carolina Militia in the War of 1812, and married Lucy Collins Simpson

of Edgefield District, South Carolina. In the early 1830s, Simpson and his wife moved from Bibb to Stewart County, in the southwestern portion of the state. Here for many years he operated a cabinet shop. He died in Lumpkin in 1884. (Helen Eliza Terrill, ed., *History of Stewart County*, vol. 1, Columbus, Ga., 1958, p. 587.)

107 Desk and bookcase

Jenkins County
1869
J. A. Brinson
Upper case: H. 24½"; W. 30¾";
   D. 9½"
Lower case: H. 34½"; W. 33"; D. 23⅞"
Primary wood: Yellow pine
Secondary wood: Yellow pine

Description: The upper case is framed with a mitered flat 1½" pine facing that projects from the top and sides. The medial shelf is set into grooves in the sides. The horizontal backboards show the marks of a circular saw and are nailed to the sides of the case. The lid of the desk section lifts to reveal a single storage compartment.

The tapered legs are joined to the frame by mortise-and-tenon joints and are pegged. On the top surface of the legs, a V-shaped cutout is seen (see Detail a). The backboard is smooth-planed, and incised is the following: "J. A. Brinson, Maker, June 16, 1869" (see Detail b). The bottom boards are both rough-sawn and circular-sawn, and are nailed in place. The desk was probably painted and has been refinished.

History: The desk was found in Millen, Jenkins County, in the eastern portion of Georgia. Although several different people with the name "J. A. Brinson" appear in nineteenth-century records of the area, it was probably made by the John A. Brinson who was listed as a carpenter, age 28, in the 1850 census of Burke County. The cemetery records of Green Fork Baptist Church in Jenkins County (partially formed from Burke in 1905) list John A. Brinson, born September 10, 1821, died December 14, 1897.

Detail a

Detail b

108 Desk and bookcase

Wilkes County
1840–60
Upper case: H. 52¼"; W. 42½"; D. 12"
Lower case: H. 29⅜"; W. 43¼";
    D. 20⅝"
Primary woods: Tulip poplar
    and yellow pine
Secondary wood: Yellow pine

Description: The cornice is made
of mitered flaring boards which are
nailed onto the top of the case. Just
beneath is a beaded block molding
strip that finishes the cornice. The
frames of the eight-paned doors are
quite thick (5/8") and are joined by
mortise-and-tenon joints and butt-
hinged to the case. The tenon goes all
the way through the frame sides. The
doors close in the center with a half-
round cover strip. The same blocked
molding as used on the cornice finishes the lower edge of the bookcase
section. The shelves are nailed into the
case from the pine sides. The tongue-
and-groove backboards of the upper
case run vertically and are nailed.

The lower case appears to be a
table, but the front of the top opens to
reveal a desk area, or well. This lift-top
is hinged directly in front of the upper
case. The lock is intact on the apron
board. The bottom boards of the desk
section run front to back. The legs are
tapered from top to bottom and are
joined to the apron by mortise-and-
tenon joints.

History: Descended in the Burdett
family, whose home place was on the
Lincolnton Road in Wilkes County.

109 Desk and bookcase

Elbert County
1840–60
Upper case: H. 58 ½"; W. 44"; D. 11 ⅝"
Lower case: H. 28 ¾"; W. 45 ⅝";
   D. 20 ¾"
Primary woods: Yellow pine and
   walnut veneer
Secondary wood: Yellow pine

Description: The cornice is comprised of two molded pieces, the lower one nailed to the case and the upper one nailed to the lower piece. A half-round bead, 1 ¼" below the lower molding, is applied to the case, framing the upper edge of the doors and wrapping around the sides. The doors butt together, with a molded strip on one door finishing the edge. There are two panes in each door, which are held in place by a medial mullion. Inside the case there are five nonadjustable shelves. The butt hinges project on the sides. The three small drawers in the upper section have half-dovetail joints top and bottom and one central full dovetail. In the back of the drawers there are two full dovetails, one at the top and one about ½" from the bottom. Most of the small brass knobs appear to be original.

Bordering the fold-over writing leaf is a crossband of walnut veneer designed to frame fabric (now missing) for the writing section. Rectangular pullouts support the writing leaf when open. The three large drawers are dovetailed in the same manner as the small ones with full dovetail joints between the half-dovetail joints top and

bottom. These drawers are supported by drawer slides on the side of the case and by dividers that are repeated in the back of the case (see Detail). The slightly rounded front stiles butt into the feet, which are shaped, extended brackets that are applied to vertical blocks. The case sides are cut out to form the sides of the feet. The beveled

lower case backboards continue down to form the back sides of the feet. The upper case backboards are not beveled but are merely placed flush with the sides of the case and nailed with square-head nails. Traces of the original paint are evident.

110 Desk and bookcase

Putnam County
1830–50
Attributed to Tucker McDade
H. 46"; W. 48"; D. 20¾"
Lower case: H. 42½"; W. 50¼";
 D. 10"
Cornice: W. 49"
Primary woods: Birch and walnut
Secondary woods: Yellow pine
 and tulip poplar

Description: The cornice is comprised
of three boards stacked one on the
other and nailed to the case. The upper and lower boards are molded and
the center one is flat. The six-paned
doors, which butt together, have
molded mullions and are joined to the
case sides with original brass hinges.
A molded strip borders the lower
edge of the separate upper case. Inside
are three nonadjustable shelves. The
horizontal backboards are set into the
rabbeted case sides and nailed with
T-head nails.

 The lower case has three drawers below the fall-front desk section.
The drawers are flanked by wide
stiles, which, below the desk level, are
hatched in a pineapple design above
a longer spiral-turned column. The
lower part of the front feet repeat
the spiral turning of the column. The
paneled sides are joined by mortise-
and-tenon joints and are pegged. The
back feet are raked extensions of the
vertically paneled backboards.

 The simulated drawer front drops
to reveal the desk section. The supporting sides of the desk section curve
down gracefully from the top of the
pigeonholes forward. The scallop-
board above the pigeonholes is part
of the casework of the desk section.
The small pigeonholes surmount a
double tier of eight small drawers
(see Detail). On the side of one of the
small drawers is written "Tucker Mc
Dade, Eatonton, Ga." In addition to
the drawer runners, a center supporting member runs front to back, under

the desk section, and tenons into the
drawer divider and through the paneled backboards.

 The wooden knobs and most of the
small brass ones, as well as the locks
and hardware, appear to be original.

History: Descended in the McDade
family. Tucker McDade, said by the
family to be the maker, was the great-
great-grandfather of Lawson Jenkin
McDade (1892–1978) of Eatonton,
from whose widow the piece was
purchased.

111 Bookcase

Stewart County
1850–60
H. 85¾"; W. 42" (body), 48½" (cornice); D. 7½" (upper case), 15¼" (lower case)
Primary wood: Yellow pine
Secondary wood: Yellow pine
Westville Village, Lumpkin, Ga.

Description: The cornice is comprised of a deep ogee molding with a flat top-board nailed on. Two inches down the case from the ogee molding is a ¼"-molded strip that acts as a frame for the top of the doors (see Figure 109). The door framings are joined by tongue-and-groove joints and glued. Each of the two upper doors is made of two glass panes separated by a medial strip. An applied half-round strip covers the door-closure, and the escutcheon is intact. The doors hinge on the side of the case. Surrounding the bottom of the upper case is a rounded molding. The doors of the lower case are paneled. The apron and the scalloped bracket feet are all cut from one piece, and the sides of the feet are formed from cutouts of the cupboard sides. Vertical corner blocks of yellow pine strengthen the front feet. The circular-sawn backboards are divided by a center 7" planed board, and are nailed on. Inside the upper case, notched-out strips on the sides allow for adjustment of the four rounded-front shelves. Flowered wallpaper of 1840–50 vintage lines the inside back of the upper case; the upper doors once had cotton fabric behind the glass, and fragments of this fabric remain (see Detail). The bookcase retains the oxidized original Spanish brown painted surface.

Multipurpose Tables and Small Stands

Each of these tables or stands performed a function in the nineteenth-century Georgia household. They were tools for easier living. They elevated some useful object or objects to a more convenient height for a person sitting or standing and they provided a surface upon which work or play could be accomplished. Among them were card tables, dressing tables, half-round tables, stretcher-based or tavern tables, folding or Pembroke tables, candlestands, lamp or light stands, and washstands. No distinctively different forms developed in the South.

Card tables, dressing tables, and half-round tables appear only occasionally in inventories, but numerous entries of tables without descriptive adjectives as to function could refer to these forms. Very few have survived. Stretcher-based or tavern tables were not listed as such on any inventories examined. A few stretcher-based tables have survived from the first decades of the century in eastern Georgia. One of these tables is known to have been used as a communion table in an early Elbert County church. In the home the stretcher-base was a multipurpose table. Early nineteenth-century advertisements in Georgia newspapers referred to Pembroke tables, but the usual inventory entry was for a folding table or a fall-leaf table. This, too, was a multipurpose table, perhaps supporting a vase of flowers or perhaps a conch shell, a "curiosity" that appeared on a number of Georgia upcountry inventories.

Stands or tables made to elevate a candle or a lamp were of two principal types: those supported by a central pedestal with a tripod base and those supported by corner legs. Few pedestal-based candlestands have survived in Georgia. The sturdier type, now called a lamp table or lamp stand or work table and having four turned or square legs, is found much more frequently today. Presumably it was more common in nineteenth-century Georgia. Inventory entries of "candle stand," "lamp stand," or even "small table" could refer to either type. A few small, square or rectangular tables having very long legs and a height of from thirty-one to thirty-six inches were examined in the survey.

In the days before indoor plumbing, washstands provided a resting place for a bowl, a bar of homemade soap, a towel, and a pitcher of water. Though Fanny Kemble referred to the form as a "wash-hand stand" in 1838, it also functioned in many households as a facility for such bathing as was done. For hand washing, the washstand was frequently placed on the veranda or near a window where the water could be thrown outside after use.

112 Table

Elbert County
1800–10
H. 27½"; W. 44"; D. 31½"
Primary wood: Yellow pine
Secondary wood: Yellow pine

Description: The wide overhanging two-board top is pegged to the apron. The corners are angled. The apron and legs are joined by mortise-and-tenon joints and are pegged. The apron is cut with side brackets. The edges of the overlapping drawer front are decorated with a ½" beaded border. The drawer front and the back are joined to the sides by half-dovetail joints top and bottom and two full dovetails between. The sides are grooved to receive the beveled drawer bottom. The runners are tenoned into, but not through, the front and back aprons.

The legs are cut in a lamb's-tongue shape as they leave the apron level and are then chamfered. The stretchers are chamfered on all four edges to within 2" of the leg. Original Spanish brown paint is evident. The drawer knob is missing.

113 Table

Morgan County
1840–50
H. 29 ¾"; W. 24" (body), 28" (top);
  D. 18" (body), 21 ⅜" (top)
Primary wood: Yellow pine
Secondary wood: Yellow pine

Description: The two-board top has cleated ends which are joined by tongue-and-groove joints and pegged. The aprons and the unusual flat tapered legs are joined by mortise-and-tenon joints and pegged. The bottom is nailed to the apron. The hinged top lifts, revealing a single storage compartment (see Detail). The piece, including the inside, is painted ochre and grained to resemble bird's-eye maple. The sapwood of the legs has caused the paint to separate, emphasizing the grain of the pine (see Figure 56).

114 Candlestand

Greene County
1860–80
H. 30"; W. 16¼"; L. 32"
Primary wood: Walnut
Secondary wood: Walnut

Description: The single-board oval top is attached to a crossed underbracing by screws. The shaft, with ring turnings at the top and close to the bottom, dowels into the underbracing. The feet are formed by undercutting two boards in bracket shapes, the top corners of which are beveled. These two boards then cross each other, fitting into slots cut in the lower edges of the shaft to which they are nailed.

The top is scrubbed and the base is varnished or shellacked.

115 Candlestand

Rabun County
1820–40
Attributed to William Cathey
H. 28"; W. 15⅝"; L. 22"
Primary wood: Birch
Secondary wood: Birch

Description: The octagonal top is attached by screws to an elongated octagonal brace into which the ring-turned shaft then tenons. The cabriole legs, with heavy knees, terminate in simple unpadded feet. The tenons of the legs are shaped as dovetails, join the slotted mortises in the shaft, and are glued.

The surface of the top is scrubbed, and the rest of the table retains its original finish.

History: Descended in the family of William Cathey of Rabun County in the mountains of extreme northeast Georgia. According to family tradition, William Cathey was the maker.

116 Table

Putnam County
1820–30
H. 28⅞"; W. 22½" (body), 28⅝"
  (top); D. 14⅞" (body), 16⅞" (top)
Primary wood: Walnut
Secondary woods: Walnut and
  yellow pine

Description: The two-board top (one 14⅞" deep, the other 2" deep) is nailed to the apron with T-head nails. The legs and apron are joined by mortise-and-tenon joints and are pegged. A delicate bead runs the length of each leg on the outside corner. Two inches below the apron the legs are cut away on the two inner surfaces to form graceful square legs. Three dovetailed joints are exposed on each side of the drawer front. The back of the drawer is constructed in the same way. The knobs appear to be original. Inside the drawer, a medial divider forms two sections. The thick sides and back of the drawer are made of walnut. The drawer bottom and the runners are of yellow pine. The drawer bottom is flush and wedged between the front, back, and sides, and nailed in. The surface finish is apparently untouched.

History: This table was handed down in the Pinkerton family, early settlers in the Rockville District of Putnam County of middle Georgia.

117 Table

Hancock County
1810–30
H. 27⅞"; W. 16⅜" (body), 20⅛" (top);
   D. 16⅜" (body), 19½" (top)
Primary wood: Walnut

Description: The top is nailed to the apron. The splayed and tapered legs are joined to the apron by mortise-and-tenon joints and are pegged. The legs taper from a width of 1 ⅜" at apron level to ⅜" at the bottom.

118 Table

Greene County
1830–40
H. 29½"; W. 17¾" (body), 23½" (top);
  D. 17¾" (body), 22" (top)
Primary woods: Walnut, cherry,
  and maple
Secondary wood: Tulip poplar

Description: The top is comprised of three boards, two wider walnut ones with a narrow strip of maple between the two. An inlaid ¼" strip of curly maple is set directly into the edge of the top on all four sides. The top is pegged to the apron. The apron sides are made of upper and lower walnut boards with a recessed strip of curly maple between them. This arrangement follows around the back so that the table is finished on all sides. The apron sections and the tapered cherry legs are joined by mortise-and-tenon joints and are pegged. A ¼"-wide, 5"-long strip of maple is set into each upper leg section, echoing the decoration of the top and the drawer front. On the cherry drawer front are three ¼" horizontal strips of curly maple. The original knobs, with little turned buttons on top, are placed along the center inlaid strip. The drawer front is rabbeted and the drawer sides nailed to it. The three-board drawer bottom is beveled on all four sides and slipped into grooves in the drawer sides. The back is grooved to match the sides and nailed, holding the beveled bottom in place.

119 Table

Oglethorpe County
1830–40
H. 29⅜"; W. 19" (body), 21" (top);
   D. 14½" (body), 16¾" (top)
Primary woods: Birch with walnut
   and light wood inlay
Secondary wood: Yellow pine

Description: The solid-board top is inlaid with a light wood double-line stringing on all four edges and is screwed to the apron from the underside. The apron, joined to the tapered legs by mortised, tenoned, and pegged construction, has a single-line inlay in the form of horizontal ovals on the sides and the back. Vertical ovals in the same line inlay flank the drawer.

The 1¼"-thick drawer front appears to have an applied molding on its edges. The molding is, in fact, formed from the solid drawer front. In the center of the drawer a large walnut diamond is inlaid; above it a second inlaid walnut diamond acting as an escutcheon fronts an original lock. On either side of the center diamond are light wood diamonds and all this framed by line inlay. The brass knob is original. The drawer front is joined by half-dovetails top and bottom with one full one between. The drawer back is joined by three full dovetails. On the side of the drawer is penciled the name "John Tenant." The drawer bottom is beveled, slipped into grooves in the sides, and nailed across the back. Runners tenon into the thick front and back aprons.

The outer sides of the legs repeat the oval tops of the line inlay flanking the drawer but taper to an inlaid cuff that surrounds the legs. Underneath the table, one leg retains blocking that has notched-V construction (see Detail a, Figure 107, and Figures 53 and 101).

History: From the estate of Miss Emma Norman, who died in 1981 at the age of 93 at Shady Nook, Nuberg, Hart County. Miss Norman's sister, Quillie Norman, wrote in 1953 of her grandfather, Thomas Jackson Maxwell:

Grandpa was a cabinetmaker as well as a farmer. When his children married there was a reserve of things he had made to help them "set up housekeeping." He died several years before Mother married, but some of the things he made were given to her. It must have been that he considered it a part of his duty to have some of his handiwork in their hope-chests. Mother had a chest, five chairs, a wardrobe, a small table, and a rolling pin. These are still here and in use. (*A Short History of the Norman-Maxwell Families*, by Quillie Norman, Shady Nook, Hartwell, Hart County, Georgia, 1953, typescript copy at Atlanta Historical Society, Atlanta, Ga.)

120 Table

Macon County
1840–60
H. 32"; W. 36"; D. 19"
Primary wood: Yellow pine
Secondary wood: Yellow pine

Description: The single-board top is cut in a half-round. The tapered legs are attached to cross braces, which are joined by mortise-and-tenon joints and are pegged. There is no front apron. Six individual pieces of wood are simply joined to form this table. The table was probably painted.

121 Table

Clarke County
1820–40
H. 28"; W. 45¾"; D. 22½"
Primary wood: Birch
Secondary wood: Yellow pine

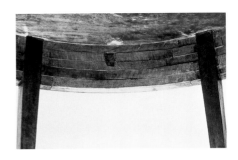

Description: The half-round top is attached to the base by screws. The framework of the apron is constructed of five stacked layers of thick pine. These laminated layers have been cut to conform to the round shape of the table and glued to each other (see Detail). The framework, faced with birch, fits into slots in the legs and is glued. The legs taper as they descend.

History: Descended in the Wilson family of Athens, Clarke County, and Calhoun, Gordon County.

122 Table

Carroll County
1840–60
Attributed to J. A. Martin
H. 29"; W. 25⅜" (body), 29⅛" (top);
  D. 20¼" (body), 23⅞" (top)
Primary wood: Yellow pine
Secondary wood: Yellow pine

Description: The two-board top is joined by a tongue-and-groove joint and nailed to the body. The apron and tapered legs are joined with mortise-and-tenon joints and pegged. The drawer front is rabbeted and the sides are nailed to it. The drawer bottoms are beveled on three sides, slipped into grooves in the sides, and nailed across the back. On the back of the drawer is penciled the name "J. A. Martin." The knob is original. On top of the drawer runners, upright drawer guides are nailed in place from the front and back of the aprons. The boards used to make this table are unusually thick, from 1" to 1¼". The table retains its original Spanish brown paint.

History: Descended in the family of Dr. Hicks Martin of the Mount Zion community of Carroll County in western Georgia near the Alabama line. Dr. J. A. Martin was said to be a son of Dr. Hicks Martin.

123 Table

Hancock County
1850–65
H. 31¾"; W. 27" (body), 32" (top); D. 21¼" (body), 24½" (top)
Primary wood: Yellow pine

Description: The top is made of two boards with a tongue-and-groove joint. It is nailed to the apron, which is inset between the legs rather than being flush with the leg surfaces. The apron and legs are mortised, tenoned, and pegged. The top 16½" section of each leg is square, chamfering into the lower turned section. Traces of the old blue surface are evident.

124 Washstand

Greene County
1830–50
H. 43½" (overall), 35¾" (shelf);
  W. 34¼" (overall), 32⅜" (body);
  D. 20½"
Primary wood: Yellow pine

Description: The two-board top is nailed to the apron. The apron and tapered legs are joined by mortise-and-tenon joints and are pegged. The pegs extrude on the inside. The splashboard is scalloped to a center crest on the back. The splashboard sides are flat, then dip, and are rounded on the front edges. The three sections of the splashboard are nailed to the side and back edges of the top. Traces of original blue-green paint remain.

125 Washstand

Clarke County
1840–50
H. 35¾"; W. 22"; D. 20½"
Primary woods: Tulip poplar and
  yellow pine

Description: The back splashboard design is halved and repeated on the side splashboards. The splashboards, joined by dovetails, are nailed to the sides of the top. The top, cut out to hold a wash bowl, is yellow pine. The rest of the piece is poplar. The sides of the body and the tapering legs are mortised, tenoned, and glued. The lower shelf is notched out at the corners to fit around the legs and is nailed to the side supports.

126 Washstand

Fulton County
1870
H. 36"; W. 19 ⅞"; D. 13"
Primary wood: Yellow pine

Description: The two-board top is cut flush with the sides. The splashboard sides are centered along the top boards and nailed. The back of the splashboard is cut in a freehand, triple-pointed design. The legs are tapered from the apron to the floor and from the apron to the top, forming the structure on which the sides and back are simply nailed. The apron is mortised across the front and nailed in place. The lower shelf is notched out at the corners to fit around the leg extension and nailed in place. The stand retains the opaque red painted surface. Written in large numbers on the backboards in the same red paint is the date "1870."

Some Nineteenth-Century Georgia Furniture Makers
A Preliminary List

The following list represents an initial effort to compile the names of furniture makers who worked in Georgia during the nineteenth century. Among the sources surveyed were the *Records of the 1820 Census of Manufacturers*, the 1850 and 1860 *U.S. Census Records* (see list of counties surveyed on page 234), the *Central Registry of Convicts (1817–68)*, and the *Militia Enrollment List, State of Georgia* (1863). From advertisements in local newspapers in towns throughout the state, many furniture makers working between 1800 and 1870 were identified. Wills and inventories from 1800 to 1870 (list of counties surveyed on page 234) were also examined in an effort to find people who had made furniture. Additional sources included personal letters, diaries, and memoirs located in special collections. *Atlanta City Directories*, published in 1859–60, 1867, 1871, 1878, and 1885, and *Georgia State Gazeteers* from 1879–80, 1881–82, and 1883–84, listed cabinetmakers and chairmakers. A number of books that focus on local, county, or state histories were also consulted. Finally, through the five-year survey effort by the Atlanta Historical Society, many pieces of furniture were located that have a family history or oral tradition of a known maker.

Many criteria entered in the decision as to which names to include. A person whose occupation was recorded as cabinetmaker, cabinet workman, chairmaker, or turner in the census records, prison registry, or militia list is listed. An individual for whom another occupation—for example, carpenter or carriage maker—was cited in the census records is included only as a second source when the name, county, age, or other census record entry appears to confirm the furniture maker identified from another source, such as a newspaper ad.

Selection of probable furniture makers from wills and inventories was based on careful scrutiny of tools listed. Since most people listed some tools, only those who had specialized cabinetmaker's tools, such as a lathe or a keyhole saw, or mentioned items such as unfinished pieces of furniture, hardware for desks, or plank for bedsteads, were included in this list. Although such stringent criteria inevitably exclude many people who did make some furniture, the primary purpose of this list is to identify those whose principal occupation was cabinetmaking.

At odds with such a statement is the fact that some individuals whose occupations were not confirmed in census records, ads, or directories as furniture makers have been included in this list. This has occurred only when a particular piece of furniture located through the survey is linked by family or oral tradition to a specific person. Many industrious people in rural Georgia made furniture when they set up housekeeping, when a daughter married, or when they simply needed it. This is one reason a definitive list of furniture makers is difficult to compile.

It is obvious that the cut-off date for examination of sources does not span the nineteenth century. The gradual progression from handmade to "factory-made" furniture involves a movement from one individual working with hand tools to build a single piece of furniture to many individuals using mechanized tools to mass-produce furniture. This list purports to include those single craftsmen as well as men working in cabinet shops still handmaking furniture. According to newspaper ads, individuals as well as craftsmen employed in cabinet shops called themselves "manufacturers" of furniture throughout the century. After 1870, furniture making reached a level of mechanization and mass production that is beyond the scope and intent of this list. Exceptions are those individuals listed in later *Directories* and *Gazeteers* as cabinetmakers, as well as makers associated with specific pieces of furniture identified through the survey.

This makers' list may serve as a guide and a tool for further study. Additional sources, census records in particular, should be examined. Several technical explanations are in order. Blank spaces on the chart indicate that a particular item of information was not available in the source cited. Note that the last column entitled "dates" has combined three areas of information: (1) date of source; (2) dates active; and (3) birth/death dates. Finally, all entries are listed as cited in the source; identical names from different sources have been combined only when other items (county, age, birthplace) coincide. Many more entries are probably repetitious; but where listings differ, no assumptions were made.

Key to Abbreviations

appr	apprentice
cabtmkr	cabinetmaker
cabt wkmn	cabinet workman
carp	carpenter
carr mkr	carriage maker
chairmkr	chairmaker
Czech	Czechoslovakia
Den	Denmark
dlr	dealer
Eng	England
Eur	Europe
fact	factory
Fr	France
furn	furniture
gen	general
Ger	Germany
gn ml	gin mill
gr ml	grist mill
Ire	Ireland
jy cabtmkr	journeyman cabinetmaker
mach	machine
matt	mattresses
Md	Maryland
Me	Maine
mfr	manufacturer
plan ml	planing mill
repr	repair
sashmkr	sashmaker
Scot	Scotland
sw ml	saw mill
Switz	Switzerland
undtkr	undertaker
uphl	upholsterer
warehs	warehouse
wheel	wheelwright
wk	work
woodwkmn	woodworkman
*	Birth Place indicates post–World War II boundaries
?	Indicates unknown date or question concerning legibility
" "	Signed piece or part of signature

Key to Sources

A	*Annals of Athens, Georgia, 1801–1901.* Augustus L. Hull (Athens, 1906)
B	*Antebellum Athens and Clarke County, Georgia.* Ernest C. Hynds (Athens, 1974)
C	*Atlanta and Environs.* Franklin M. Garrett, 3 vols. (New York, 1954)
D	*The Cabinetmakers of America.* Ethel H. Bjerkoe (New York, 1957)
E	*Cyclopedia of Georgia.* Ed. Allen D. Candler & Clement A. Evans, 4 vols. (Atlanta, 1906)
F	*Pioneer Citizens' History of Atlanta, 1833–1902.* (Atlanta, 1902)
G	Dunn Correspondence (AHS Survey)
H	Hopkins Family Papers, GDAH
J	AHS Correspondence
SS	*Soil of the South*, vols. 2, 3, 5. (Columbus, Ga., 1852, 1853, 1855)
W&I	Wills & Inventories, GDAH
CRC	*Central Registry of Convicts, 1817–1869.* RG 21-1-5, GDAH
Mil Lt	*Militia Enrollment List, State of Georgia.* Act of December 14, 1863. Microfilm Library, GDAH
Cen Mfr	*Records of the 1820 Census of Manufacturers.* Microcopy No. 279RG29, GDAH
Census	*United States Census: 1850, 1860.* Microfilm Library, GDAH
AHS Sv	Atlanta Historical Society Survey
Gaz	*Georgia State Gazeteer.* Sholes' 1879–80 Sholes' 1881–82 Estill and Weatherbe's 1883–84
newsp ad	newspaper advertisement
City Dir	*Atlanta City Directory.* Williams', 1859–60 Barnwell's, 1867 Hanleiter's, 1871 Sholes', 1878 Weatherbe's, 1885
GDAH	Georgia Department of Archives and History

N.B. Those dates listed as "1861–75" do not reflect continous advertisements for each consective year.

Maker's Name	Occupation	Town	County	Age	Birth Place	Source(s)	Dates: 1) source 2) active 3) birth/death
Adams							
Armstrong & Adams	furn dlr-mfr	Acworth	Cobb			Gaz	1) 1881–82
Adams, Anthony	wheel-chairmkr		Taylor	73	SC	census	1) 1860
Adams, John	cabtmkr	Savannah	Chatham			D	2) 1807
"Adams, R. N."	maker	Milledgeville	Baldwin			AHS Sv	
Adams, Robert N.	cabtmkr		Chatham	30	Ga	census	1) 1850
Adams, Robert N.?	cabtmkr		Baldwin	40	Ga	census	1) 1860
Adamson, J. C.	plan ml-furn	Jonesboro	Clayton			Gaz	1) 1883–84
Albertson	mfr-whse-rtl furn	Columbus	Muscogee			newsp ad	2) 1857
Albertson, Flynn & Co.							
Alexander, James	cabtmkr	Washington	Wilkes		Eur	newsp ad	2) 1810–13
Alford, Kinchin	cabtmkr		Hancock			W&I	1) 1815
Allen	chair-cabtmkr	Savannah	Chatham			newsp ad	2) 1806–10
Richmond & Allen							
Allen, F. H.	cabtmkr	Jasper	Pickens			Gaz	1) 1881–84
Alliff, John	cabtmkr		Bulloch			W&I	1) 1865–66
Allisen, Charles	cabtmkr		Muscogee	40	NY	census	1) 1860
Anderson, Andrew P.	cabtmkr		Chatham	47	NY	census	1) 1850
Anderson, Arthur	cabtmkr		Glynn			W&I	1) 1808
Anderson, John M.	cabtmkr	Savannah	Chatham			newsp ad	2) 1796–1802
							3) ?–1802
Andrew, G. B.	cabtmkr		Henry	53	Ga	census	1) 1860
Andrews, S. S.	chairmkr	Goloid	Screven			Gaz	1) 1881–82
Ansley, Benjamin	cabtmkr	Savannah	Chatham			newsp ad	2) 1809–1811
Hewitt & Ansley	cabtmkr	Savannah	Chatham			newsp ad	2) 1806
Ansley, Columbus C.	cabtmkr	Smithville	Lee			Gaz	1) 1879–84
"Ansley, Jole"	maker	Lula	Hall			AHS Sv	2) 1800–30
Anthony, C. W.	cabtmkr	Brass	Towns			Gaz	1) 1883–84
Armstrong, John	furn mfr-undtkr	Acworth	Cobb			Gaz	1) 1883–84
Armstrong	furn dlr-mfr	Acworth	Cobb			Gaz	1) 1879–82
Armstrong & Adams							
Armstrong & Smithson							
Arnold, John W.	cabt wkmn		Bibb	18	Ga	census	1) 1860
Arnold, P. E.	cabtmkr	Palmetto	Fulton			AHS Sv	
Arnold, William M.	cabtmkr	Atlanta	Fulton			Gaz	1) 1879–84
Autry, Jacob	cabtmkr		Clarke			B	2) 1841–50
Awtry, I? (or J?)	cabt work		Coweta	55		Mil Lt	1) 1863
Aycock, W. C.	furn-plan-sw ml	Whitesburgh	Carroll			Gaz	1) 1881–84
Aymiar, George	cabtmkr		Glynn	39	NY	census	1) 1860
Bacon, Henry C.	cabtmkr	Savannah	Chatham			Gaz	1) 1879–80
Bacon, Samuel	cabtmkr	Blackshear	Pierce			Gaz	1) 1883–84
Bagardus, Henry	cabtmkr		Chatham	33	NY	census	1) 1860
Bailey, Newton L.	maker	Heardmont	Elbert			AHS Sv	2) c. 1850
Bailey, William	turner		Upson	54	Ga	census	1) 1860
Bain, Arthur	maker		Bulloch			W&I	1) 1827
Bain, J. A.	turner	Columbus	Muscogee			newsp ad	2) 1833
Baker, D. M.	woodwkmn		Heard	43	SC	Mil Lt	1) 1863

Maker's Name	Occupation	Town	County	Age	Birth Place	Source(s)	Dates: 1) source 2) active 3) birth/death
Baker, James	cabtmkr		Cherokee	44	SC	census	1) 1850
Balkcom, Robert Percival	maker	Macon	Bibb			AHS Sv	2) c. 1850
Ballard, T. W.	cabtmkr-gn-gr-sw ml	Dekle	Thomas			Gaz	1) 1881–82
Banfield, Charles	cabtmkr		DeKalb	40	Ger	census	1) 1860
Banfield, John	cabtmkr		Richmond	25	Ga	census	1) 1860
Barbour, William	turner		Chatham	72	Eng	census	1) 1860
Barlow, Elias	chairmkr		Montgomery	52	SC	census	1) 1850
Barnes, W.	cabtmkr	Savannah	Chatham			newsp ad	2) 1819
"Barr, T. G."	maker		Stewart			AHS Sv	
Barr, Thomas	carp		Stewart	45	SC	census	1) 1850
Bart, Charles	cabtmkr		Fulton	55		Mil Lt	1) 1863
Bartel, John	turner-wheel		Columbia			newsp ad	2) 1814
Barton, Billy	chairmkr	Walnut Grove	Walton			AHS Sv	
Barton, Shad[1]	chair seating	Walnut Grove	Walton			AHS Sv	
Bausch, John G.	cabtmkr	Columbus	Muscogee			Gaz	1) 1883–84
Bazer, Edward	cabtmkr		Hancock			W&I	1) 1805
Beall, A. H.	cabtmkr		Upson	23	Ga	census	1) 1860
Beatty, Henry	chairmkr		Chatham	18	Ire	census	1) 1860
Beaufield, John	cabtmkr		Richmond	25	Ga	census	1) 1860
Beck, Jesse	chairmkr		Morgan			Cen Mfr	1) 1820
Beeks, James A.	chair mfr-gn-plan ml	Griffin	Spalding			Gaz	1) 1883–84
Bell, J. W.	cabtmkr		Decatur	27	NC	census	1) 1850
Bell, John	cabt wkmn		Pike	18		census	1) 1850
Bell, John	cabt wkmn		Jasper	27	Ga	census	1) 1860
Bell, William J.	cabt wkmn		Clarke	23	Ga	census	1) 1860
Bellah, Moses	cabtmkr		Clarke			W&I	1) 1809
Bellamy, A.	carr-cabt-sash mkr	Griffin	Spalding			newsp ad	2) 1855–56
Bellamy, Alex	cabtmkr		Spalding	49	Ga	census	1) 1860
Bennet, Richard	cabtmkr		Richmond	40	NY	census	1) 1850
Bennett, William	maker		Franklin			AHS Sv	2) c. 1870
Bennett, William A.	farmer		Lowndes	25	Ga	census	1) 1850
Bennett, William J.	carp		Cherokee	34	SC	census	1) 1850
Bennitt, William A.	cabtmkr		Berrien			W&I	1) 1864
Benson, Thomas J.	cabtmkr		Richmond	32	SC	census	1) 1860
Benton, John	cabtmkr		Pike	38		census	1) 1850
Benton, John	cabtmkr		Spalding	47	Ga	census	1) 1860
Berry, N. W.	cabtmkr		Whitfield	36	SC	census	1) 1860
Berryhill, William C.	cabtmkr		Richmond	50	Pa	census	1) 1850
Betty, Sanford	turner		DeKalb	26	Ga	census	1) 1860
Bissenger, Aton?	cabtmkr		Cobb	39	Ger	census	1) 1850
Bliley, Frances X.	cabtmkr	Atlanta	Fulton			City Dir	1) 1878
Blocker, Hercules	cabtmkr	Augusta	Richmond			Gaz	1) 1883–84
Bloodsworth, W. B.	cabtmkr		DeKalb	43	SC	census	1) 1860
Bloodworth, Wm. R.	cabtmkr		DeKalb	33	SC	census	1) 1850
Blount, Stephen	chairmkr	Savannah	Chatham		SC	D	3) 1761–1804

Maker's Name	Occupation	Town	County	Age	Birth Place	Source(s)	Dates: 1) source 2) active 3) birth/death
Boader, George W. Perry	turner		Gwinnett	24	SC	census	1) 1850
Boady, Christi	cabtmkr		Chatham	30	NY	census	1) 1860
Bobin, A.	cabtmkr		Cass[2]	45	Scot	census	1) 1860
Bogarders, H. L.	cabtmkr		Chatham	59	US	Mil Lt	1) 1863
Bogardus, H. S.	cabtmkr		Chatham	50	NY	census	1) 1850
Bogardus, Henry[3]	clerk		Chatham	23	NY	census	1) 1850
Boggs, James R.	cabtmkr	Lexington	Oglethorpe			Gaz	1) 1878–80
Bohnerferd, Chas.	cabtmkr	Atlanta	Fulton			City Dir	1) 1859
	undtkr-furn repr	Atlanta	Fulton			newsp ad	2) 1873
Bohnefeld, Chas.	undtkr	Atlanta	Fulton			City Dir	1) 1867
	undtkr-furn dlr	Atlanta	Fulton			City Dir	1) 1871
Bolen, Felix	chairmkr		Decatur	45	Ga	census	1) 1860
Bolling, William	cabtmkr		Bibb	22	Tenn	census	1)1860
Bond Bond & Joiner	cabtmkr	Drayton	Dooly			Gaz	1) 1879–80
Bonnenberge, Christian	cabtmkr		Richmond	36	Ger	census	1) 1860
Bonner A. Bonner & H. Ridley	cabtmkr	Columbus	Muscogee			Gaz	1) 1879–80
Bonner, Robt. Hicks	cabtmkr		Hancock			W&I	1) 1806
Boon, Tyra	chairmkr		Cherokee	63	NC	census	1) 1850
Boran, Jesse	cabtmkr		Hancock			W&I	1) 1803
Bowman, John C.	cabt wkmn		Bibb	42	Mass	census	1) 1860
Bracewell, J. R. Bracewell & Clark	furn mfr	Atlanta	Fulton			Gaz	1) 1883–84
Bradford, William	cabt wkmn		Sumter	30	Ga	census	1) 1860
Bradford, William M.	chairmkr		Sumter	30		Mil Lt	1) 1863
Bradley, E. A.	cabtmkr		Bibb	43	Conn	census	1) 1850
Bradley, Timothy	carp-cabtmkr		Richmond	31	Ire	CRC	2) 1845
Brainard, Serone	cabtmkr		Muscogee	47	NY	census	1) 1850
Brannan, John	cabtmkr	Atlanta	Fulton			City Dir	1) 1859
Brannon, W.	chair fact-gr ml	Mimosa	Walker			Gaz	1) 1883–84
Branon, John	cabtmkr		Fulton	24	Ga	census	1) 1860
Brevard Hicks & Brevard	cabtmkr	Cartersville	Bartow			Gaz	1) 1881–84
Brewer, Samuel	cabtmkr		Wilkinson	31	Ga	CRC	2) 1844
Brickell, Nicholas	cabtmkr		Coweta	26	NC	census	1) 1850
Brickman, Theodore	cabtmkr	Savannah	Chatham			Gaz	1) 1881–82
Bridges, Nathan T.	cabt wkmn		Gwinnett	22		census	1) 1850
Bridges, William	cabtmkr		Webster	50		census	1) 1860
Bridges, Wilson	cabtmkr		Franklin	58	NC	census	1) 1850
"Brinson, J. A."	maker		Burke			AHS Sv	2) 1869
Brinson, John A.	carp		Burke	28		census	1) 1850
	mechanic		Burke	39	Ga	census	1) 1860
Britton, John B.	cabtmkr	Pine Log	Bartow			Gaz	1) 1879–80
Broadnax, Richard	appr cabt trade		Richmond	16	Ga	census	1) 1860
Brock, S. F.	cabtmkr		Hall	31	NC	census	1) 1850
Bronson, Zenos?	chair-cabtmkr	Lexington	Oglethorpe			Cen Mfr	1) 1820

Maker's Name	Occupation	Town	County	Age	Birth Place	Source(s)	Dates: 1) source 2) active 3) birth/death
Brooknes, Chas. F.	cabtmkr		Walker	47	SC	census	1) 1850
Brown Brown & Wood	chair-cabtmkr	Macon	Bibb			newsp ad	2) 1824–36
Brown	carp		Richmond	40	Va	census	1) 1850
Brown, A. O.	turner	Macon	Bibb			newsp ad	2) 1837
Brown, George W.	cabtmkr		Early	35	Conn	census	1) 1850
	cabtmkr		Clay[4]	45	Conn	census	1) 1860
	cabtmkr		Clay	49		Mil Lt	1) 1863
Brown, J. M. Lawrenceville Cabinet Manufactory	cabtmkr	Augusta	Richmond			newsp ad	2) 1850
Brown, John	chairmkr	Chestnut Gap	Fannin			Gaz	1) 1883–84
Brown, Lolson? A.	cabtmkr		Banks	31	NC	census	1) 1860
Brown, Nathaniel	Windsor chairmkr	Savannah	Chatham			newsp ad	2) 1803
					Pa	D	3) 1777–1803
Brown, Owen T.	cabt wkmn		Terrell	25	NC	census	1) 1860
Brown, William	chairmkr		Washington			Cen Mfr	1) 1820
Brown, William R.	cabt mfr	Macon	Bibb			newsp ad	2) 1831
Brownin, Willy	chair seating		DeKalb	77	SC	census	1) 1860
Bruckman, Theodore	cabtmkr		Chatham	47	Ger	Mil Lt	1) 1863
Brumslow, Isaac	chairs		Forsyth	45	SC	census	1) 1850
Brumby, J. R. Brumby & Bro.	chair mfr	Marietta	Cobb			Gaz	1) 1881–84
Brumby, T. M. Brumby & Bro.	chair mfr	Marietta	Cobb			Gaz	1) 1881–84
Brunett, William J.	carp		Cherokee	46	SC	census	1) 1860
"Bryan, J. G."	maker		Stephens			AHS Sv	2) 1873
Bryant, M. T.	cabtmkr	Melville	Chattooga			Gaz	1) 1879–84
Bryon, F. M.	cabtmkr		Pike	35	Va	census	1) 1850
Buchanan, Micajah	maker		Sumter			AHS Sv	2) c. 1820
Buchanan, William H.	cabtmkr		Clarke			B	2) 1851–60
	cabtmkr		Clarke	30	NC	census	1) 1850
	cabtmkr		Clarke	41	NC	census	1) 1860
Buckner, Joel	cabtmkr		Hancock			W&I	1) 1812
Buggs, James R.	cabtmkr		Oglethorpe	43	Ga	census	1) 1860
Buggs, Richard	cabtmkr		Oglethorpe	18	Ga	census	1) 1860
Burney, William	cabtmkr		Cobb	56	Ga	census	1) 1850
Burnley, Isreal	cabtmkr-fmr		Wilkes		Va	AHS Sv	
Burns, Jerry	furn mkr	Savannah	Chatham			Gaz	1) 1881–82
Burton, William	turner		Greene	43	Ga	CRC	2) 1843
Bush, James Z.	cabtmkr	Wrightsville	Johnson			Gaz	1) 1881–82
Bussel, George	cabtmkr		Madison	57	Ga	Mil Lt	1) 1863
Byers, J. A.	cabtmkr	Ball Ground	Cherokee			Gaz	1) 1883–84
Cadle, Fiedlen	chairmkr		Stewart	39	SC	census	1) 1850
Cagle, Elijah	cabt wkmn		Murray	28	Tenn	census	1) 1850
Cagle, Martin	maker	Cagletown	Cass			AHS Sv	2) c. 1860
Calflatch, Adaline[5]	chair bottomer		Richmond	40	Fr	census	1) 1860

Maker's Name	Occupation	Town	County	Age	Birth Place	Source(s)	Dates: 1) source 2) active 3) birth/death
Calflatch, John	cabtmkr		Richmond	47	Ger	census	1) 1860
Calhoun, D. W.	cabt wkmn		Floyd	45	SC	census	1) 1850
Callahan, William	cabtmkr	Woodville	Greene			Gaz	1) 1879–80
Camel, Robert	chairmkr		Cherokee	18	Ga?	census	1) 1850
Cameron, Hiram	furn dlr-cabtmkr	Columbus	Muscogee			Gaz	1) 1883–84
Cameron, Thomas	cabtmkr		Fulton	20	SC	census	1) 1860
Camervin, Gilbert C.	cabtmkr		Macon	31	NC	census	1) 1860
Camp	sw ml-furn-mach shop	Puckett Station	Coweta			Gaz	1) 1883–84
Camp and Cureton							
Camp, E. N.	furn mfr	Puckett Station	Coweta			Gaz	1) 1881–82
"Camp, William M."	maker		Fulton			AHS Sv	
Campbell, J.	turner		Baldwin	39	Ire	census	1) 1860
Cann, B.	cabtmkr		Fulton	45		Mil Lt	1) 1863
Carithers, John M.	cabtmkr		Madison	44	Ga	census	1) 1860
Carne, John	chairmkr	Savannah	Chatham			newsp	2) 1803
Carpenter, G.	cabtmkr	Savannah	Chatham			newsp ad	2) 1811
Carpenter, J.							
G. & J. Carpenter							
Capers, Morgan	chairmkr	Savannah	Chatham			newsp ad	2) 1799
Carrel, John G.	cabt		Hall	29	SC	census	1) 1850
Carup, Hosea N.	cabtmkr		Gordon	34	Ga	census	1) 1860
Casady, Elbert[6]	cabtmkr		Walker	24	Tenn	census	1) 1860
Casady, Richard	cabtmkr		Walker	52	Va	census	1) 1860
Castleberry, M. T.	furn mfr	Atlanta	Fulton			newsp ad	2) 1873–74
M. T. Castleberry & Co.							
Cathey, Samuel B.	cabt wkmn		Walker	27	Tenn	census	1) 1850
Cathey, William	maker	Tiger	Rabun			AHS Sv	
Cathey, Wm. H.	farmer		Union	36	NC	census	1) 1850
Cawley, Frederick	turner		Pike	42	SC	census	1) 1850
Chaffe, Daniel	cabtmkr		Richmond	35	Mass	census	1) 1850
Chamberlain, E.	cabtmkr		Bibb	25	Mass	census	1) 1850
Chambers, Charles E.	furn mfr	Carrollton	Carroll			Gaz	1) 1879–84
Chase, C. W.	cabtmkr	Cartersville	Bartow			Gaz	1) 1883–84
Checehere, D.	cabtmkr		Randolph	24	NC	census	1) 1850
Cheek, W. H.	cabtmkr	Bowersville	Hart			Gaz	1) 1879–82
"Chesnut, Alexander"	maker	"Decatur"	DeKalb		Ga	AHS Sv	3) 1809–81
Childres, Thomas	cabt appr		Clarke	20	Ga	census	1) 1860
Chivers, C. H.	cabtmkr		Bibb	45	Ga	census	1) 1850
Christian, G. W.	chairs		Elbert	36		census	1) 1850
Christian, W.	cabtmkr		Webster	38	Ga	census	1) 1860
Clark, David	cabtmkr		Muscogee	43	Mass	CRC	2) 1855
Clark, David	carp	Milledgeville	Baldwin	38	Mass	census	1) 1850
Clark, David	cabtmkr		Chatham	49	Ga	census	1) 1860
Clark, E. F.	furn mfr	Atlanta	Fulton			Gaz	1) 1883–84
Bracewell & Clark							
Clark, James	cabtmkr		Fayette	28	Va	CRC	2) 1855

Maker's Name	Occupation	Town	County	Age	Birth Place	Source(s)	Dates: 1) source 2) active 3) birth/death
Clark, Jesse	cabtmkr	Atlanta	Fulton			City Dir	1) 1859
Clark, John L.	cabtmkr		Chatham	58	NY	census	1) 1860
Clark, William	cabtmkr	Savannah	Chatham			Gaz	1) 1881–82
Clarke, Jesse	cabtmkr	Atlanta	Fulton			F	1) 1902
	cabtmkr	Atlanta	Fulton			F	2) 1851
Clarke, John	cabtmkr	Atlanta	DeKalb	39	Va	census	1) 1850
Clarke, Kinsey	cabt wkmn		Lumpkin	20	SC	census	1) 1850
Clayton, James	maker		Carroll			AHS Sv	2) 1837
Clem, James	chairmkr		Richmond	60	SC	census	1) 1850
Clements, David	maker		Hancock			W&I	1) 1802
Clower, D. M.	cabtmkr		Clarke			B	2) 1841–50
Coffin, H.	cabtmkr-undtkr	Augusta	Richmond			newsp ad	2) 1852
Coffin, Hilary	cabtmkr		Richmond	58	Fr	census	1) 1850
Cohen, Salmon	cabtmkr		Spalding	21	Ger	census	1) 1860
Coker, Reese	furn mfr	Acworth	Cobb			Gaz	1) 1883–84
"Coleman, Joseph W."	maker		Oglethorpe			AHS Sv	2) 1846
Coleman, Phillip	cabt wkmn		Cherokee	47	SC	census	1) 1850
Coleman, W.	chairmkr		Cass	30	Ga	census	1) 1860
Colflesh, Irving	cabtmkr		Fulton	22	NY	census	1) 1860
Colley, John Tillery	cabtmkr		Newton		Ga	AHS Sv	3) 1810–31
Collier, W.	cabtmkr		Coweta	50	NC	census	1) 1850
Colson	lumber-chair mfr-gn-gr ml	Enecks	Screven			Gaz	1) 1883–84
Gordy and Colson							
Comfort, James	cabtmkr appr		Baldwin	17	Mass	census	1) 1860
Companiac, Theodore	cabtmkr		Chatham	27		census	1) 1850
Compaynae?, John	cabtmkr		Muscogee	37	Ga	census	1) 1860
Compton, Hampton	maker		Sumter			W&I	1) 1850
Coneboy, John	chairmkr		Habersham	70		census	1) 1850
Conn, G. M.	cabtmkr		Chatham	51	NY	Mil Lt	1) 1863
Conn, George M.	cabtmkr		Chatham	45	NJ	census	1) 1860
Conner, James	chairs		Forsyth	41	Ga	census	1) 1850
Conner, James M.	chairmkr	Fort Buffington	Cherokee			Gaz	1) 1881–82
Cook, Elijah	chairmkr	Savannah	Chatham			D	3) 1784–1817
Cook, I. B.	cabtmkr		Fulton	21	Ga	census	1) 1860
Cook, J.	cabt wkmn		Floyd	37	SC	census	1) 1860
Cook, Peter	cabt wkmn		Bibb	35	Ger	census	1) 1860
Cooper, Henry	cabtmkr	Savannah	Chatham			Gaz	1) 1881–82
Cooper, John	chairmkr	Savannah	Chatham		Mass	D	3) 1763–1808
Cooper, Silas	Windsor chairmkr	Savannah	Chatham			newsp ad	2) 1801–11
"Cooper, W. B."	maker		Madison			AHS Sv	
Cooper, William	sawyer		Madison	30	Ga	census	1) 1850
Cooper, William	carp		Burke	27	SC	census	1) 1860
Cottingham, John T.	cabt appr		Talbot	19	Ga	census	1) 1860
Cough, Ferdinand	turner		Chatham	47	Ger	census	1) 1860
Coupee, Charles	cabt-furn mfr	Macon	Bibb			newsp ad	2) 1831
Crane, Benjamin	maker		Morgan			W&I	1) 1823

Maker's Name	Occupation	Town	County	Age	Birth Place	Source(s)	Dates: 1) source 2) active 3) birth/death
Crews, Thomas	cabt wkmn		Murray	51		census	1) 1850
Crocker, J. J.	cabtmkr	Reed Creek	Hart			Gaz	1) 1879–82
Cromwell, A. F.	cabtmkr		Walker	40	Va	census	1) 1850
Crossman, Wm. H.	furn wareroom-mfr	Columbus	Muscogee			newsp ad	2) 1852
Crow, I.	chairmkr		Hall	80	SC	census	1) 1860
Cruse, Stephen	cabtmkr		Coweta	35	Ga	census	1) 1850
Cubbedge, Stephen J. M.	cabtmkr		Chatham	34		census	1) 1850
Culberson, David H.	carpenter		Coweta	39	Ga	census	1) 1850
Cunningham, T. B.	furn mfr	Bowersville	Hart			Gaz	1) 1881–82
Cureton	sw ml-furn-mach shop	Puckett Station	Coweta			Gaz	1) 1883–84
Camp and Cureton							
Curry, Duncan	maker		Decatur			W&I	1) 1847
Curtis, John M.	carr mkr-furn-undtkr	Thomson	McDuffie			Gaz	1) 1879–80
Cutter, Howard	cabt wkmn		Bibb	27	Ga	census	1) 1860
Dace, J. D. B.	chairmkr	Keyton	Calhoun			Gaz	1) 1883–84
Daily, J. G.	cabt wkmn		Floyd	25	Ire	census	1) 1850
Dalton, John	shop joiner		Jackson	65	NC	census	1) 1850
Daniel, Andrew J.	cabtmkr		Coweta	22	NC	census	1) 1850
Daniel, Martin	carp		Upson	40	SC	census	1) 1850
	chairmkr		Upson	50	SC	census	1) 1860
Daniel, Samuel	cabinet		Richmond	33	NY	census	1) 1850
Daniel, William	turner	Macon	Bibb			newsp ad	2) 1837
Dans, Van	cabt		Gwinnett	27	SC	census	1) 1850
Darne, Henry	cabtmkr		Richmond	22	Ger	census	1) 1850
Davant, G. S.	cabtmkr	Penfield	Greene			Gaz	1) 1881–84
Davis, A. A.	turner		DeKalb	33	SC	census	1) 1860
Davis, Henry	maker		Bulloch			W&I	1) 1856
Davis, James	cabtmkr		DeKalb	34	Eng	census	1) 1860
Davis, Wesley	maker		Gilmer			AHS Sv	
Deaton, W. H.	maker	Shakerag	DeKalb			AHS Sv	2) 1827–28
						AHS Sv	3) 1810–9?
Deas, James M.	carp		Dooly	38		census	1) 1850
Dees, James M.	cabtmkr	Drayton	Dooly			Gaz	1) 1879–80
DeGraaf, S. M.	furn-uphl-undtkr-mattress mfr	Augusta	Richmond			Gaz	1) 1879–80
Delay, H. R.	chairmkr	Augusta	Richmond			newsp ad	2) 1850
Lawrenceville Cabinet Manufactory							
Delay, Hiram	cabtmkr		Fulton			W&I	1) 1857
DeLay, Hiram R.	cabtmkr	Decatur	DeKalb	43	SC	census	1) 1850
Dempsey, J. J.	cabtmkr	Sonora	Gordon			Gaz	1) 1879–82
Denkam?, S. M.	chairmkr		Harris	23	Ga	census	1) 1860
Densler, Henry	chairmkr	Savannah	Chatham			newsp ad	2) 1794–1802
Densler, William	chairmkr	Savannah	Chatham			newsp ad	2) 1806
						newsp ad	3) ? –1811

Maker's Name	Occupation	Town	County	Age	Birth Place	Source(s)	Dates: 1) source 2) active 3) birth/death
Dermott, R.G.	cabtmkr	Leliaton	Coffee			Gaz	1) 1881–82
Derten, Ben	cabtmkr		Bibb	17	Ga	census	1) 1850
Derucker, Elain	cabt wkmn		Bibb	28	Ga	census	1) 1860
Desimick, Joseph	chairmkr		Richmond	19		census	1) 1850
Dewerg?, Oneziene?	cabtmkr		Chatham	22	Ga	census	1) 1860
Dicks, William E.	cabtmkr		Clarke	43	Tenn	census	1) 1860
Dickson, Thomas J.	maker		Hancock			W&I	1) 1864
Dickson, William E.	cabtmkr		Clarke	33	Tenn	census	1) 1850
	furn		Clarke			B	2) 1851–61
	cabtmkr	Athens	Clarke			newsp ad	2) 1856
Dimerol?, Jesse	chairmkr-turner		Richmond			Cen Mfr	1) 1820
Dimons	cabtmkr	Augusta	Richmond			newsp	2) 1819
Dismuke, Ben	chairmkr	Gibson	Glascock			AHS Sv	
Dismuke, Ben	chairmkr	Gibson	Glascock			AHS Sv	2) 1860
Dismuke, Reuben	chairmkr		Richmond	66	Ga	AHS Sv	2) 1860
Dixon, Christopher C.	cabtmkr		Chatham	30	Ga	census	1) 1860
Dixon, William D.	cabtmkr		Chatham	21	Ga	census	1) 1860
Dixon, Wm. E.	cabtmkr		Clarke			B	2) 1851–60
D'lamater, Abraham	cabtmkr	Savannah	Chatham			D	2) 1803–27
Dobbs, M.	chairmkr		Cass	70	Ga	census	1) 1860
Doney, George	cabt wkmn		Bibb	24	Ger	census	1) 1860
Dorling, Jacob	cabtmkr		Richmond	28	Va	census	1) 1860
Dorsey, J. Wallace & Co.	undtkr-cabtmkr	Savannah	Chatham			Gaz	1) 1883–84
Douglas, George	cabt worker		Bibb	45	Ga	census	1) 1850
Douglas, J. M.[7]	appr		Bibb	16	Ga	census	1) 1850
Dover, S. W.	cabtmkr	Rabun	Clayton			Gaz	1) 1879–84
Dreoksel, Christopher	cabtmkr		Murray	34	Ger	census	1) 1850
Ducker, W. N.	cabt shop-furn wareroom	Rome	Floyd			newsp ad	2) 1859
	cabtmkr		Floyd	33	Ky	census	1) 1860
Ducker, Wm. N.	cabtmkr	Atlanta	Fulton			City Dir	1) 1867
Duggan	maker		Stewart?			AHS Sv	
Duggan, Michael	turner		Chatham	38	Ire	census	1) 1850
Duncan, G. W.	chairmkr		Catoosa	27	Ga	census	1) 1860
Duncan, M. A.	chairmkr	Air Line	Hart			Gaz	1) 1879–80
Dunkin, O. F.	cabtmkr		DeKalb	22	Ga	census	1) 1860
Dunn, Alexander H.[8]	cabtmkr		Fayette		SC	J	3) 1814–89
Dunn, E.[8]	cabtmkr		Henry		SC	J	2) 1850
						J	3) 1802–?
Dunn, Frederic Clermont[9]	cabtmkr		Fayette		Ga	J	3) 1861–94
Dunn, Frederick W.	cabtmkr		Cherokee	34	Ga?	census	1) 1850
Dunn, Henry Clay[9]	cabtmkr		Henry		Ga	J	3) 1844–63
Dunn, Henry (NMN)[9]	cabtmkr		Fayette		Ga	J	3) 1865–?
Dunn, Stephen[8]	cabtmkr		Henry		SC	J	3) 1807–?
Dunn, W.	cabinet		Henry	43	SC	census	1) 1850
Dunn, W. F.	cabtmkr	Hassler's Mill	Murray			Gaz	1) 1881–82

Maker's Name	Occupation	Town	County	Age	Birth Place	Source(s)	Dates: 1) source 2) active 3) birth/death
Dunn, William	cabtmkr		Henry		SC	J	3) c. 1740–c. 1830
Dunn, William[8]	cabtmkr		Henry		SC	J	3) 1807–?
Dunn, William Samuel[9]	cabtmkr		Henry		Ga	J	3) 1841–1906
Durand, S. A.	cabtmkr	Decatur	DeKalb			Gaz	1) 1879–80
						Gaz	1) 1883–84
Durham, George	cabt-chair shop	Decatur	DeKalb	17	Ga	census	1) 1850
Dusch, Leopold	cabtmkr		Richmond	27	Ger	census	1) 1850
Dutton, Thos. W.	cabtmkr-shop	Columbus	Muscogee			newsp ad	2) 1833
Dye, Thomas	cabt shop	Griffin	Spalding			newsp ad	2) 1854
Dyer, A. A.	gen store-furn mfr-gn	Yellow River	Gwinnett			Gaz	1) 1883–84
Dyer, Augustus	carp		Morgan	24		census	1) 1850
Dyer, Bluford	cabtmkr		Jackson	44	SC	census	1) 1850
Easley, Warham	cabtmkr	Athens	Clarke			newsp ad	2) 1808
	furn		Clarke			B	2) 1800–10
Ebert, Conrad	cabtmkr		Thomas	40	Ger	census	1) 1850
Edleman?, Frank	cabtmkr		Cobb	29	Ger	census	1) 1860
Edmonds, Augustus	appr cabt trade		Richmond	17	Ga	census	1) 1860
Elliott, Alfred	cabtmkr		Bibb	25	NC	CRC	2) 1826
Ellis, Madison	cabtmkr		Cass	22	NC	census	1) 1860
Elsworth, Samuel	cabtmkr		Chatham	38	Eng	CRC	2) 1820
"Ely, John W. M."	maker		Clarke			AHS Sv	2) 1836
Emerick, David H.	cabtmkr appr		Clarke	23	NC	census	1) 1860
Emfinger, G. O.	cabtmkr		Baldwin	18	Ga	census	1) 1860
Engle, John	appr cabtmkr		Richmond	17	Ga	census	1) 1860
Englehart, C.	cabtmkr		Chatham	40	Ger	census	1) 1850
Englehart, D.	cabtmkr		Chatham	40	Ger	census	1) 1850
Enzenger, Joseph	cabtmkr		Chatham	29	Ger	census	1) 1860
Enzenger, Matthew	cabtmkr		Chatham	27	Ger	census	1) 1860
Evans, Henry	cabtmkr		Whitfield	26	SC	census	1) 1860
Fail, Isaac M.	turner		Lowndes	43		census	1) 1850
Falvy, Dennis	cabtmkr	Savannah	Chatham			Gaz	1) 1881–82
Faran, James	chairmkr		Muscogee	32	Ire	census	1) 1850
Faris? Faris? & Miller	cabtmkr-turner	Savannah	Chatham			newsp ad	2) 1817–19
Faris, George G.	cabtmkr	Savannah	Chatham			D	2) 1823
Faust, Johan	maker		Elbert		Ger	AHS Sv	2) 1810
Fearney, Thomas	cabtmkr		Chatham	28	Ire	census	1) 1850
Fell, Isaac	cabtmkr-uphl	Savannah	Chatham		Eng	D	3) 1759–1818
Fenser, Augustus	cabtmkr		Richmond	38		Mil Lt	1) 1863
Ferguson, Alex	cabtmkr		Cass	48	Va	census	1) 1850
Ferguson, Dougald	cabtmkr		Chatham	22	Ga	census	1) 1860
Ferguson, Dugald	undtkr-cabtmkr-bell hanger		Chatham			Gaz	1) 1881–82
Fetters, Jacob	cabtmkr		Muscogee	33	Ger	census	1) 1850
Feuser, Carl A.	cabtmkr	Augusta	Richmond			Gaz	1) 1879–84

Maker's Name	Occupation	Town	County	Age	Birth Place	Source(s)	Dates: 1) source 2) active 3) birth/death
Fields, W. B.	furn fact-gn-gr-sw ml	Yellow River	Gwinnett			Gaz	1) 1879–82
Finch, William	cabtmkr		Richmond	29	SC	census	1) 1860
Fincher, William C.	cabtmkr	Snapping Shoals	Newton			Gaz	1) 1879–80
Fisher, George	cabtmkr		Fulton	38	Ger	census	1) 1860
	cabtmkr-shop	Atlanta	Fulton			City Dir	1) 1867
Fitts, E. M.	cabtmkr	Whitesburgh	Carroll			Gaz	1) 1879–80
Fittz, Tandy W.	cabt wkmn		Madison	44	Ga	census	1) 1860
Flaherty, Daniel	cabtmkr		Richmond	27	Ire	census	1) 1850
Flanigan, Wm.	cabtmkr		Chattahoochee			W&I	1) 1856
Fletcher	cabtmkr		Dade	43	NC	census	1) 1860
Floyd Frieze & Floyd	cabt shop	Washington	Wilkes			newsp ad	2) 1868
Floyd, Ansel C.	cabt wkmn		Madison	26	Ga	census	1) 1850
Floyd, D. S.	chairmkr	Decatur	DeKalb	25	Tenn	census	1) 1850
Floyd, Enoch	chairmkr		Jackson			Cen Mfr	1) 1820
Floyd, John D.	cabt wkmn		Wilkes	22	Ga	census	1) 1860
Floyd, S. S.	chair seating		DeKalb	35	SC	census	1) 1860
Floyd, McLa?	carp		Wilkes	39	Va	census	1) 1850
Flynn Albertson, Flynn & Co.	mfr-whse-rtl furn	Columbus	Muscogee			newsp ad	2) 1857
Flynn, F. W.	cabtmkr		Muscogee	30	Ire	census	1) 1860
Flynn, F. W.	cabtmkr		Catoosa	30	Ire	census	1) 1860
Flynn, F. W.	cabtmkr	Atlanta	Fulton			City Dir	1) 1867
Flynn, R. B.	cabtmkr		Catoosa	32	Ire	census	1) 1860
Folkner, B.	turner		Fulton	28	Scot	census	1) 1860
Foran, Patrick	cabtmkr		Muscogee	35	Ire	census	1) 1850
Foran, Patrick	cabtmkr		Muscogee	39	Ire	census	1) 1860
Forbis, L. R.	cabtmkr	Snapping Shoals	Newton			Gaz	1) 1879–80
Forsyth, John J.	cabt wkmn		Bibb	53	SC	census	1) 1860
Forsythe, Henry E.	cabtmkr		Chatham	18	Ga	CRC	2) 1838
Foster, David	cabtmkr	Billow	Carroll			Gaz	1) 1879–82
Frasier, John	chairmkr		Mitchell	48	Ga	census	1) 1860
Fraxel, Christopher	cabtmkr		Richmond	45	Ger	census	1) 1860
Frayell, W. H.	cabtmkr		Fulton	26	Va	census	1) 1860
Freeman, J. Wesley	maker	Sylvania	Screven			AHS Sv	
Freeze, John	cabt wkmn		Wilkes	44	Ger	census	1) 1860
Friese, John	cabtmkr	Sparta	Hancock			Gaz	1) 1879–80
Frieze Frieze & Floyd	cabt shop	Washington	Wilkes			newsp ad	2) 1868
"Frost, Sam"	cabtmkr	"Athens"	Clarke			AHS Sv	2) "1844"
Frost, Samuel	cabtmkr-cabt warehs	Athens	Clarke			newsp ad	2) 1834
	cabtmkr		Clarke			B	2) 1831–40
	furn		Clarke			B	2) 1841–50
	cabtmkr-auctioneer-justice of the peace	Athens	Clarke			A	2) c. 1879
Fuller, William	cabtmkr		Wilkinson	43	Ga	census	1) 1860

Maker's Name	Occupation	Town	County	Age	Birth Place	Source(s)	Dates: 1) source 2) active 3) birth/death
Furguson, William	cabtmkr		Chatham	42	SC	census	1) 1850
Furman, Augustus	cabtmkr		Richmond	32	Ger	census	1) 1860
Gaely, John	cabtmkr		Murray	34	Ger	census	1) 1850
Gailey, A.	cabtmkr	Clarksville	Habersham			Gaz	1) 1879–82
Galley, Andrew, Jr.	cabt wkmn		Habersham	47	SC	census	1) 1850
Gaines, R. L.	wheel-cabtmkr	Hickory Flat	Cherokee			Gaz	1) 1881–84
R. L. Gaines & Sons							
Gallagher, Charles	cabtmkr		Bibb	20	Ga	census	1) 1860
Gammersh, Augustus	cabtmkr		Chatham	36	Ger	census	1) 1860
Gardner, John S.	cabtmkr		Richmond	42	NY	census	1) 1850
Gardner, Joseph	cabtmkr		Wilkes	38	SC	census	1) 1850
Gardner, William J. M.	cabtmkr	Powers	Terrell			Gaz	1) 1879–80
Garibold	maker	Athens	Clarke		Italy	AHS Sv	
Garibold, J. A.	furn	Athens	Clarke			Gaz	1) 1883–84
Garmon, P.	cabtmkr		Catoosa	40	Ire	census	1) 1860
Garner, J. C. C.	cabtmkr		Catoosa	22	Ga	census	1) 1860
Garrett, J. M.	cabtmkr	Bowden	Carroll			Gaz	1) 1879–80
Garrison, H. P.	cabtmkr-plan ml-physician	Nail's Creek	Banks			Gaz	1) 1879–80
Garry, James	cabtmkr		Chatham	18	Ire	census	1) 1850
Gary, Nicholas	turner		Hancock	53	Va	census	1) 1850
Gavis, Jacob	cabt wkmn		Bibb	21	Ger	census	1) 1860
Gazzaway, D. T.	miller-cabtmkr	Cove City	Whitfield			Gaz	1) 1879–80
Gibbs, C. B.	cabt wkmn		Whitfield	33	Tenn	census	1) 1860
Gilbert	plan ml-bedstead mfr	Atlanta	Fulton			F	2) 1853
Gilbert & Strong							
Gilleland, Rev. W. J.	box-furn mfr	Boltonville	Fulton			Gaz	1) 1879–80
Gillum, Robert	cabtmkr		Floyd	28	SC	census	1) 1860
Gilmer, Anthony	cabtmkr		Greene	51	SC	census	1) 1850
Girardy, C. E.	chairmkr					SS	2) 1853
C. E. Girardy & Co.							
Godfrey, Francis H.	cabt-gig making shop	Macon	Bibb			newsp ad	2) 1826
Golden, Abraham	chairmkr		Marion	69	SC	census	1) 1860
Golding, Lewis A.	cabt work-wheel		Wilkinson	49	Ga	census	1) 1860
Golding, Vincent	cabtmkr-wheel		Wilkinson	31	Ga	census	1) 1860
Goldsmith, William	cabtmkr		Cass	36	SC	census	1) 1850
Gollizr, John	cabtmkr		Richmond	22	Ger	census	1) 1850
Golucki, Edward	master cabtmkr		Wilkes	34	Ger	census	1) 1860
Goodwin, Franklin H.	cabtmkr		Cass	17	Ga	census	1) 1850
Goodwin, John W.	chairmkr		Richmond	35	SC	census	1) 1860
Gordon, Richard	cabtmkr		Washington			Cen Mfr	1) 1820
Gordy	lumber-chair mfr-gn-gr ml	Enecks	Screven			Gaz	1) 1883–84
Gordy and Colson							
Gordy, W. A.	cabtmkr	Enecks	Screven			Gaz	1) 1883–84
Gore, Michael	cabtmkr	Yorkville	Paulding			Gaz	1) 1879–84

Maker's Name	Occupation	Town	County	Age	Birth Place	Source(s)	Dates: 1) source 2) active 3) birth/death
Gosline Gosline & Heaton	cabtmkr	Douglasville	Douglas			Gaz	1) 1879–80
Goss, Hamilton	cabtmkr		Newton	39		census	1) 1850
Gotte, Joseph	cabtmkr		Chatham	28	Ger	census	1) 1860
Gouldsmith, R.	cabtmkr	Atlanta	Fulton			City Dir	1) 1867
Gouldsmith, Richard	cabtmkr		Cass	35	SC	census	1) 1850
Gouldsmith, William	cabtmkr	Cassville	Cass			newsp ad	2) 1854
Graham, R. W. Harris & Graham	cabtmkr	Dallas	Paulding			Gaz	1) 1879–80
Green, Josiah	cabtmkr		Chatham	23		census	1) 1850
Green, Thomas	cabtmkr		Lowndes	38	Eng	census	1) 1850
Green, William H.	maker		Union			W&I	1) 1865
Green, William W. G.	cabtmkr	Columbus	Muscogee			Gaz	1) 1881–82
Greggs, Rodum?	cabtmkr		Troup	21	Ga	census	1) 1850
Gregory, William	wheel-chairmkr		Washington			Cen Mfr	3) 1820
"Griest, W. P."	cabtmkr		Habersham?			AHS Sv	
Griggs, Junius Augustus	builder-wood-metal		Habersham		Ga	AHS Sv	2) 1869
Grimm, Frederick	cabtmkr		Bibb	38	Ger	census	1) 1860
Guild, Nathaniel	cabtmkr	Savannah	Chatham		Mass	D	3) 1778–1805
Gunn, John	cabtmkr		Chatham	30	Ger	census	1) 1860
Guntz, Gabert	cabtmkr		Chatham	39	Switz	census	1) 1860
Guntz, Gifford	cabtmkr		Chatham	35	Switz	census	1) 1860
Habersetzer, Martin	cabtmkr		Chatham	32	Fr	census	1) 1860
Haily, J. T.	gr-sw ml-furn-thread fact	Woodstock	Cherokee			Gaz	1) 1879–82
Hain, Samuel C.	cabt wkmn		Murray	45	NC	census	1) 1850
Haisten, W. J.	chair mfr	Humboldt	Dougherty			Gaz	1) 1879–80
Haley, A. E.	woodwkmn		Newton	50	NC	Mil Lt	1) 1863
Hall, James A.	cabtmkr shop	Macon	Bibb			newsp ad	1) 1832
	turner	Macon	Bibb			newsp ad	1) 1837
Hamell, John	cabtmkr		Randolph	28	NY	census	1) 1850
Hamilton, James	maker	Griffin				W&I	1) 1830
Hammond, Samuel	cabtmkr	Athens	Clarke			newsp ad	1) 1845
Haney, L. B.	cabt-chair shop	Decatur	DeKalb	22		census	1) 1850
Harmon, John	chairmkr		Hall			AHS Sv	3) c. 1835
Harper, James	cabtmkr		Pike	30		census	1) 1850
Harris, Claiborne	cabtmkr		Forsyth	67	Ga	census	1) 1860
Harris, John P.	cabtmkr		Oglethorpe	20	Va	census	1) 1850
Harris, M. A. Harris & Graham	cabtmkr	Dallas	Paulding			Gaz	1) 1879–80
Harris, N.	cabtmkr	Wood Lawn	Murray			Gaz	1) 1879–80
Harris, R. W.	cabtmkr	Clarksville	Habersham			newsp ad	2) 1845–46
Harris, Robert Williamson	maker					AHS Sv	3) 1810–?
Harris, Thompson	turner		Clinch	66	NC	census	1) 1850
Harris, William W.[10]	cabtmkr		Forsyth	28	Ga	census	1) 1850
Harrison, John	turner		Chatham	35	Eng	census	1) 1850
Harrison, John F.	cabtmkr		Forsyth	33	NC	census	1) 1850

Maker's Name	Occupation	Town	County	Age	Birth Place	Source(s)	Dates: 1) source 2) active 3) birth/death
Harrison, William	turner		Chatham	56	Eng	census	1) 1850
Harrison, Wm. L.	wooden ware-turning-bucket mfr	Sandersville	Washington			newsp ad	2) 1863
Harrisson, Jim	maker	Philomath-Rayle	Oglethorpe			AHS Sv	2) c. 1840–60
Harvey, Edward J.	cabt wkmn		Bibb	17	Ga	census	1) 1860
Harvey, Thomas	cabt appr		Talbot	18	Ga	census	1) 1860
Haslet, James	chairmkr	Savannah	Chatham			newsp	2) 1803
Hasper, J. W.	chairmkr		Harris	24	Ga	census	1) 1860
Hastings, W. J.	chair mfr	Humboldt	Dougherty		Ga		1) 1881–82
Hatcher, Charles	cabtmkr	Bolton	Fulton			Gaz	1) 1883–84
Hatsuck, Fred	cabtmkr		Whitfield	29	Ger	census	1) 1860
Hawkins, S. L.	maker		Taylor			W&I	1) 1864
Hawks, William B.	cabinet		Hall	36		census	1) 1850
Hayes, Sammy	maker	Rocky Mount	Meriwether			AHS Sv	2) c. 1850
Haynes, Reuben	carp	Atlanta	DeKalb	48	NC	census	1) 1850
	cabtmkr					C	2) c. 1845
						C	3) 1800–?
Haynes, Thomas	carr-chairmkr		DeKalb			W&I	1) 1854
Haynes, Thomas	cabt-chairmkr		Fulton			W&I	1) 1854
Hays, A. C.	cabtmkr	Atlanta				City Dir	1) 1867
Healy, Jeremiah	cabtmkr		Richmond	26	Mass	CRC	2) 1819
Heath, Cliff	maker		Schley			AHS Sv	
Heath, William	cabtmkr	Pine Log	Bartow		Ire?	AHS Sv	2) c. 1885
Heath, William T.	wheel		Cass	23	Ga	census	1) 1850
Heaton Gosline & Heaton	cabtmkr	Douglasville	Douglas			Gaz	1) 1879–80
Heller, Adam	cabtmkr	Savannah	Chatham			Gaz	1) 1881–82
Hemrick, David	cabtmkr	Athens	Clarke			Gaz	1) 1881–84
Henderson, R. H.	woodwkmn		Henry	36	Ga	Mil Lt	1) 1863
Henderson, Thomas	cabtmkr		Chatham	29	Ire	census	1) 1850
	cabtmkr-undtkr		Chatham	40	Ire	census	1) 1860
	cabtmkr		Chatham	46	Ire	Mil Lt	1) 1863
Henderson, Thomas J.	cabtmkr	Conyers	Rockdale			Gaz	1) 1879–82
Henderson, William	cabtmkr		Gordon	39	Tenn	census	1) 1850
Henson, James B.	child		Gordon	4	Ga	census	1) 1860
	blacksmith					AHS Sv	3) 1856–?
Herfel, John A.	cabtmkr		Greene	22	Ger	census	1) 1860
Hermann, Peter	cabtmkr		Chatham	54	Ger	census	1) 1860
Hermes, Wm. D.	cabtmkr		Bibb	29	Ga	census	1) 1850
Hermon, Peter	turner		Chatham	40	Ger	census	1) 1850
Herring, Elijah	maker		Madison		Ga	AHS Sv	2) c. 1830
						AHS Sv	3) ? –1864?
Hewitt, John	cabtmkr	Savannah	Chatham			D	2) 1801
Hewitt & Ansley	cabtmkr	Savannah	Chatham			newsp ad	2) 1800–1806
Hewitt & Mandeville	cabt wareroom	Savannah	Chatham			newsp ad	2) 1808
Hickman, Alexander	cabtmkr		Paulding	43	Va	census	1) 1850
Hickman, J. T.	cabtmkr		Upson	39	Ga	census	1) 1860

Maker's Name	Occupation	Town	County	Age	Birth Place	Source(s)	Dates: 1) source 2) active 3) birth/death
Hicks Hicks & Brevard	cabtmkr	Cartersville	Bartow			Gaz	1) 1881–84
Hightower, H.	cabtmkr	Cochran	Pulaski			Gaz	1) 1879–80
Hightower, James	lathe		Union			W&I	1) 1853
Hightower, Wm. T.	cabtmkr		Rabun	32	Ga	census	1) 1860
Hilburn, R. M.	cabtmkr		Whitfield	34	SC	census	1) 1860
Hill, John C.	cabtmkr		Clay	23	Ga	census	1) 1860
Hiller, Adam	cabtmkr	Savannah	Chatham			Gaz	1) 1879–80
Hineman, Frederick	cabtmkr		Chatham	38	Switz	census	1) 1850
Hines, Samuel	cabtmkr		Thomas	37	Conn?	census	1) 1850
Hinman, G. Hinman, G. B.[11] Hinman & Son	furn mfr	Atlanta	Fulton			Gaz	1) 1883–84
Hinman, George	furn mfr	Atlanta	Fulton			Gaz	1) 1881–82
Hinman, J. W.	cabtmkr	Atlanta	Fulton			newsp ad	2) 1880
Hinman, J. W.	furn fact	Augusta	Richmond			newsp ad	2) 1885
Hitz, Jacob	cabtmkr		Chatham	27	Ger	census	1) 1860
Hochslatter, Charles	cabtmkr		Randolph	29	Ger	census	1) 1860
Hodges, David Hodges, Joseph R.[12] D. Hodges & Son	furn mfr-lumber dlr	Osceola	Oconee			Gaz	1) 1879–82
Hodgins, Martin	cabtmkr		Chatham			D	2) 1779–1814
Hodistire, M.	cabtmkr		Chatham	47	Fr	Mil Lt	1) 1863
Hogan, C. H.	cabtmkr		Bibb	26	NY	census	1) 1850
Hogan, Jeter A.	maker		Sumter			W&I	1) 1863
Hohenstein, Adam	cabtmkr		Chatham	40	Ger	census	1) 1860
Holbert, J. S.	cabtmkr		Habersham	36	Pa	census	1) 1850
Holden, T. J.	cabtmkr	Wynn's Mill	Henry			Gaz	1) 1879–82
Holder, William W.	cabtmkr		Habersham	23	Ga	CRC	2) 1848
Holland, Elisha	cabtmkr		Clarke			B	2) 1841–50
Holland, R. J.	cabtmkr		Walker	33	Ga	census	1) 1860
Holly, Hiram G.	chairmkr	Decatur	DeKalb	23		census	1) 1850
Holly, Hiram J.	chairmkr	Atlanta		23	Ga	C	
Holmes, Clark	cabt wkmn		Floyd		Mass	census	1) 1860
Holmes, J. H.	maker		Stewart			AHS Sv	2) c. 1800
Holmes, Warren H.	cabt wkmn		Floyd	33		census	1) 1850

Homan, E. T.
 	
  Moore & Homan's
  Variety Works
	furn mfr-turning-sawing	Thomasville	Thomas			newsp ad	2) 1857–58

Honeycut, Edmund	cabinet		Forsyth	50	SC	census	1) 1850
Honeycut, James S.[13]	cabinet		Forsyth	24	Ga	census	1) 1850
Honeycut, Thomas C.[13]	cabinet		Forsyth	16	Ga	census	1) 1850
Hopkins, John R.	turner-farmer-wheel		Gwinnett		Ga	H H	2) c. 1855–70 3) c. 1835–1909
Houghton, S.	cabtmkr	Savannah	Chatham			newsp ad	1) 1801–08
Houseley, W. H.	cabtmkr		Richmond	55	Ga	census	1) 1860

Maker's Name	Occupation	Town	County	Age	Birth Place	Source(s)	Dates: 1) source 2) active 3) birth/death
Houser, G. W.	cabtmkr		Catoosa	28	Tenn	census	1) 1860
Houstein, Adam	cabtmkr		Chatham	30	Ger	census	1) 1850
Houston, Cal	cabtmkr		Fulton	23	Tenn	census	1) 1860
Houston, Edward J.	cabtmkr	Nacoochee	White			Gaz	1) 1879–84
Hoy, William	cabtmkr	Fairburn	Campbell			Gaz	1) 1881–84
Hudson, John R.	cabtmkr	Dean	Haralson			Gaz	1) 1881–84
Huff, Francis	cabtmkr?	Griffin	Spalding			newsp ad	2) 1854
Hughes, C. A.	maker		Cherokee			AHS Sv	
Hughes, Gabriel	cabtmkr		Lumpkin	26	SC	census	1) 1850
Humeston, Joy	Windsor chairmkr	Savannah	Chatham			newsp ad	2) 1800–1804
Humphreys, Amasa	cabt warehsman-cabtmkr	Savannah	Chatham			newsp ad	2) 1818–20
Humphreys & Lynch	cabtmkr-uphl	Savannah	Chatham			newsp ad	2) 1817
Hunt, Clifford	coach-chairmkr	Savannah	Chatham			D	2) 1785–1810
Hunter, John	maker		Union			AHS Sv	
Hunter?, W. M.	cabt wkmn		Carroll	29	Ga	census	1) 1860
Hunter, William G.	maker		Brooks			W&I	1) 1864
Huntington, Henry	cabtmkr		Baldwin	24	Eng	census	1) 1860
Hurst, Stephen	turner		Screven	20		census	1) 1850
Hutchins, Jonathan W.	cabinet		Forsyth	21	SC	census	1) 1850
Hutson, William	chairmkr		Jackson			Cen Mfr	1) 1820
Inglet, Andrew J.	chairmkr		Richmond	29		census	1) 1850
Irving, George	cabtmkr		Morgan			Cen Mfr	1) 1820
Jack, Sam'l	cabinet		Walker	31	NC	census	1) 1850
Jackson, Elias	cabt wkmn		Murray	33	NC	census	1) 1850
Jackson, William	chairmkr		Cherokee	55	SC	census	1) 1860
Jarrell, Nancy Ann	maker		Monroe			AHS Sv	2) c. 1895
Jarrold, W. R.	woodwkmn		Upson	24	Ga	census	1) 1860
Jefferson, R. J.	maker	Columbus	Muscogee			SS	2) 1852
Jenkins, Stephen	turner		Burke			Cen Mfr	1) 1820
Jett, John G.	turner		DeKalb	23	Ga	census	1) 1860
Jett, Stephen L.	cabt wkmn		Carroll	28	Ga	census	1) 1860
Jobson, Giles T.	cabt wkmn		Bibb	32	Ga	census	1) 1860
Johns, John	cabt wkmn		Bibb	20	Ger	census	1) 1860
Johnson, A.	cabtmkr		Catoosa[14]	37	Tenn	census	1) 1860
Johnson, Abijah	cabtmkr		Walker	27	Tenn	census	1) 1850
	undtkr-cabtmkr	Ringgold	Catoosa			newsp ad	2) 1872
	undtkr-cabtmkr	Ringgold	Catoosa			Gaz	1) 1879–84
Johnson, Anderson B.	furn-lumber	Cuthbert	Randolph			Gaz	1) 1879–80
Johnson, Benjamin	chairmkr		Baldwin	55	SC	census	1) 1860
Johnson, Frank M.	bedstead mfr	Bowersville	Hart			Gaz	1) 1883–84
Johnson, J. A.	chairmkr		Newton	46	Ga	census	1) 1860
Johnson, James	turner		Pulaski			Cen Mfr	1) 1820
Johnson, Thomas	cabtmkr		Cass	29	NC	census	1) 1860
Johnson, William Beverly	cabtmkr	Ellaville	Schley			AHS Sv	2) c. 1880
Johnston, Andrew	turner	Flat Shoals	DeKalb	34	SC	census	1) 1850
Johnston, Benjamin N.	cabtmkr		Liberty	34	SC	census	1) 1850

Maker's Name	Occupation	Town	County	Age	Birth Place	Source(s)	Dates: 1) source 2) active 3) birth/death
Joiner	cabtmkr	Drayton	Dooly			Gaz	1) 1879–80
Bond & Joiner							
Jones, Alexander	carp		Richmond	28		census	1) 1850
	carp		Richmond	40	Ga	census	1) 1860
	cabtmkr		Richmond	38	Ga	CRC	2) 1860
Jones, Jonathan	chairmkr		Decatur	54		census	1) 1850
Jones, Robert W.	cabtmkr		Telfair	65	SC	census	1) 1850
Jordan, T.	turner		Baldwin	24	Ire	census	1) 1860
Jourdan, Henry	turner		Bibb	22	Ga	census	1) 1860
Kah, John J.	cabt wkmn		Bibb	45	Ger	census	1) 1860
Kahlflieush, John H.	cabtmkr		Thomas	23	NY	CRC	2) 1861
Kalbfleisch, John	chairmkr		Richmond	38	Ger	census	1) 1850
Kaufman, Joseph	cabtmkr-furn repr	Sandersville	Washington			newsp ad	2) 1852
Kaufman, Solomon							
Joseph & Solomon Kaufman							
Kay, R. W.	justice-cabtmkr	Fair Mount	Gordon			Gaz	1) 1881–84
Kearly, John	cabtmkr	Atlanta				City Dir	1) 1867
Keener, G.	cabtmkr	LaGrange	Troup			newsp ad	2) 1843
Keller?, Andrew	bedstead mkr		Lumpkin	23	SC	census	1) 1850
Kelly, Jos. E.	furn repr-cabtmkr	Sandersville	Washington			newsp ad	2) 1852
Kelly, Joseph	cabtmkr		Talbot	31	Eng	CRC	2) 1849
Kelly, L. H.	cabtmkr		Catoosa	20	Ga	census	1) 1860
Kelly, L. W.	cabtmkr		Whitfield	18	US	census	1) 1860
Kenfield, Lester	cabtmkr		Baldwin	28	Mass	census	1) 1860
Kennedy, Benjamin Franklin	cabtmkr		Crawford			AHS Sv	2) c. 1867
Kennedy, James	cabtmkr		Chatham	48	Ire	census	1) 1850
Kennedy, James	cabtmkr		Chatham	58	NY	census	1) 1860
Kennedy, S. B.	bedstead-chair mfr	Atlanta	Fulton			Gaz	1) 1883–84
Ristine, May & Co.							
Kennedy, William	maker		Crawford			AHS Sv	2) c. 1895
Ketchum?, William H.	joiner		Murray	39	Va	census	1) 1850
Key, William, Sr.	chairmkr		Forsyth	48	NC	census	1) 1850
Kilpatrick, Spencer	carpenter		Richmond	15		census	1) 1850
King, J. M. D.	cabtmkr		Chattooga	30	NC	census	1) 1860
King, James H.	cabt mason		Houston	29	Ga	census	1) 1860
King, James R.	gn-cabtmkr	Roswell	Cobb			Gaz	1) 1879–82
King, Samuel	chairmkr		Greene			W&I	1) 1818
King, Thomas R.	cabtmkr		Baker	23		census	1) 1850
Kinney, James R.	cabtmkr	Cassville	Bartow			Gaz	1) 1879–80
Kirkpatrick	furn mkr-repr	Atlanta	Fulton			newsp ad	2) 1857
Morgan, Kirkpatrick & Co.		Decatur	DeKalb				
Kirkpatrick, M.[15]	maker	Atlanta				SS	2) 1855
Kirksey, Andrew J.	maker		Taylor			W&I	1) 1863
Kirsch, John	chairmkr		Richmond	25	Ger	census	1) 1850
Kirsch, John	cabtmkr		Richmond	28	Ger	census	1) 1850
Kirsch, John N.	chairmkr		Richmond	35	Fr	census	1) 1860
Klasing, August	cabtmkr	Rome	Floyd			Gaz	1) 1883–84

Maker's Name	Occupation	Town	County	Age	Birth Place	Source(s)	Dates: 1) source 2) active 3) birth/death
Knight. J. E.	cabtmkr	Valdosta	Lowndes			Gaz	1) 1879–80
Knight, J. H.	cabtmkr	Valdosta	Lowndes			Gaz	1) 1879–80
Knight Bros.							
Knight, Francis B.	cabt wkmn		Bibb	25	Ger	census	1) 1860
Knight, Richard W.	cabtmkr	Augusta	Richmond			Gaz	1) 1883–84
Knight, Thomas	chairmkr	Decatur	DeKalb	32	SC	census; C	1) 1850
Kraft, Henry	undtkr-cabtmkr	Sandersville	Washington			newsp ad	2) 1863
Laden, J. G.	cabtmkr		Hall	32	SC	census	1) 1850
Laden, L. C.	cabtmkr		Hall	18	Ga	census	1) 1850
Ladivez, Charles	cabtmkr		Richmond	30	Ga	census	1) 1860
Lancaster, T. C.	cabtmkr-carp	Hatcher's Station	Quitman			Gaz	1) 1883–84
Landsdale, Alfred M.	cabtmkr		Greene	39	NC	census	1) 1850
Langford, Thos.	cabt-chair shop	Decatur	DeKalb	22		census	1) 1850
Lankford, Edward P.	chairmkr	New Hope	Paulding			Gaz	1) 1879–84
Lanier, Noel	chairmkr	Guyton	Effingham			AHS Sv	3) 1811–90
Lanier, Thomas Washington	maker	Oliver	Screven			AHS Sv	3) 1840–1913
Lansdell, Alfred	cabtmkr		Floyd	50	NC	census	1) 1860
Lansdell, W. S.[16]	cabtmkr		Floyd	19	Ga	census	1) 1860
Lash, Joseph	cabtmkr		Calhoun	56	NC	census	1) 1860
	cabtmkr		Calhoun	59		Mil Lt	1) 1863
	cabtmkr	Albany	Dougherty			newsp ad	2) 1857
	cabtmkr	Morgan	Calhoun			Gaz	1) 1879–84
Laurance, William	cabtmkr	Blairsville	Union			Gaz	1) 1881–82
Lawerence, William	cabtmkr	Blairsville	Union			Gaz	1) 1883–84
Laveliss, M.	cabtmkr		Cass	42	SC	census	1) 1860
Leakman, Charles W.	cabtmkr		Jones	28	Ga	census	1) 1860
Lee, W. B.	furn mfr-repr	Covington	Newton			newsp ad	2) 1895
W. B. Lee & Co.							
Lenier?, J.?	cabtmkr		Pike	25		census	1) 1850
Levain, Isaac	turner		Chatham	23	Ire	census	1) 1860
Levall, Robert T.	cabtmkr		Coweta	24	Ga	census	1) 1850
Leverett, Thomas	maker		Union			W&I	1) 1826
Levin, Albert	cabtmkr		Chatham	36	Ger	census	1) 1850
Lewis	maker		Stewart			AHS Sv	
Lewis, M.	cabtmkr	Morgan	Calhoun			Gaz	1) 1881–84
Lillingsworth?, Matthew C.	cabtmkr		Washington	21	Ga	census	1) 1850
Lindsey, Joseph	cabtmkr		Franklin	21	SC	census	1) 1860
Lippman, Andrew	cabtmkr		Whitfield	45	Ger	census	1) 1860
	cabtmkr		Whitfield	48	Ger	Mil Lt	1) 1863
Llewellyn, W.	chairmkr	Gillsville	Banks			Gaz	1) 1883–84
Lloyd, Sidney	cabtmkr	Columbus	Muscogee			Gaz	1) 1879–80
Lockey, John P.	cabt shop	Columbus	Muscogee			newsp ad	2) 1833
John P. Lockey & Co.							
Loden, J. G.	cabtmkr		Hall	32	SC	census	1) 1850
Loden, J. N.	cabtmkr		Hall	43	SC	census	1) 1860
Lodge, Alfred J.	turner		Chatham	32	Del	census	1) 1860
"Lofitt, G. W."	maker		Clarke?			AHS Sv	

Maker's Name	Occupation	Town	County	Age	Birth Place	Source(s)	Dates: 1) source 2) active 3) birth/death
Logley, James	cabt wkmn		Murray	60?	Tenn	census	1) 1850
Long, Henry W.	cabtmkr		Gilmer	43	SC	census	1) 1850
Lord, William	cabtmkr		Banks	42	SC	census	1) 1860
Loveless, M.	cabtmkr	Cartersville	Bartow			Gaz	1) 1881–84
Lucks, LaFayette	cabtmkr		Cass	25	Tenn	census	1) 1850
Lumpton, James	cabtmkr		Floyd	49	Va	census	1) 1860
Lyon, Jesse	cabtmkr		Newton	22		census	1) 1850
Lyon, Jessee L.	cabtmkr		Campbell	32	SC	census	1) 1860
Lynch, Cornelius	maker		Stewart			AHS Sv	
Mabrey, Jesse P.	cabt wkmn		Floyd	60?	NC	census	1) 1850
Mabry, Warren M.	chairmkr		Franklin	31	Ga	census	1) 1860
Mabury, Lesser	cabtmkr		Floyd	70	NC	census	1) 1860
McAllister, H. H.	cabtmkr	Albany	Dougherty			Gaz	1) 1879–80
McAllister & Mroczkowsky							
McCall, Edward J.	turner		Clarke	35	Pa	census	1) 1860
McCarter, John	cabtmkr		Cobb	54	SC	census	1) 1850
McCary?, George G.	cabtmkr		Murray	56	NC	census	1) 1850
McCinsey, C.	cabtmkr		Floyd	18	Tenn	census	1) 1850
McClafresh, William S.	cabtmkr		Cobb	35	Md	census	1) 1850
McClendon, David	cabtmkr		Chatham	20	Ire	census	1) 1850
McCleskey, Thomas J.	cabt making	Macon	Bibb			newsp ad	2) 1826
McCleskey, Thomas J.	cabtmkr		Chatham	55	SC	census	1) 1850
McClesky?, Thomas J.	cabtmkr		Chatham	66	SC	census	1) 1860
McCollough, Robert	cabtmkr		Henry	33	NC	census	1) 1860
MacCombs, A. T.	woodwkmn		Heard	46	SC	Mil Lt	1) 1863
McConough, James	cabtmkr		Chatham	35	Ire	census	1) 1860
McCormac, John	cabtmkr		Bibb	17	NY	census	1) 1850
McCown, Robert	cabtmkr	Atlanta	Fulton			City Dir	1) 1867
McCoy, Dugal	turner		Randolph	45	NC	census	1) 1850
McCoy, Isaac	chairmkr		Muscogee	70	NC	census	1) 1850
McCracken, William D.	cabtmkr		Newton	57	NC	census	1) 1850
McCrackin, W. L.	cabtmkr		Newton	62	NC	census	1) 1860
Macrae, William	cabtmkr	Savannah	Chatham			newsp ad	2) 1819–20
McCutchen, B. A.	cabtmkr		Whitfield	34	Ga	census	1) 1860
"McDade, Tucker"	cabtmkr	"Eatonton"	Putnam			AHS Sv	2) c. 1830–35
McFarland, William S.	cabtmkr		Chatham	39	Ga	census	1) 1860
McGill, Neil	chair mfr	Perry's Mill	Tattnall			Gaz	1) 1881–82
McGinnis, J. L.	cabtmkr	Atlanta	DeKalb	36	NC	census	1) 1850
McGregor, Daniel	maker	Mt. Vernon	Montgomery			AHS Sv	2) c. 1835
McGuire, J. E.	chairmkr-sw ml	Lithonia	DeKalb			Gaz	1) 1881–82
McGuire, J. H. C.	chairmkr-sw ml	Lithonia	DeKalb			Gaz	1) 1881–82
McGuire, John	chair mfr-gr-plan ml	Centreville	Gwinnett			Gaz	1) 1883–84
McKay, Andrew J.	chairmkr	Banksville	Banks			Gaz	1) 1879–80
McKay, Billy	maker	Macon?	Bibb			AHS Sv	2) c. 1855
McKinnon, Thomas B.	maker		Glynn			W&I	1) 1808
McKinsey, C.	chairmkr	Langtry	Emanuel			Gaz	1) 1883–84
McKinsey, S.	chairmkr	Langtry	Emanuel			Gaz	1) 1883–84

Maker's Name	Occupation	Town	County	Age	Birth Place	Source(s)	Dates: 1) source 2) active 3) birth/death
McKinsey, W. E.	chairmkr	Langtry	Emanuel			Gaz	1) 1883–84
McLane, Alpheus T.	cabtmkr		Clarke	22	SC	census	1) 1860
McLaughlin, George	maker		Oglethorpe			AHS Sv	
	farmer		Oglethorpe	52	Ga	census	1) 1850
	farmer		Oglethorpe	62	Ga	census	1) 1860
McLean Williams & McLean	dlr-furn mfr	Atlanta	Fulton			newsp ad	1) 1862
McLellan, William	cabtmkr		Cass	25	Scot	census	1) 1850
McLemore, Chesly B.	maker		Montgomery			AHS Sv	2) c. 1850
McLemore, Chesley B.	farmer		Emanuel	36	SC	census	1) 1850
McLemore, Chesley B.	farmer		Montgomery	46	Ga	census	1) 1860
McLisky, John[17]	cabtmkr		Wilkes			Cen Mfr	1) 1820
McMichael, John C.	editor-furn mfr-dlr	Barnesville	Pike			Gaz	1) 1881–82
McMichael, S. C.	cabtmkr		Randolph	37	Ga	census	1) 1860
McMillian, James	cabtmkr		Richmond	27	SC	census	1) 1860
McMinn, Richard	cabtmkr		Bibb	28	Ire	census	1) 1850
McNag, Hugh	turner		Richmond	21	Ire	census	1) 1860
Magan, Peter	cabtmkr		Chatham	30	Ga	census	1) 1860
Maguire Maguire & Bros.	gr-plan ml-chair mfr	Centreville	Gwinnett			Gaz	1) 1881–82
Malatour, M.	cabtmkr		Cass	24	Ger	census	1) 1850
Malcolm, Barrett	maker		Morgan			AHS Sv	2) c. 1830
Malony, John B.	cabt wkmn		Gwinnett	75	Ire	census	1) 1850
Mamard, Lewis	cabt worker		Bibb	18	Ga	census	1) 1850
Mandeville Hewitt & Mandeville	cabt wareroom	Savannah	Chatham			newsp ad	2) 1808
Martin, A. B.	turner		Carroll	49	SC	census	1) 1850
"Martin, J. A."	maker	Mt. Zion	Carroll			AHS Sv	
Martin, J. A.	carp	Little Creek	Haralson			Gaz	1) 1883–84
Martin, J. M.	cabtmkr		Hall	26	Ga	census	1) 1860
Martin, J. Millen	appr cabtmkr		Richmond	14	Ga	census	1) 1860
Martin, James A.	student		Carroll	11	Ga	census	1) 1860
Martin, John G.	turner		Fulton	36	Ga	census	1) 1860
Martin, William	chairmkr		Cherokee	46	SC	census	1) 1850
Mastenn, H. M.	furn mfr	Simsville	Carroll			Gaz	1) 1879–80
Mathews, James	maker		Morgan			W&I	1) 1815
Maund, Lexington	cabt appr		Talbot	21	Ga	census	1) 1860
May, Edwin F. Ristine & May	bedstead-chair mfr	Atlanta	Fulton			Gaz City Dir	1) 1879–82 1) 1885
May, John	cabtmkr		Muscogee	40	NC	census	1) 1860
Mayne, W. H.	cabtmkr		Gwinnett	41	SC	census	1) 1860
Mayne, William H.	cabtmkr		Gwinnett	31	SC	census	1) 1850
Lawrenceville Cabinet Manufactory	cabtmkr	Augusta	Richmond			newsp ad	2) 1850
Mayo, David	master cabtmkr		Wilkes	72	Mass	census	1) 1860
Meano, Peter A.	maker	Savannah	Chatham			newsp ad D	2) 1787 3) ?–1824

Maker's Name	Occupation	Town	County	Age	Birth Place	Source(s)	Dates: 1) source 2) active 3) birth/death
Medcalf, James	cabtmkr		Gordon	30	Ga	census	1) 1860
Meeks, Edward C.	cabt-chairmkr	Savannah	Chatham			newsp ad	2) 1794–1801
						D	3) ?–1806
Mehathy, Thomas	turner		Gwinnett			Cen Mfr	1) 1820
Mereland, John	cabtmkr	Macon	Bibb			newsp ad	2) 1832
Merk, James	cabtmkr		Murray	36	SC	census	1) 1850
Merritt, William	maker		Greene			W&I	1) 1826
Mertins, W. H.	cabtmkr		Chatham	30	Ger	census	1) 1850
Meyers, Rufus	gr ml-chair fact	Gerber	Walker			Gaz	1) 1883–84
Michael, Casper	cabtmkr		Muscogee	32	Ger	census	1) 1850
Middleton, Stephen S.	furn mfr	Hampton	Henry			Gaz	1) 1883–84
Miller Faris? & Miller	cabtmkr-turner	Savannah	Chatham			newsp ad	2) 1817–19
Miller, A. J. A. J. Miller & Son	furn mfr	Atlanta	Fulton			newsp ad	2) 1888
Miller, A. J. A. J. Miller & Co.	undtkr-cabtmkr	Savannah	Chatham			newsp ad	1) 1862–83
Miller?, Hiram	cabt wkmn		Newton	23	NC	census	1) 1850
Miller, Jacob	cabtmkr		Chatham	59		census	1) 1850
Miller, Osborne	carr mkr		Houston	28	Ga	census	1) 1860
Miller, Osborne H.	gn mfr-furn-carr mkr	Fort Valley	Houston			Gaz	1) 1879–84
Miller, Peter	cabtmkr	Savannah	Chatham			AHS Sv	2) 1798–1810
						newsp ad	2) 1803–10
						W&I; D	3) 1763–1810
Miller, Thomas	cabt wkmn		Newton	23	NC	census	1) 1850
Miller, Thomas, Sr.	cabtmkr		Greene	45		census	1) 1850
Millhauser, Anselun	cabtmkr		Chatham	35	Ger	census	1) 1860
Mills, Charles W. Mills & Sumter	furn mfr-importing-undtkr	Rome	Floyd			newsp ad	2) 1859
Mills, John P.	cabtmkr		Habersham	28		census	1) 1850
Millsap, Sol	chair mkr		Cass	47	Tenn	census	1) 1850
Millsaps, Peter	cabtmkr		Gilmer	45	Tenn	census	1) 1850
Mitchell, Wm. L.	furn		Clarke			B	2) 1851–61
Mitcher, Maradit	cabt wkmn		Floyd	64	SC	census	1) 1860
Mixon, Elijah	carr mkr	Oxford	Newton	54	NC	census	1) 1850
	maker	Oxford	Newton			AHS Sv	3) 1796–1873
Monds, Wm.	maker	Macon	Bibb			SS	2) 1852
Moon, B. I.	cabtmkr	Harmony Grove	Jackson			Gaz	1) 1879–82
Moon, Benjamin Franklin	maker-farmer	Bowdon	Carroll			AHS Sv	
Moon, Bird	farmer		Madison	18	Ga	census	1) 1850
Moon, Bird Isaac	furn mkr-farmer		Madison			AHS Sv	3) 1845–82?
Moon, Vincent	chair mkr		Henry	42	Ga	census	1) 1860
Moor?, Henry	cabtmkr		Troup	38	Ger	census	1) 1850
Moore, C. G. Moore & Homan's Variety Works	furn mfr-turning-sawing	Thomasville	Thomas			newsp ad	2) 1857–58

Maker's Name	Occupation	Town	County	Age	Birth Place	Source(s)	Dates: 1) source 2) active 3) birth/death
Moore, Elijah S.	cabtmkr		Cobb	20	Ga	census	1) 1850
Moore, Gordon J.	cabtmkr		Troup	30	Ga	census	1) 1850
Moore, H. A.	gr ml-chair fact	Franklin	Heard			Gaz	1) 1883–84
H. A. & J. J. Moore							
Moore, Henry	chair mfr	Merrill	Heard			Gaz	1) 1883–84
Moore, J. J.	gr ml-chair fact	Franklin	Heard			Gaz	1) 1883–84
H. A. & J. J. Moore							
Moore, J. J.	gr ml-chair mfr	Texas	Heard			Gaz	1) 1883–84
J. J. Moore & Co.							
Moore, John	chairmkr	Sunny Side	Spalding			Gaz	1) 1879–80
Moore, R. T.	cabt wkmn	Floyd		37	Ga	census	1) 1860
Moore, Robert	cabtmkr	Summerville	Chattooga			Gaz	1) 1879–84
Moore, Robert	woodwkmn		Coweta	57		Mil Lt	1) 1863
Moore, Robt.	carp		Coweta	42	SC	census	1) 1850
Moore, Roderick R.	wheel-chairmkr		Columbia	57		Mil Lt	1) 1863
Moreland, James	cabtmkr		Crawford	60	SC	census	1) 1860
Morgan	furn mkr-repr	Atlanta	Fulton			newsp ad	2) 1857
Morgan, Kirkpatrick & Co.		Decatur	DeKalb				
Morgan, Enoch[18]	cabtmkr	Decatur	DeKalb		Mass	C	3) 1804–43
Morgan, J.	lawyer-chairmkr	Decatur	DeKalb	50	Mass	census	1) 1850
Morgan, J.	furn mkr	Decatur	DeKalb			C	2) 1844
J. & L. S. Morgan	chairmkr	Decatur	DeKalb			newsp ad	2) 1852
Morgan, Joseph[18]	cabtmkr	Decatur	DeKalb		Mass	C	3) 1800–1854
Morgan, L. S.	furn mkr	Decatur	DeKalb		Mass	C	2) 1844
Morgan, L. L. [sic]	cabt-chairmkr		DeKalb	45	Mass	census	1) 1850
J. & L. S. Morgan	chairmkr	Decatur	DeKalb			newsp ad	2) 1852
Morgan, Lawrence Sterne[18]	cabt-chairmkr	Decatur	DeKalb		Mass	C	2) 1850
						C	3) 1806–62
Morrell, W.	cabtmkr	Savannah	Chatham			D	2) 1824
Morris, Caswell D.	cabtmkr	Clinton	Jones			Cen Mfr	1) 1820
Morris, George	turner		Baldwin	40	Wales	census	1) 1860
Morris, John Z.[19]	appr turner		Baldwin	16	Pa	census	1) 1860
Morris, Thomas J.	maker		Carroll			W&I	1) 1863
Morrison, Matthew	cabtmkr		Richmond	23	SC	census	1) 1850
Morton, E. L.	master cabtmkr		DeKalb	39	SC	census	1) 1860
Morton, Edward L.	cabtmkr		Coweta	29	SC	census	1) 1850
Morton, Marshall	chairmkr		Coweta			newsp ad	2) 1852
Moss, Ephraim	cabtmkr		Richmond	28	NC	census	1) 1850
Moyers, F. D.	cabtmkr		Floyd	22	Tenn	census	1) 1850
Mroczkowsky, T. K.	cabtmkr	Albany	Dougherty			Gaz	1) 1879–80
McAllister & Mroczkowsky							
Mullins, John	cabtmkr	Canton	Cherokee			newsp ad	2) 1897
Muncus, William N.	chairmkr		Muscogee	32	NC	census	1) 1850
Murphy, Milton	bedstead-coffin-sash-door maker	Athens	Clarke			newsp ad	2) 1854
Myers, Henry	cabtmkr	Peachtree Shoals	Henry			Gaz	1) 1879–84
Myers, Lewis	cabtmkr		Muscogee	35	Ger	census	1) 1860

Maker's Name	Occupation	Town	County	Age	Birth Place	Source(s)	Dates: 1) source 2) active 3) birth/death
Nabors, James B.	cabt wkmn		Jackson	55	SC	census	1) 1860
Nabors, William	cabt wkmn		Clarke	62	SC	census	1) 1860
Nash, Simon W.	turner		Berrien	46	SC	census	1) 1860
Neeler, William	cabtmkr		Clarke	39	Ga	census	1) 1850
Nelmns, F. M.	cabtmkr	Rocky Creek	Gordon			Gaz	1) 1879–80
Nelson, H. T.	turner	Augusta	Richmond			newsp ad	2) 1857
Nelson, Nicholas	cabtmkr		Early			Cen Mfr	1) 1820
Newmark, Meyer	cabtmkr		Chatham	50	Ger	census	1) 1860
Newton, E. L.	furn		Clarke			B	2) 1851–61
Nichols, Charles	cabtmkr		Richmond	18	SC	census	1) 1860
Nichols, Joseph	Windsor chairmkr	Savannah	Chatham			D	2) 1800
Nichols, Sam'l[20]	cabtmkr		Richmond	27	NY	CRC	2) 1826
Nisbet, F. M.	wood turner		Whitfield	21	Tenn	census	1) 1860
Noel, Jobe	turner		Randolph	78	NC	census	1) 1850
Norman, J. S.	cabtmkr	Hopewell	Colquitt			Gaz	1) 1883–84
Norris, James	chairmkr	Salt Springs	Douglas			Gaz	1) 1879–80
Norris, Robert	maker		Hancock			W&I	1) 1826
Nungazer, Nathaniel A.	cabtmkr		Chatham	27		census	1) 1850
	cabtmkr		Chatham	37	Ga	census	1) 1860
Obear, J. W.	cabtmkr	Reed Creek	Hart			Gaz	1) 1879–82
Oliver, C. S.	wareroom-cabt shop	Athens	Clarke			newsp ad	2) 1846
Oliver, S. C.	furn		Clarke			B	2) 1841–50
Olmstead, Edward H.	cabtmkr		Chatham	31		census	1) 1850
Ohegan, H.	cabtmkr		Catoosa	24	Ire?	census	1) 1860
Osborne, C. H.	furn mfr-dlr-chair mfr	Griffin	Spalding			Gaz	1) 1881–82
Osborne&Wolcott		Griffin	Spalding			Gaz	1) 1883–84
Owens, M. C.	furn mfr	Hickory Flat	Cherokee			Gaz	1) 1881–82
Owensby, Thomas F.	chairmkr		Henry	20	Ga	census	1) 1860
Padgett, L. Frank	furn-mattress mfr	Augusta	Richmond			Gaz	1) 1883–84
Page, Thomas	cabtmkr	Savannah	Chatham			D	2) 1783–1828
Page, William	maker		Glynn			W&I	1) 1827
Painter, William	cabtmkr		Richmond	29	Eng	census	1) 1860
Pander, J. P.	cabtmkr		Union	70	NC	census	1) 1850
Parish, W. L.	cabtmkr		Catoosa	32	Ga	census	1) 1860
Parker, J. J.	cabtmkr	Persimmon	Rabun			Gaz	1) 1883–84
Parker, Joshua	chairmkr		Newton	61	ND?	census	1) 1850
Parkes, Johnson	chair seating		DeKalb	45	Ga	census	1) 1860
Parks, James	maker		Greene			W&I	1) 1825
Parks, Muses	cabtmkr		Macon	57	NC	census	1) 1860
Parrish, James	maker		Berrien			W&I	1) 1865
Parrs, B. W.	bed maker	Atlanta				City Dir	1) 1859
Parsons Trimmier & Parsons	cabtmkr	Ringgold	Catoosa			Gaz	1) 1879–84
Paterson, L. H.	cab		Hall	34	SC	census	1) 1850
Patrick, Churchwell	maker		Stewart			AHS Sv	
Patrick, Joshua	cabtmkr		Butts	31	Tenn	census	1) 1850

Maker's Name	Occupation	Town	County	Age	Birth Place	Source(s)	Dates: 1) source 2) active 3) birth/death
Patterson, Samuel M.	turner		Chatham	20	Ire	CRC	2) 1820
Paul, George	cabtmkr		Houston	30	Ger	census	1) 1860
Payne, William	cabt wkmn		Bibb	25	Mass	census	1) 1860
Payton, J. N.	cabtmkr	Bowdenville	Carroll			Gaz	1) 1879–80
Pearson, Uncle Jesse	chairmkr		Wilkinson			AHS Sv	
Pebbles, D. H.	cabtmkr		Henry	22	SC	census	1) 1850
Peck, James	coach-chairmkr	Savannah	Chatham			D	3) 1783–1812
Peek	cabtmkr		Stewart			AHS Sv	
Peters, Alexander	cabtmkr		Glynn	27	Ger*	census	1) 1860
Petty, D. F.	wheel-cabtmkr-turner	Columbus	Muscogee			newsp ad	2) 1857
Philipe, Jackson	cabtmkr?		Stewart	28		census	1) 1850
Philips, William M.	cabtmkr		Paulding	25		census	1) 1850
Phillips, Joel	chairmkr		Hart	23	SC	census	1) 1860
Phillips, Joel	chairmkr	Bowersville	Hart			Gaz	1) 1879–80
Phillips, William	chairmkr	Bowersville	Hart			Gaz	1) 1879–80
Pierce, Alfred J.	chairmkr					AHS Sv	
Pierce, Jesse Payton	maker	Irwinton	Wilkinson			AHS Sv	3) 1872–1957
Platt, C. A.	furn-mattress	Augusta	Richmond			Gaz	1) 1879–80
Platt Bros.	maker-undtkr	Augusta	Richmond			newsp ad	2) 1865
Platt, Charles A.	furn mfr	Augusta	Richmond			newsp ad	2) 1850–54
	maker					SS	2) 1853
	furn mfr		Richmond	36		census	1) 1850
	cabtmkr		Richmond	45	Conn	census	1) 1860
Platt, Col. Chas. A.	cabtmkr	Augusta	Richmond		NY	E	3) ?–1887
Platt, Jacob B.	cabtmkr		Richmond	33	NY	census	1) 1860
Platt, W. L.	furn-mattress	Augusta	Richmond			Gaz	1) 1879–80
Platt Bros.	maker-undtkr	Augusta	Richmond			newsp ad	2) 1865
Plunket, James W.	cabtmkr		Gwinnett	19	Ga	census	1) 1850
Plunkett, Silas P.	cabt wkmn		Bibb	26	Ga	census	1) 1860
Porter, William C.	cabtmkr		Talbot	29	Ga	census	1) 1860
Posten, Robert	chairmkr		Fayette	71	NC	census	1) 1850
Pournell, W. F.	furn repr-cabtmkr	Sandersville	Washington			newsp ad	2) 1852
Powell, Charles H.	cabtmkr		DeKalb	30	Mass	census	1) 1860
Powell, Uriah M.	cabtmkr	Dawson	Terrell			Gaz	1) 1879–84
Powers, William	cabtmkr	Thomaston	Upson			newsp ad	2) 1836
Powledge, John Augustus	maker		Meriwether			AHS Sv	2) c. 1850
Prather, E. C.	furn-wheel	Hogansville	Troup			Gaz	1) 1883–84
Prather & Rosser							
Presley, J.	cabtmkr	Cromer's	Franklin			Gaz	1) 1879–80
Priestley, Edward	cabtmkr	Savannah	Chatham			newsp ad	2) 1803
Proctor, Sampson	turner		Burke	39		census	1) 1850
Pruitt, Eli	chairmkr		Cherokee	45	SC	census	1) 1850
Pye, John	maker	Pleasantville	Talbot			AHS Sv	3) 1823–85
Quintill, Charles	cabtmkr		Richmond	30	Ger*	census	1) 1860
Ragsdale, David	cabtmkr		Coweta	22	Va	census	1) 1850
Rambo, John	cabtmkr		Baldwin	29	Ga	CRC	2) 1842

Maker's Name	Occupation	Town	County	Age	Birth Place	Source(s)	Dates: 1) source 2) active 3) birth/death
"Rankin, L. R."	maker		Hancock			AHS Sv	
Raufman, J.	cabtmkr		Bibb	23	Ger	census	1) 1850
Raufman, S.	cabtmkr		Bibb	25	Ger	census	1) 1850
Raushenberg, Fredrick	turner		Murray	17	Ger	census	1) 1850
Rawlings, Moody	maker		Hancock			W&I	1) 1804
Raynal, Pierre N.	uphl-cabtmkr	Savannah	Chatham			Gaz	1) 1883–84
Read, John	chairmkr		Chatham	26		census	1) 1860
Readmond, Jeremiah	cabt wkmn	Savannah	Chatham			D	2) 1802–28
Rector, Benjamin	cabtmkr		Murray	63	Va	census	1) 1860
Reeds, H.	cabtmkr		Upson	52	NC	census	1)1860
Reepel, George	cabt wkmn		Madison	54	Ga	census	1) 1860
Reichert, Frederick	furn-wallpaper-mattress mfr	Macon	Bibb			Gaz	1) 1883–84
Reick, Louis	cabtmkr		Richmond	25	Ger	census	1) 1860
Reid, Lon	chairmkr					AHS Sv	
Reynolds, Alexander	cabtmkr		Bibb	40	Pa	CRC	2) 1842
Reynolds, Eli(z)?	cabt-chair shop		DeKalb	19		census	1) 1850
Reynolds, John	repr-paint-gild chairs	Athens	Clarke			newsp ad	2) 1835
Reynolds, John	chairmkr	Warrenton	Warren			AHS Sv	
Reynolds, John	carp		Warren			census	1) 1850
Reynolds, John	wood machinist		Warren	46	Ga	census	1) 1860
Reynolds, John[21]	carp		Warren	17	Ga	census	1) 1860
Reynolds, Peter	cabtmkr		Chatham	22	Fr	census	1) 1860
Reynolds, Thomas	cabt wk	Decatur	DeKalb	25		census	1) 1850
Reynolds, Thomas S.	cabt wk	Fairburn	Fulton			AHS MS	3) 1815–1917
Rhudy, W. A.	carp	Rome	Floyd			newsp ad	1) 1889
Richards, John	turner		Burke			Cen Mfr	1) 1820
Richards, Robert	cabtmkr		Chatham	30		census	1) 1850
	cabtmkr		Chatham	42	Ga	census	1) 1860
Richards, William C.	cabt wkmn		Bibb	37	Ga	census	1) 1860
Richardson, David	maker		Clarke			W&I	1) 1828
Richmond Richmond & Allen[22]	chair-cabtmkr	Savannah	Chatham			newsp ad	2) 1806–10
Ridley, H. A. Bonner & H. Ridley	cabtmkr	Columbus	Muscogee			Gaz	1) 1879–89
Riggs, William	cabtmkr-uphl	Savannah	Chatham			newsp ad	2) 1804–10
Riley, Jimmy	preacher		Elbert			AHS Sv	
Riley, James	farmer		Hall	61	Va	census	1) 1850
Risner, I.? W.	cabtmkr		Whitfield	22	Tenn	census	1) 1860
Ristine, John S. Ristine & May Ristine, May & Co.[23]	bedstead-chair mfr	Atlanta	Fulton			City Dir Gaz	1) 1885 1) 1879–84
Roady, Nicholas	chair seating		DeKalb	68	SC	census	1) 1860
"Roane, F. G."	maker	Lexington	Oglethorpe			AHS Sv	
Robertson, M. L.	cabtmkr	Dean	Haralson			Gaz	1) 1881–82
Robilliard, Samuel	turner	Savannah	Chatham			D	2) 1766–1806

Maker's Name	Occupation	Town	County	Age	Birth Place	Source(s)	Dates: 1) source 2) active 3) birth/death
Rohman, John	cabtmkr		Bibb	37	Ger	census	1) 1850
Rollison, James	cabtmkr	Augusta	Richmond			Gaz	1) 1883–84
Rooks, Joel	cabt wk		Walton	50	Ga	census	1) 1860
Roomsu?, Jacob	cabtmkr		Stewart	37	Switz	census	1) 1850
Rooney, L.	cabt business		Muscogee	34	Pa	census	1) 1850
	furn store	Columbus	Muscogee			newsp ad	2) 1877
Sammis & Rooney	cabt warehs-shop	Columbus	Muscogee			newsp ad	2) 1853–55
Ross, Thomas	cabtmkr		DeKalb	20	Tenn	CRC	2) 1855
Rosser, W. C.	furn-wheel	Hogansville	Troup			Gaz	1) 1883–84
Prather & Rosser							
Rosseter, White	maker		Clarke			W&I	1) 1828
Rosy, Joseph F.	cabtmkr		Chatham	26	Fla	census	1) 1850
Rote, Mayer	cabtmkr	Atlanta	Fulton			City Dir	1) 1859
Rote, Michael	cabtmkr		Fulton	30	Ga	census	1) 1860
Rotes	cabtmkr	Atlanta	Fulton			City Dir	1) 1859
Rouse, Willie	chairmkr		Hall	37	NC	census	1) 1860
Rowe, James E.	maker		Bulloch			W&I	1) 1862
Rowlin, William	cabtmkr		Pike	25	NY	census	1) 1850
Ruis, Thomas	cabtmkr		Richmond	23	Ga	census	1) 1860
Runnell, Frances	cabtmkr		Richmond	33	Czech*	census	1) 1860
Rush, Abraham	chairmkr		Talbot	34	SC	census	1) 1850
Russal, John	cabt wkmn		Pulaski	62	Ger?	census	1) 1860
Russel, George	cabt wkmn		Madison	44	Ga	census	1) 1850
Rutherford, Babel	laborer		Lowndes	22	Ga	census	1) 1850
Rutherford, Babel	farmer		Berrien	28	Ga	census	1) 1860
Rutherford, Babel Jackson	maker		Berrien			AHS Sv	3) 1830–82
Rutledge, W.	cabt wk		Henry	52	SC	census	1) 1850
Ryan, Sherman	cabinet		Hall	39	Ire	census	1) 1850
Sammis, Richard	cabt business		Muscogee	41	NY	census	1) 1850
Sammis & Rooney	cabt warehs-shop	Columbus	Muscogee			newsp ad	2) 1853–55
Sandwich, Thomas	musical instrument-cabtmkr	Augusta	Richmond			newsp ad	2) 1796–1800
Sasnett, Richard	maker		Hancock			W&I	1) 1810
Satterfield, James J.	cabt wkmn		Cherokee	61	SC	census	1) 1860
Saulsbury, Henry	cabt-turner business	Macon	Bibb			newsp ad	2) 1832
Saunders, Thomas M.	cabtmkr		Muscogee	47	Ga	census	1) 1850
Savarison, William P.	cabtmkr		Murray	60	NC	census	1) 1860
Saye, R. W.	builder-contractor-mfr-repr furn	Athens	Clarke			newsp ad	2) 1879
R. W. Saye & Sons							
Schafer, Charles	cabt wkmn		Bibb	55	Ger	census	1) 1860
Schaub, John	cabtmkr		Richmond	32	Ger	census	1) 1850
Schramin, Fredrick	cabtmkr		Chatham	28	Ger	census	1) 1850
Scott, Isaac	cabtmkr	Hamilton X Roads	McDuffie			Gaz	1) 1881–82
Scott, J. T.	cabtmkr	Columbus	Muscogee			newsp ad	2) 1856
Scott, John	cabtmkr	Savannah	Chatham			newsp ad	2) 1806–9
						newsp ad	3) ?–1808

Maker's Name	Occupation	Town	County	Age	Birth Place	Source(s)	Dates: 1) source 2) active 3) birth/death
Scott, John L.	cabtmkr		Newton	21	Ga	census	1) 1860
Scotte, J.	chairmkr		Paulding	47	SC	census	1) 1860
Scroggins, John	cabtmkr		Washington			Cen Mfr	1) 1820
Seawell, J. B.	furn-lumber mfr-sw-gr-carding-ml	Travis	Habersham			Gaz	1) 1883–84
Self, Thomas M.	cabtmkr		Laurens			Cen Mfr	1) 1820
Shaw, Alfred	furn dlr		Morgan	34	Ga	census	1) 1860
Shaw, Alfred	mfr-dlr-cabt shop-warehs	Madison	Morgan			newsp ad	2) 1842–47
Shaw, Caleb T.	mechanic		Franklin	46	Mass	census	1) 1850
	cabtmkr		Franklin	55	Mass	census	1) 1860
Shaw, L. C.	carr-wagon mkr	Albany	Dougherty			newsp ad	2) 1858
Shaw, S. S. Shaw & Co.	bedroom furn-chairs	Madison	Morgan			newsp ad	2) 1883
Shaw, Sebastian	cabtmkr		Morgan	32	Ger	census	1) 1860
Shaw, William P.	cabt wkmn		Bibb	23	Ga	census	1) 1860
Sheets, Linville W. D.[24]	chairmkr		Chatham	21	Va	CRC	2) 1844
Shick, George	cabtmkr	Savannah	Chatham			newsp ad	2) 1807–11
Shields, M. A.	cabtmkr	Senoia	Coweta			Gaz	1) 1881–82
Shockley, Benjamin	turner		Greene	22	Ga	CRC	2) 1819
Shomaker, Adam	chairmkr		Gwinnett	78	NC	census	1) 1850
Shoultz, Carl	cabtmkr		Chatham	30	Ger	census	1) 1850
Shultze, William	cabtmkr		Richmond	38	Ger	census	1) 1860
Shumate, A. H. P.	turner		DeKalb	39	Ga	census	1) 1860
Shuther, S. S.	cabtmkr	Eatonton	Putnam			Gaz	1) 1879–84
Sibbles, William	appr cabtmkr		Richmond	15	Ga	census	1) 1860
Siggers, William	cabtmkr		Jackson	60	NC	census	1) 1860
Sikes, G. N.	cabtmkr		Muscogee	35	Va	census	1) 1860
Silcox, J.	furn mfr	Augusta	Richmond			newsp ad	2) 1851
Silver, John	cabtmkr		Richmond	43	Eng	census	1) 1850
Simmons, Jas. W.	maker		Hancock			W&I	1) 1869
Simmons, Robert	cabtmkr		Muscogee	36	NC	census	1) 1850
Simpson, Edward	cabtmkr	Augusta	Richmond			Gaz	1) 1881–82
Simpson, Edward D.	cabtmkr	Augusta	Richmond			Gaz	1) 1883–84
Simpson, Miles B.	cabt wkmn		Hall	38	SC	census	1) 1860
Simpson, Miles Berry	cabtmkr		Hall		SC	newsp	3) 1820–92
Simpson, Thomas	furn dlr	Lumpkin	Stewart			Gaz	1) 1883–84
Simpson, Thomas W.	cabtmkr		Stewart		Tenn	AHS Sv	3) 1796–1884
Simpson, W. M.	furn mfr	Absalom	Hall			Gaz	1) 1881–82
Simpson, Wm.	cabtmkr		Wilkes		Va	AHS Sv	3) 1778–?
Sims, Iverson W.	uphl-cabtmkr	Senoia	Coweta			Gaz	1) 1883–84
Sims, J. W.	cabtmkr	Senoia	Coweta			Gaz	1) 1879–80
Singer, Johann	maker	Americus	Sumter			AHS Sv	
Singleton, Jerimiah	turner		Pike	24		census	1) 1850
Singleton, William	cabtmkr		Richmond	30	Eng	census	1) 1860
Sisemore, Henry	turner		Banks	28	Ga	census	1) 1860
Skipper, Mathew	cabtmkr		Chatham	30	NJ	census	1) 1850

Maker's Name	Occupation	Town	County	Age	Birth Place	Source(s)	Dates: 1) source 2) active 3) birth/death
Sleck, Jacob	cabt wkmn		Bibb	26	Ger	census	1) 1860
Sloan, F. A.	furn-lumber mfr	Red Clay	Whitfield			Gaz	1) 1881–82
Sloan, John A.	cabt wkmn		Bibb	45	SC	census	1) 1860
Smith, Binckney	cabtmkr		Baldwin	24	SC	census	1) 1860
Smith, Bird	chairmkr		Jackson	47		Mil Lt	1) 1863
Smith, Birde	chairmkr		Jackson	30	SC	census	1) 1860
Smith, Ezekial	maker	Sumter				W&I	1) 1853
Smith, George	cabtmkr		Campbell	29	Ga	census	1) 1860
Smith, George	cabt wkmn		Bibb	25	Ger	census	1) 1860
Smith, J. M.	furn		Clarke			B	2) 1851–61
Smith, Jesse	carp		Newton	73	Va	census	1) 1850
Smith, Jesse	chairmkr		Newton	76	Va	census	1) 1860
Smith, Jonathan	bedstead mkr		Lumpkin	44	SC	census	1) 1850
Smith, Michael W.	cabtmkr		Walker	36	NC	census	1) 1850
Smith, Rollins	cabtmkr		Morgan			Cen Mfr	1) 1820
Smith, Samuel	cabtmkr		Baker	45	SC	census	1) 1850
Smith, Samuel	furn mfr	Albany	Dougherty			newsp ad	2) 1854–58
Smith, William	cabt wkmn		Floyd	45	SC	census	1) 1850
Smith, William	chairmkr		Morgan			Cen Mfr	1) 1820
Smith, William B.	turner		Laurens			Cen Mfr	1) 1820
Smith, Z.	wagon-chairmkr	Claude	Washington			Gaz	1) 1883–84
Smithson							
Armstrong & Smithson	furn dlr-mfr	Acworth	Cobb			Gaz	1) 1879–80
Snead, W. H.	cabtmkr	Nashville	Berrien			Gaz	1) 1879–80
Sparks, Albert G.	cabtmkr	Camp Creek	Union			Gaz	1) 1879–84
Sparks, J. M.	cabtmkr		Catoosa	16	Ga	census	1) 1860
Sparks, L. E. G.	cabtmkr		Catoosa	20	Ga	census	1) 1860
Sparks, Ludlow	cabtmkr	Atlanta	Fulton			City Dir	1) 1867
Sparks, Ludlow E.	cabtmkr	Atlanta	Fulton			Gaz	1) 1879–80
Weinmeister & Sparks							
Speidtel?, Christian	cabt wkmn		Bibb	26	Ger	census	1) 1860
Spencer, Joseph	cabtmkr		Gilmer	27	NC	census	1) 1860
Spencer, Perry	maker		Stewart			AHS Sv	2) 1856
Spencer, Samuel	cabtmkr		Gilmer	40	NC	census	1) 1860
Spinks, Rolly	chairmkr		Harris	65	Ga	census	1) 1860
Spitz, L. J.	cabtmkr	Thomasville	Thomas			Gaz	1) 1881–84
Spivey, George M.	cabt wkmn		Terrell	20	Ga	census	1) 1860
Stapper, Matthew	cabtmkr		Chatham	30	NJ	census	1) 1850
Stavaland, John Obed	maker	Boston	Thomas			AHS Sv	3) 1806–83
Stavaland, Benjamin F.[25]	maker	Boston	Thomas			AHS Sv	3) 1830–63
Stephens, Harry	chairmkr	Crawfordville	Taliaferro			AHS Sv	
Stephens, Washington D.	chairmkr		Carroll			W&I	1) 1856
Stephenson, John	cabtmkr	Billow	Carroll			Gaz	1) 1879–84
Stetier?, Joseph	chairmkr		Carroll	33	Ga	census	1) 1860
Stewart, George W.	cabtmkr	Lily Pond	Gordon			Gaz	1) 1879–80
Stewart, J. E.	cabtmkr		Hancock	42	SC	census	1) 1860
Stewart, James S.	cabtmkr		Cass	59	SC	census	1) 1850

Maker's Name	Occupation	Town	County	Age	Birth Place	Source(s)	Dates: 1) source 2) active 3) birth/death
Stewart, John A.	cabtmkr		Sumter	37	SC	census	1) 1850
Stewart, Samuel	turner	Savannah	Chatham			D	2) 1789–1820
Stidham, B. F.	furn mfr	Flowering Branch	Hall			Gaz	1) 1883–84
Stitt, Job	maker	Tallapoosa	Haralson		Ill	AHS Sv	2) c. 1895
Stocker, John D.	furn mfr	Atlanta	Fulton			Gaz	1) 1883–84
Stone, George	cabtmkr		Chatham	29	Ger	census	1) 1850
Stone, Jonathan	chairs		Forsyth	30	SC	census	1) 1850
Stow, George	cabtmkr	Savannah	Chatham			D	2) 1800–1827
Strand, Manson	cabtmkr		Floyd	40	Ga	census	1) 1860
Strange, Owen	cabtmkr	Savannah	Chatham			D	2) 1776–1814
Richmond & Allen						newsp ad	2) 1809–12
Strong	plan ml-bedstead mfr	Atlanta	Fulton			F	2) 1853
Gilbert & Strong							
Stroup, Levi	cabtmkr		Cass	38	SC	census	1) 1850
Stuart, Samuel J.	cabtmkr		Greene	66	SC	census	1) 1860
Stunt, Robert	cabtmkr		Chatham	26	Eng	census	1) 1860
Sulenberzor?, A. R.	cabtmkr		Catoosa	43	Va	census	1) 1860
Sullivan, David H.	cabt wkmn		Bibb	30	Ire	census	1) 1860
Sullivan, James	turner		Chatham	26		census	1) 1850
Summons, James B.	maker		Laurens			W&I	1) 1856
Sumter, J. M.	cabtmkr		Floyd	39	NC	census	1) 1850
"Sumter, James"	furn mfr	Rome	Floyd			AHS Sv	
Sumter, James M.	furn mfr-importing-undtkr	Rome	Floyd			newsp ad	2) 1859
Mills & Sumter							
Sumter, Thomas Web	cabtmkr		White	74	NC	census	1) 1860
Sumter, William L.	cabtmkr		Floyd	23	NC	census	1) 1850
Sumter, William L.	cabtmkr		White	33	NC	census	1) 1860
Syneh, Daniel	cabt wkmn		Dougherty	39	Va	census	1) 1860
Tate, Asi	cabt wkmn		Cherokee	63	SC	census	1) 1860
Tayler, James	cabtmkr		Bibb	63	Ga	census	1) 1850
Tayler, William[26]	cabtmkr		Bibb	33	Ga	census	1) 1850
Taylor, Alfred	cabtmkr		Newton	45	NC	census	1) 1860
Taylor, E. P.	furn dlr	Macon	Bibb			newsp ad	2) 1876–80
W. & E. P. Taylor							
Taylor, James	cabt mfr-uphl	Macon	Bibb			newsp ad	2) 1833–38
Taylor, W.	furn dlr	Macon	Bibb			newsp ad	2) 1876–80
W. & E. P. Taylor							
Taylor, William	cabt wkmn		Bibb	42	Eng	census	1) 1860
"Taylor, William"	maker	Oconee	Washington			AHS Sv	2) c. 1850
Tenant, John	farmer		Franklin	35	SC	census	1) 1850
"Tenant, John"	maker	Hartwell	Hart			AHS Sv	
Thiess, W.	cabtmkr	Savannah	Chatham			D	2) 1797–1817
Thomas, John	chair mkr		Murray	40	NC	census	1) 1850
Thomas, P. M.	cabtmkr	Camp Creek	Union			Gaz	1) 1879–84
Thomas, William	cabtmkr		Bibb	30	SC	census	1) 1860
Thompson	cabt-chairmkr		DeKalb	16		census	1) 1850

Maker's Name	Occupation	Town	County	Age	Birth Place	Source(s)	Dates: 1) source 2) active 3) birth/death
Thompson, James C.	cabt-chairmkr		DeKalb	19	Ga	census	1) 1850
Thompson, John H.	cabt wkmn		Murray	50	Va	census	1) 1850
Thompson, Lucius L.	cabtmkr	Cedartown	Polk		Ga		1) 1881–84
Thompson, Young H. J.	turner		Coweta	26	Ga	census	1) 1860
Thweatt, John T.	maker					SS	2) 1852
Tilton, Nathan R.	cabtmkr	Athens	Clarke			Gaz	1) 1879–84
Tinney, Thos. J.	cabtmkr		Coweta	36	SC	census	1) 1850
Tondee, Peter	cabtmkr	Savannah	Chatham			AHS Sv	2) c. 1800
Torrance, James	cabtmkr		Burke			Cen Mfr	1) 1820
Trawick, Lunsford	maker		Clarke			W&I	1) 1810
Trimmier Trimmier & Parsons	cabtmkr	Ringgold	Catoosa			Gaz	1) 1879–84
Trone, A. E.	cabtmkr		Troup	28	Pa	census	1) 1850
Trope, Lewis	cabtmkr		Taliaferro	41	Eur	census	1) 1850
	cabtmkr		Taliaferro	55	Ger	Mil Lt	1) 1863
Trowbridge, John Trowbridge, H. T. John Trowbridge & Son	furn mfr	Atlanta	Fulton			Gaz	1) 1883–84
Tucker, David	cabtmkr	Marietta	Cobb	22	Ga	census	1) 1850
Tucker, Edmund	cabtmkr	Columbus	Muscogee			Gaz	1) l879–82
Tucker, William	cabtmkr	Columbus	Muscogee			Gaz	1) 1879–84
Tufts, Warren N.	cabt wkmn		Bibb	25	Mass	census	1) 1860
Tweedy, John	cabtmkr	Augusta	Richmond			newsp ad	2) 1852
Tyre, Michael	cabtmkr		Chatham	34	Ger	census	1) 1860
Tyson, K. P.	carp		Coweta	21	Ga	census	1) 1850
Tyson, Kinchen P., Jr.	master cabtmkr		Spalding	35	Ga	census	1) 1860
Tyson, W. A.	furn dlr	Griffin	Spalding			newsp ad	2) 1860
Tyson, W. A.	furn dlr		Spalding	30	Ga	census	1) 1860
Untz, George	cabtmkr		Chatham	46	Ger	Mil Lt	1) 1863
VanBuren, Jasper	maker	Clarksville	Habersham			SS	2) 1852
	maker	Clarksville	Habersham			AHS Sv	2) c. 1850
Vaughn, Joseph	wagon-cabtmkr	Cuthbert	Randolph			Gaz	1) 1883–84
Vaughn, William	chairmkr		Cherokee	37	SC	census	1) 1850
	cabt wkmn		Cherokee	47	SC	census	1) 1860
Vaugnby, Frank	cabt worker		Murray	25	Ger	census	1) 1850
Vernbes, Fusk	cabtmkr		Murray	30	Ger	census	1) 1860
Verner, James	chairmkr		Murray	35	Pa	census	1) 1850
Vitenger, Witey	cabtmkr		Cass		Ger	AHS Sv	2) c. 1848
Voelker, Wm.	cabtmkr	Augusta	Richmond			Gaz	1) 1879–82
Wade, W. H.	cabtmkr		Lumpkin	44	SC	Mil Lt	1) 1863
Wade, William	cabt wkmn		Lumpkin	30	SC	census	1) 1850
Waite, J. I.	contractor-builder-furn-undtkr	Eastman	Dodge			Gaz	1) 1883–84
Walcot, Walter	cabtmkr		Newton	52	Conn	census	1) 1850
Walcot, William	cabtmkr		Newton	21	Me	census	1) 1850
Waldrop, Hiram	chairmkr		Lumpkin	47	SC	census	1) 1860
Wales, Thomas	cabtmkr	Santa Luca	Gilmer			Gaz	1) 1879–80

Maker's Name	Occupation	Town	County	Age	Birth Place	Source(s)	Dates: 1) source 2) active 3) birth/death
Walker, Abner	chairmkr	Porter Springs	Lumpkin			Gaz	1) 1881–84
Walker, J. D.	cabtmkr		Newton	26	NC	census	1) 1860
Walker, John W.	cabtmkr		Richmond	58	Va	census	1) 1860
Walker, John W.	cabtmkr		Whitfield	33	Tenn	census	1) 1860
Wallace, Lorenza D.	chairmkr		Talbot	45		census	1) 1850
Wallace, W. Wallace & Co.	undtkr-cabtmkr	Savannah	Chatham			Gaz	1) 1883–84
Wallace, W. R.	sw ml-cabtmkr	Doraville	DeKalb			Gaz	1) 1883–84
Wallan, Albert	master cabtmkr		Richmond	40	Czech	census	1) 1860
Wallbohn, Daniel	cabtmkr		Muscogee	50	Ger	census	1) 1850
Wallis, Thomas G.	cabtmkr?		Gwinnett	23	NC	census	1) 1850
Ward, Thomas	chair bottomer		Richmond	21	SC	census	1) 1860
Ward, W.	cabtmkr		Whitfield	54	NY	Mil Lt	1) 1863
Waren, I. M.	cabtmkr		Fulton	48	Ga	census	1) 1860
Warner, Joseph	cabtmkr		Fulton	40	Ga	census	1) 1860
Warren, James M.	cabtmkr		Newton	38		census	1) 1850
Warren, Jesse Wiggins	cabtmkr		Newton	17	Ga	census	1) 1850
Watson, Elias	cabtmkr		Coweta	21	Ga	census	1) 1850
Watson, William	turner		Randolph	45	Ga	census	1) 1850
Waurstgen, Henry	cabtmkr		Muscogee	44	Den	census	1) 1850
Weatherington, Furney	cabt work		Campbell	52	NC	census	1) 1850
Weaver, Thos. G.	cabtmkr		Troup	36	Ga	census	1) 1850
Webb, Charles C.	cabtmkr	Clinton	Jones			Cen Mfr	1) 1820
Webb, John H.	cabt wkmn		Whitfield		Ga	census	1) 1860
Webb, John N.	cabtmkr		Upson	39	Md	census	1) 1850
Weimazr, Conrad	cabtmkr	Atlanta	Fulton			City Dir	1) 1867
Weinmeister, Henry Weinmeister & Sparks	cabtmkr	Atlanta	Fulton			Gaz	1) 1879–80
Wellborn, C. R.	cabtmkr		Newton	32	Ga	census	1) 1860
Wellborn, J. M.	cabtmkr		Newton	34	Ga	census	1) 1860
Wellman, George	turner		Chatham	24	Me	census	1) 1860
Werner, Ferdinand J.	cabtmkr	Atlanta	Fulton			City Dir	1) 1859
West, Lanier	cabtmkr		Richmond	31	Pa	census	1) 1860
Wethersby, Joshua	cabtmkr		Richmond	16	SC	census	1) 1860
Whatley, Elbert L.	chairmkr		Troup	50	Ga	census	1) 1850
Whatley, James G.	maker		Union			W&I	1) 1865
Wheeler, Scott	turner		Burke			Cen Mfr	1) 1820
Whitaker, Edward	chairmkr		Columbia	35	Ga	CRC	2) 1858
Whitaker, William	cabtmkr	Marthasville	DeKalb		NC	F	1) 1902
	cabtmkr-furn mfr-coffins					C	2) 1845
						F	3) ?–1866
Whitaker, William	carp	Atlanta	DeKalb	44	NC	census	1) 1850
	carp	Atlanta	Fulton	53	NC	census	3) 1860
White, Daniel	cabt finisher		Richmond	20	Ga	census	1) 1860
White, E. J.	cabtmkr-shop	Columbus	Muscogee			newsp ad	1) 1833
White, Elijah	cabtmkr	Athens	Clarke			newsp	1) 1809

Maker's Name	Occupation	Town	County	Age	Birth Place	Source(s)	Dates: 1) source 2) active 3) birth/death
White, H. V.	cabtmkr	Bowdenville	Carroll			Gaz	1) 1879–80
White, J. S. W.	cabtmkr	Columbus	Muscogee			newsp ad	2) 1833
White, Noah	chairmkr	Loudsville	White			Gaz	1) 1879–80
Whitehead, L. C.	cabtmkr	Travis	Habersham			Gaz	1) 1883–84
Whitehead, T. L.	cabtmkr	Travis	Habersham			Gaz	1) 1883–84
Whitinger, John	cabt work		Camden?	49		Mil Lt	1) 1863
Whitley, J. N.	chairmkr	Windsor	Walton			Gaz	1) 1883–84
Whitman, Robert G.	cabtmkr		Burke	27	SC	census	1) 1860
Whitmire, B.	turner		Hall	36	Ga	census	1) 1860
Wiggins, Jesse	cabtmkr		Fulton	27	SC	census	1) 1860
		Atlanta				City Dir	1) 1859; 1867
		Atlanta	Fulton			Gaz	1) 1879–80
Wilkerson, Elam	chairmkr		Coweta	25	NC	census	1) 1850
Wilkins?, Leroy	cabtmkr		Greene	20		census	1) 1850
Wilkins, S. H.	cabtmkr		Richmond	30	SC	census	1) 1860
Wilkins, Thaddeus M.	cabtmkr		Chatham	23	Ga	census	1) 1860
Wilkins, Thaddeus M.	cabtmkr	Savannah	Chatham			Gaz	1) 1879–80
Wilkinson, Columbus	cabt-chair shop	Decatur	DeKalb	20	Ga	census	1) 1850
Willers, Henry	cabtmkr-wareroom	Columbus	Muscogee			newsp ad	2) 1847
Willey, John	cabtmkr	Decatur	DeKalb	17		census	1) 1850
Williams Williams & McLean	dlr-mfr furn	Atlanta	Fulton			newsp ad	2) 1862
Williams, A. J. A. J. & J. S. Williams	maker		DeKalb			SS	2) 1855
Williams, Elbert L.	cabtmkr		Whitfield	19	Tenn	census	1) 1860
Williams, F. A.	mfr-dlr furn-matt	Atlanta	Fulton			City Dir	1) 1859
	mfr-dlr furn-uphl	Atlanta	Fulton			newsp ad	2) 1859
Williams, G. L.	cabtmkr		Whitfield	27	Tenn	census	1) 1860
Williams, H. M.	carp-furn	Flowery Branch	Hall			Gaz	1) 1883–84
Williams, J. S. A. J. & J. S. Williams	maker		DeKalb			SS	2) 1855
Williams, John	cabtmkr		Banks	57	NC	census	1) 1860
Williams, John	turner		Camden	20	NJ	CRC	2) 1820
Williams, R. M.	cabtmkr	Buena Vista	Marion			Gaz	1) 1879–80
Williams, Robert	chairmkr		Franklin	66	Ga	CRC	2) 1847
Williams, William E.	cabtmkr		Talbot	31	Ala	census	1) 1860
Williamson, William[27]	cabtmkr		Glynn	33	Eng	CRL	2) 1849
Wilsch, J. E.	cabtmkr	Harmony Grove	Jackson			Gaz	1) 1881–82
Wilson, Abraham B.	farmer-chairmkr		Murray	56		census	1) 1850
Wilson, J. E.	cabtmkr	Harmony Grove	Jackson			Gaz	1) 1879–80
Wilson, James F.	cabt wkmn		Clarke	30	Ga	census	1) 1860
Wilson, James R. C.	cabtmkr		Coweta	15	SC	census	1) 1850
Wilson, Levi	turner		Brooks	70	Ga	census	1) 1860
Wilson, Levi	maker		Berrien			W&I	1) 1867
Wilson, Moses W.	maker		Glynn			W&I	1) 1840
Wilson, S. W.	maker		Hancock			W&I	1) 1863
Wilson, W.? J.	cabtmkr		Catoosa	27	NC	census	1) 1860

Maker's Name	Occupation	Town	County	Age	Birth Place	Source(s)	Dates: 1) source 2) active 3) birth/death
Windham, G. W.	carp-bedsteads	Augusta	Richmond			newsp ad	1) 1855
Windham, George	carp		Richmond	23	SC	census	1) 1850
Windham, George W.	carp		Chatham	35	SC	census	1) 1860
Witt, J. M.	cabtmkr	Quitman	Brooks			Gaz	1) 1881–84
Witter, Henry	cabtmkr	Atlanta	Fulton			City Dir	1) 1867
Wofford, Ira	cabtmkr		Gordon	38	SC	census	1) 1850
Wofford, Ira	chairmkr	Blue Spring	Gordon			Gaz	1) 1881–84
Wolcott, W. W.	furn mfr-dlr	Griffin	Spalding			Gaz	1) 1881–82
Osborne & Wolcott	chair mfr	Griffin	Spalding			Gaz	1) 1883–84
Wood	chair-cabtmkr	Macon	Bibb			newsp ad	1) 1824
Brown & Wood							
Wood, Bradley	maker	Macon	Bibb			SS	1) 1852
Bradley Wood & Co.							
Wood, Granville	cabt merchant		Bibb	35	Conn	census	1) 1850
Wood, Grenville	cabtmkr		Bibb	45	Conn	census	1) 1860
Wood Bros. & Co.	cabt-chairmkr	Macon	Bibb			newsp ad	2) 1855–76
T. & G. Wood	cabt wkmn	Griffin	Spalding			newsp ad	1) 1856
Wood, Philip	cabt-carp		Wilkinson	31	NY	census	1) 1860
Wood, Seth G.	carp	Macon	Bibb			newsp ad	2) 1861–62
Wood Bro. & Co.							
Wood, Thomas	cabt wkmn	Macon	Bibb			newsp ad	1) 1833–65
T. & G. Wood	furn mfr	Griffin	Spalding			newsp ad	1) 1856
Wood, William	cabtmkr		Clarke	40	Eng	census	1) 1860
Wood, Wm.	cabtmkr		Clarke			B	2) 1851–61
Wood, William	cabtmkr	Athens	Clarke			newsp ad	2) 1854–56
Woodall, Drary	turner-farmer		Murray	50	SC	census	1) 1850
Woods, Rufus Peoples	maker	Franklin	Heard			AHS Sv	2) c. 1863
Woodside, B. F.	cabtmkr	Atlanta	Fulton			City Dir	1) 1867
Woodson, John C.	cabtmkr		Bibb	38	Ga	census	1) 1860
Woody, William	furn mfr	Joy	Lumpkin			Gaz	1) 1881–84
Worner, Ferdinand	cabt worker	Atlanta	DeKalb	30	SC	census	1) 1850
"Wright, L. C."	maker					AHS Sv	2) c. 1865
Wright, Wm. H.	cabtmkr		Coweta	30	Ga	census	1) 1850
Wright, Zacheus	maker		Green			W&I	1) 1840
Wylly, W. A. J.	cabtmkr	Chatham		31		census	1) 1850
Yates	cradles-carr-child chairs	Augusta	Richmond			newsp ad	1) 1855
York, James	cabtmkr		Cobb	22	Ga	census	1) 1850
York, William	chair		Forsyth	44	SC	census	1) 1850
Young, James	maker		Bulloch			W&I	1) 1861
Young, John F.	cabtmkr		Walker	41	Tenn	census	1) 1850
Zimmerman, I. C.	cabtmkr		Upson	28	Va	census	1) 1860
Zimmerman, J. C.	cabtmkr		Upson	22	Va	census	1) 1850
	cabtmkr		Upson	31	Va	census	1) 1860

Notes:
1. Son of Billy Barton
2. The name of Cass Co. was changed in 1861 to Bartow Co.
3. Son of H. S. Bogardus
4. Clay Co. was created from parts of Early and Randolph Cos. in 1854
5. Wife of John Calflatch
6. Son of Richard Casady
7. Son of George Douglas
8. Son of William Dunn (c. 1740–c. 1830)
9. Son of Alexander H. Dunn
10. Son of Claiborne Harris
11. Son of G. Hinman
12. Son of David Hodges
13. Son of Edmund Honeycut
14. Catoosa Co. was formed in 1853 out of Walker Co.
15. Probably James M. Kirkpatrick, brother-in-law of Lawrence Sterne Morgan
16. Son of Alfred Lansdell
17. Possibly John M. Lisky
18. Joseph, Enoch, and Lawrence Sterne Morgan are brothers
19. Son of George Morris
20. Alias Sam'l N. Smith
21. Son of John Reynolds, wood machinist
22. Joined by Owen Strange
23. Joined by S. B. Kennedy
24. Alias Linville W. D. Dickson
25. Son of John Obed Stavaland
26. Son of James Tayler
27. Alias William Robinson

Counties Surveyed: 1850 and 1860 Census Records

Appling	Clinch	Forsyth	Jasper	Morgan	Taliaferro
Baker	Cobb	Franklin	Jefferson	Murray	Tattnall
Baldwin	Columbia	Gilmer	Jones	Muscogee	Telfair
Bibb	Coweta	Glynn	Laurens	Newton	Thomas
Bryan	Crawford	Gordon	Lee	Oglethorpe	Troup
Bulloch	Dade	Greene	Liberty	Paulding	Twiggs
Burke	Decatur	Gwinnett	Lincoln	Pike	Union
Butts	DeKalb	Habersham	Lowndes	Pulaski	Upson
Calhoun	Dooly	Hall	Lumpkin	Putnam	Walker
Camden	Dougherty	Hancock	Macon	Rabun	Walton
Campbell	Early	Harris	Madison	Randolph	Ware
Carroll	Effingham	Heard	Marion	Richmond	Warren
Cass	Elbert	Henry	McIntosh	Screven	Washington
Chatham	Emanuel	Houston	Meriwether	Stewart	Wayne
Chattooga	Fayette	Irwin	Monroe	Sumter	Wilkes
Cherokee	Floyd	Jackson	Montgomery	Talbot	Wilkinson
Clarke					

Additional Counties Surveyed: 1860 Census Records Only

Banks	Clay	Fannin	Mitchell	Quitman	Webster
Berrien	Clayton	Fulton	Miller	Schley	White
Brooks	Coffee	Glascock	Milton	Spalding	Whitfield
Catoosa	Colquitt	Haralson	Pickens	Taylor	Wilcox
Charlton	Dawson	Hart	Pierce	Terrell	Worth
Chattahoochee	Echols	Johnson	Polk	Towns	

Counties Surveyed: Wills and Inventories, 1800–1870

Baker	Chattahoochee	Dougherty	Gwinnett	Macon	Towns
Baldwin	Chattooga	Effingham	Habersham	Morgan	Troup
Banks	Cherokee	Elbert	Hancock	Oglethorpe	Union
Berrien	Clarke	Fannin	Haralson	Rabun	Upson
Bibb	Clay	Floyd	Harris	Schley	Walker
Brooks	Clayton	Franklin	Heard	Screven	Warren
Bulloch	Columbia	Fulton	Jasper	Spalding	Webster
Burke	Cobb	Gilmer	Johnson	Stewart	White
Camden	Coffee	Glascock	Laurens	Sumter	Whitfield
Carroll	Dawson	Glynn	Liberty	Taylor	Wilkes
Catoosa	Dooly	Gordon	Lowndes	Terrell	Wilkinson
Chatham	Decatur	Greene			

Lenders to the Exhibition

Mr. and Mrs. Billy F. Allen

Mr. James E. Allen

Mr. and Mrs. Jack P. Atkinson

Atlanta Historical Society (Tullie Smith House Restoration)

Carolyn J. Bennett

Stewart County Historical Commission (Bedingfield Inn, Lumpkin, Ga.)

Dr. and Mrs. Charles G. Boland

Mr. and Mrs. R. L. (Cotton) Boswell

Mr. and Mrs. James Braithwaite

Dr. J. T. Bryson

John A. Burrison

Mr. and Mrs. J. David Chesnut

Susan and Carl Cofer

Thomas F. Collum

Mrs. Thomas Allen Dixon Jr.

Mrs. Naomi Henson Farnham

Mr. and Mrs. Robert McAlpine Goodman Jr.

Mr. and Mrs. Holcombe T. Green Jr.

Mr. and Mrs. William W. Griffin

Louis Turner Griffith

Mr. and Mrs. Vernon Halliday (Brazier family)

Mr. and Mrs. Paul M. Hawkins

James T. and Mabel R. Hicks

Mrs. Robert Hodges and Mr. and Mrs. Collins Sullivan

Jarrell Plantation, State Historic Site, Department of Natural Resources (Juliette, Ga.)

Mrs. James F. Jenkins

Mr. and Mrs. Taylor B. Knox

Dr. and Mrs. James E. Lee

Deanne and Jarvin Levison

Mr. and Mrs. James Mills Jr.

Alexander H. Stephens Memorial, State Historic Site, Department of Natural Resources (Crawfordville, Ga.)

Mr. and Mrs. John Trammell McIntyre

Mr. and Mrs. William M. Matthews

Mercer University (Macon, Ga.)

Margaret Norris

Dr. and Mrs. Robert F. Norton

Mr. William Parker Jr.

Mrs. Bill Pettit

Frank B. Pierce

Dr. and Mrs. W. Harrison Reeves

Mrs. Marian Pierce Russell

Mr. and Mrs. Tony L. Shank

Mrs. Elizabeth Ross Sherrod

Mr. and Mrs. William Smith

Mr. and Mrs. Andrew Sparks

Mrs. John Cleves Symmes

Mrs. William Tate

John R. Tompkins and Lee D. Spence

Traveler's Rest, State Historic Site, Department of Natural Resources (Toccoa, Ga.)

Uncle Remus Museum, Inc. (Eatonton, Ga.)

Westville Village: by gift or loan of Castleberry, Crittendon, and House Families, Citizens of Chattahoochee Co. (Lumpkin, Ga.)

Sidney F. Wheeler

James A. Williams

Mrs. Lewis Shelton Woodson

Mr. and Mrs. Kendall Zeliff

Mrs. Norma W. Watterson

Several lenders who wish to remain anonymous

Exhibition Committees

Steering Committee

Florence P. Griffin

William W. Griffin

Paul M. Hawkins

Sally W. Hawkins

Deanne D. Levison

William L. Pressly

Statewide Committee

William N. Banks, Newnan

John A. Burrison, Atlanta

Mills B. Lane IV, Savannah

Sue McLendon Moye, Lumpkin

Nancy Fraser Parker, Atlanta

Andrew Sparks, Atlanta

Jane Campbell Symmes, Madison

Eliot Wigginton, Rabun Gap

James A. Williams, Savannah

Professional Advisory Committee

Wendell D. Garrett, Editor and Publisher, the magazine *Antiques*, New York, New York; Chairman

Charles F. Hummel, Deputy Director for Collections, the Henry Francis du Pont Winterthur Museum, Wilmington, Delaware

Jessie J. Poesch, Professor, History of Art, Newcomb College, Tulane University, New Orleans, Louisiana

Bradford Rauschenberg, Curator, Museum of Early Southern Decorative Arts, Winston-Salem, North Carolina

David B. Warren, Associate Director, the Museum of Fine Arts, Houston, Texas